THE SPORTS BOOK FOR BOYS 9-12

FOOTBALL, BASEBALL, AND BASKETBALL: THE HISTORY OF EACH GAME, BIOGRAPHIES OF THE GREATEST PLAYERS OF ALL TIME, STORIES OF AMAZING GAMES, AND INCREDIBLE FACTS

3 BOOKS IN 1

JIMMY MCCALL

TOMOKAI RIVER

© Copyright 2023 Jimmy McCall - All rights reserved.

The content contained within this book may not be reproduced, duplicated, or transmitted without direct written permission from the author or the publisher.

Under no circumstances will any blame or legal responsibility be held against the publisher, or author, for any damages, reparation, or monetary loss due to the information contained within this book. Either directly or indirectly.

Legal Notice

This book is copyright protected. This book is only for personal use. You cannot amend, distribute, sell, use, quote or paraphrase any part, or the content within this book, without the consent of the author or publisher.

Disclaimer Notice

Please note the information contained within this document is for educational and entertainment purposes only. All effort has been executed to present accurate, up to date, and reliable, complete information. No warranties of any kind are declared or implied. Readers acknowledge that the author is not engaging in the rendering of legal, financial, medical or professional advice. The content within this book has been derived from various sources. Please consult a licensed professional before attempting any techniques outlined in this book.

By reading this document, the reader agrees that under no circumstances is the author responsible for any losses, direct or indirect, which are incurred as a result of the use of the information contained within this document, including, but not limited to, — errors, omissions, or inaccuracies.

CONTENTS

THE FOOTBALL BOOK FOR BOYS 9-12
Jimmy McCall

Introduction	3
1. The History of Football	7
2. How the Game is Played	21
3. The Greatest of All Time	31
Quarterback: Tom Brady	33
Running Back: Walter Payton	39
Wide Receiver: Jerry Rice	45
Offensive Lineman: Anthony Muñoz	53
Defensive Lineman: Reggie White	59
Linebacker: Lawrence Taylor	65
Defensive Back: Ronnie Lott	71
4. Amazing Games	75
5. Fun Facts About Football	105
Conclusion	111

THE BASEBALL BOOK FOR BOYS 9-12
Jimmy McCall

Introduction	115
1. The History of the Game	119
2. How the Game is Played	133
3. The Greatest of All Time	141
Pitcher: Walter Johnson	143
Catcher: Johnny Bench	149
First Baseman: Lou Gehrig	155
Second Baseman: Jackie Robinson	161
Shortstop: Cal Ripken, Jr.	167
Third Baseman: Mike Schmidt	171
Outfielder: Babe Ruth	175
4. The Greatest Games of All-Time	181
5. Did You Know? Amazing Baseball Facts	201
Conclusion	207

THE BASKETBALL BOOK FOR BOYS
9-12
Jimmy McCall

Introduction	211
1. The History of Basketball	213
2. How the Game Is Played	225
3. The Greatest of All Time	237
Magic Johnson	241
Michael Jordan	245
LeBron James	249
Tim Duncan	253
Kareem Abdul-Jabbar	259
Kobe Bryant	263
Stephen Curry	267
Shaquille O'Neal	271
Wilt Chamberlain	275
Larry Bird	279
Baby Goats	283
4. Amazing Games	285
5. Incredible Facts	305

THE FOOTBALL BOOK FOR BOYS 9-12

THE HISTORY OF THE GAME, BIOGRAPHIES OF THE GREATEST PLAYERS OF ALL TIME, STORIES OF AMAZING GAMES, AND INCREDIBLE FACTS

JIMMY MCCALL

INTRODUCTION

The smell of fresh green grass on game day. The sound of fans cheering and screaming when your team runs out of that tunnel. The incredible feeling of scoring the winning touchdown and having players lift you on their backs and the crowd chanting your name. Going out after the game and celebrating with your friends and family.

Yup, that all happened for me. The thrill of playing football was one of the greatest feelings in the world. But that's not even close to how it all started.

Instead, it was the smell of dirty jerseys, the taste of mud in my mouth, cold water running down my body in the shower, and the sound of coaches screaming obscenities in my ear.

But you know what? That was just as good, because it was all football.

It was my first day playing. I was 14 and signed up to play on the junior varsity high school team because my friends urged me to. I was more of a soccer and baseball guy but loved watching football on television. I was a huge Notre Dame fan growing up and Lou Holtz was my favorite coach. He motivated me to want to put the pads on and play.

Back in the 80s and early 90s, Notre Dame football was life for me. They were a national championship contender every year, and I was always glued to the television on Saturdays. "Rudy" was my favorite movie ever and I even had the fantastic opportunity to fly from Florida to South Bend, Indiana to watch a Notre Dame game.

I knew the game from watching it, but didn't really know anything about playing it other than when my brother and I would be in the back yard as kids, pretending we were Joe Montana and Jerry Rice.

That first day I really played football was a rude awakening. It was Florida in August and someone had turned the water on. No, not a water fountain – I mean water from the heavens. It rained, then rained some more. For five days, we practiced in pouring rain and ran around the field in inch-deep water and mud. Our white jerseys had turned black by the end of practice on day one, but we had to wear those black jerseys for the next four days.

But that was football, and it felt great. That first week, I fell in love with the game. I played running back and defensive back for four years in high school. I played three sports–football, baseball, and soccer–but football was by far my favorite. The energy you got from playing and the excitement of game day was like nothing else.

While I was good and started for my varsity team, I didn't have the talent to make it to the collegiate level. But I did do some coaching at the high school level and spent some time as a football journalist when I became an adult.

There's a reason why the world seems to stop on Saturdays and Sundays when football comes on. Stadiums fill up to capacity and the atmosphere is electric. Fans love the sport. Tom Brady once said, "Football is unconditional love," and there couldn't be a more true quote. Baseball has long been America's favorite pastime, but these days, football has become the most popular sport in America.

As I said earlier, I am in love with football. I'm not just a fan of Notre Dame and the Tampa Bay Buccaneers…I'm a fan of the game and the history of it. The truth is, baseball, basketball, and hockey haven't really changed much over the course of history, but football has gone through an incredible evolution from when it was first invented. The game you see on television today isn't the game it once was. It has improved over time and continues to become more popular every year.

In this book, we will explore football and find out what has made the game so accepted over time. How is it played and how has that changed? We will also examine the players and the amazing moments that have helped make it the most watched sport in America.

1

THE HISTORY OF FOOTBALL

WHERE WAS FOOTBALL BORN?

If you ask most people around the world where football was invented, they'll tell you England. After all, "football" to most people globally is what we Americans call soccer. In truth, England **IS** the birthplace of football, although Central America, China, Scotland, Greece, and Rome all have claimed to be the inventors of the game.

In December 1863, The Football Association in London, led by Ebenezer Cobb Morley, formed rules and organized the sport that eventually spread around the world. While people had been kicking a ball for hundreds of years before the 1800s, this would be the first time it had teams and rules and a field with goals with lines drawn. The organization also created an official soccer ball to be used for games.

At this point, you might be saying, "Stop! That's soccer, not football!" But the truth is that American football started with soccer and gradually evolved into our style of football based on rule adjustments from soccer and another sport, called rugby, that also started in England in 1823. If you are familiar with rugby, you know that the game is similar to American football, with tackling, kicking, and passing.

Football competitions in America first started at college universities, using pure "soccer style" rules, not at professional stadiums, which didn't even exist until the 1900s. On Nov. 6, 1869, Princeton and Rutgers got together to play what is widely recognized as the first ever football game in New Brunswick, New Jersey, using the same rules created by The Football Association and even using a soccer ball. The game included physicality like we see on the gridiron today, but players were not allowed to pass the ball using their hands, only their feet. The game would spread to other schools in the Northeast, with the exception of Harvard, who preferred their own style of football–a style that more closely resembled rugby.

Harvard played with their own rules and created what was known as "The Boston Game," a sport that was a hybrid of rugby and soccer. They used a more egg-shaped ball and players were allowed to use their hands and feet to pass it. In 1875, Harvard and Yale played the first organized football game using the new rugby style rules and the game caught on with spectators. In 1876, they added the crossbar to the goal posts that we see today. The Harvard-Yale football rivalry is claimed by some to be the greatest rivalry in sports and is simply referred to as "The Game."

When first introduced in the U.S., the field for football was 120 yards long and 75 yards wide, with 25 players on each side. When the goalposts were added in 1876, the field was shortened to today's dimensions of 125 x 53⅓ yards (same as today) and the number of players on the field was reduced to 15 on each side.

Harvard's new rules were well received, and other universities began using them. But over the next two decades, the game would undergo a massive change with the help of a Yale medical student who wanted to put his own American spin on it.

"THE FATHER OF AMERICAN FOOTBALL"

As more schools adopted Harvard's style of rugby and soccer, many individuals came up with ideas to change the game. One of those with high aspirations was Walter Camp, a Yale football player and medical student who graduated in 1881.

Camp loved football but wanted to make the game more exciting and implement more offense and defense, and less "scrumming." His goal was to expand the new sport; he proposed a series of new rules and guidelines to the Intercollegiate Football Association (IFA) to be used at college stadiums all across America.

Camp had become a member of the IFA as a freshman in 1877 and worked with the association for 15 years to create the new game. While he didn't propose to drastically change it from the traditional hybrid football rules that Harvard first started using, he made some critical changes that would forever change the game. By 1892, the IFA fully adopted Camp's football game and administered the rules to be used in all college football games across the nation. Camp would go on to become known as "The Father of American Football."

Camp left his medical studies to work for his family's clock business, but in 1888, he became the first head football coach at Yale, and worked for no pay. In his time as coach, the team won 67 games and lost only two. He went on to coach for Stanford in 1892, and again from 1894-95. He finished his career with a record of 79-5-3 and was inducted into the College Football Hall of Fame in 1951.

THE RULES

First and foremost, Camp did away with the opening "scrummage" that rugby uses, where players gather in the middle of the field and fight for the ball, almost like the game "Kill the Carrier" that kids play. Instead, he created the line of scrimmage where one team lines up across from the other and possesses the ball, trying to work the ball down the field. Teams were given three tries, known as "downs," to gain five yards, and if they failed to get those yards, they'd have to give the ball up to the other team.

Camp also invented the 11-man team and created many of the positions we are familiar with today. He helped create the quarterback, the halfback, and blockers known as lineman. Quarterbacks were in charge of calling signals and yelling the word "hike" to receive the ball from the snapper, known today as the center of the offensive line.

The quarterbacks of the past weren't like they are now, however. They simply were the captain of the offense, the one who took the snap and directed where the ball went. They did not throw it forward, only handed it off or pitched it to the player next to them.

The scoring system also changed. If a player crossed the line with the ball to score a touchdown, it was worth two points. If they were able to then kick it over the goal posts afterward, they would be given four points. A regular field goal was worth five points. These rules would be changed in 1909 when a touchdown would be worth the six points we have today, and with the point after worth one point and the field goal three points.

COLLEGE FOOTBALL VS. PRO FOOTBALL

If you ever saw *Leatherheads,* a comedy starring George Clooney and John Krasinski, you may have laughed at the movie's depiction of college football in the early 1900s, because it portrays it as much bigger than professional football. At the beginning of the movie, we see a packed stadium of fans watching Princeton University play a game while a professional game is being played with just a handful of fans on an open field, and one of those fans is a cow!

While the movie is only "loosely" based on a true story and exaggerates public empathy for professional football, it is accurate in portraying college football as dominant and preferred over professional football for a long time. It was also accurate in showing that professional football was a complete failure at first and struggled to stay alive.

As college football gained popularity, however, people looked for a way to take the game to the next level and form a professional league, where players could get paid for their talent. After Camp changed the rules, which had fully taken effect by 1892, the first professional club was born, when Yale player and graduate Puff Heffelfinger became the first professional football player. He would play for the Allegheny Athletic Association and be paid a salary of $500.

More clubs would slowly form, and the first organized professional game took place in 1895 between the Latrobe Athletic Association and Jeannette Athletic Club. Most clubs had rosters that changed weekly. Players came and went. Guys went from working in oil refineries and factories to playing a few weeks of professional football to make a quick $50 and would then return to work after the club went bankrupt. It was ever-changing.

Simply put, professional football was very unorganized in the late 1800s and early 1900s, and as a whole, was failing. Crowds were small, players had other blue-collar jobs, and teams would fold because they were losing money. The best players and coaches were found at the college level, not the professional level. So fans went to college games because that was where the real excitement was. The talent level of the professionals was amateur compared to the college players.

Baseball even got involved in the early 1900s and tried to form football teams, but that failed. The clubs then migrated from playing in Pittsburgh to playing in the Midwest. They looked for a universal location that would appease clubs and settled on Ohio.

The move to Ohio was met with some success, and financial backers became interested in putting money into the league. Crowds slowly grew. In 1919, Canton Bulldogs owner Ralph Hay saw an opportunity to form actual teams and move professional football forward. He organized a meeting, with Canton, Ohio as the center of professional football. (Today, Canton is the site of the Pro Football Hall of Fame). The real purpose behind Hay's meeting was to sell his automobile dealership, but he would end up selling a lot more than that.

Ten franchises, the first-ever franchises of a real professional football league, met to discuss opening an organized league. Those franchises were the Racine Cardinals, the Cleveland Tigers, the Dayton Triangles, the Hammond Pros, the Muncie Flyers, the Rock Island Independents, the Rochester Jeffersons, the Akron Pros, the Decatur Staleys, and Hay's team, the Canton Bulldogs.

These teams probably sound unfamiliar because only two of them survived over time. Racine would soon make its way to Chicago, St. Louis, and then Phoenix to become what is today the Arizona Cardinals. Decatur would also move to Chicago and today are known as the Chicago Bears.

Looking for a way to keep professional football alive, these men created their own league. They formed the American Professional Football Conference; soon, other representatives from other cities joined in, 11 teams in four states were formed, and the association was named to the American Professional Football Association (APFA). There were 14 total teams–the Buffalo All-Americans, Chicago Tigers, Columbus Panhandles, and Detroit Heralds were added to the 10 named above.

But professional football also needed stars to help their game… and they got it. First, Jim Thorpe, a famous Olympian and star baseball player, joined the Canton Bulldogs and fans began buying tickets to watch him play. Then in 1920, George Halas purchased the Decatur Staleys, which were on the verge of folding. Halas bought the team, moved it to Chicago, and changed the name to the Chicago Staleys, and then shortly after that, the Chicago Bears.

Halas would play a key role in keeping professional football alive. He helped teams that were on the verge of folding to stay in business. More teams were formed, including the New York Giants and the Green Bay Packers, founded by player-coach Curly Lambeau. In 1922, the name of the APFA was changed to the National Football League (NFL). The Green Bay Packers, however, were ousted from the NFL that same year because they illegally used college players. Luckily, Curly Lambeau was able to have his team reinstated by paying the $50 fine.

Another instrumental team in keeping professional football alive was the Duluth Eskimos (in the movie *Leatherheads* they were called the Duluth Bulldogs). Duluth helped sell the game across the country, becoming the first team to wear a logo on their uniform.

"If it wasn't for the Duluth Eskimos, the NFL wouldn't be around today," Chuck Frederick said, the author of the book *Leatherheads of the North*. "The NFL would have gone bankrupt like so many other upstart leagues. There was too much competition."

The Eskimos recruited star graduates from college to help sell their sport, one of whom was Ernie Nevers. Nevers was a fullback who helped attract crowds that professional football had never seen before. Duluth showcased him to other towns in 1926 and 1927 before he transferred to play for Chicago.

Another star college player, Harold "Red" Grange from Illinois also decided to give professional football a try and helped popularize the sport with his stardom. Grange played for the Bears and attracted more than 39,000 fans in Chicago, 35,000 in Philadelphia and 70,000 at the Polo Grounds in New York. Prior to Nevers and Grange coming along, professional football was only averaging about 500-1,000 spectators per game. These two men played a huge role in popularizing the sport. Slowly, the NFL was gaining traction.

Returning to the movie *Leatherheads*, John Krasinski's character Carter Rutherford's story is based on a combination of Grange's and Nevers' story. Grange became professional football's first rich player, and when college players saw the success he had, they realized for the first time that a player could make a living simply playing football and doing advertisements.

THE EVOLUTION OF THE NFL

The NFL continued to grow over time but teams would still form and fold. In 1932, when they instituted the NFL Championship, only 8 teams existed in the NFL–the Giants, Cardinals, Bears, Packers, Boston Braves, Portsmouth Spartans, Staten Island Stapletons, and Brooklyn Dodgers. The Braves would ultimately relocate to Washington and becoming the Redskins (today the Commanders). Portsmouth would move to Detroit and change their name to the Lions. The Dodgers and Stapletons would fold in the 1930s.

In 1933, the Philadelphia Eagles were formed, along with the Pittsburgh Pirates, which would eventually become the Steelers. In 1937, the Cleveland Rams were created, but they would soon relocate to Los Angeles and become the Los Angeles Rams.

By the start of World War II, there were 10 teams–the Dodgers, Giants, Eagles, Steelers, Redskins, Bears, Cardinals, Rams, Lions, and Packers. In 1936, the NFL introduced the Draft, where pro teams would select college players to join their teams.

In 1946, however, shortly after World War II, a new professional football league was formed, called the All-America Football Conference (AAFC). The purpose of the new league was to challenge the NFL. They attracted their own crop of talent and formed eight teams–including the San Francisco 49ers and the Cleveland Browns.

Eventually the two leagues would merge, but would have separate conferences and championships. The Eastern Division was renamed The American Football Conference while the western division was named The National Football Conference. Three years later, they became simply the Eastern and Western Conferences. The Baltimore Colts also joined. The American Conference was comprised of the Cardinals, Browns, Giants, Eagles, Steelers, and Redskins, while the

National Conference included the Bears, Yanks (folded in 1951), Lions, Packers, 49ers, and Colts.

Things were going well until 1959, when a group of businessmen who called themselves "The Foolish Club" decided to form their own league. The Club was frustrated with the NFL's efforts to block them from buying a team, so they formed their own league–The American Football League (AFL). The league consisted of eight teams: the Boston Patriots (now the New England Patriots), the Buffalo Bills, the Houston Oilers, the Dallas Texans (soon to become the Kansas City Chiefs), the Denver Broncos, the Los Angeles Chargers, the New York Titans (who would later become the Jets), and the Oakland Raiders. Meanwhile, the NFL, still split into two conferences, added two new expansion teams, the Dallas Cowboys and Minnesota Vikings.

The last major changes to the league came at the end of the 1960s. Beginning in 1966, the AFL and NFL decided to create a championship game between the two leagues, which would eventually be called The Super Bowl. The Chiefs and Packers played in the first ever AFL vs. NFL Championship Game. The NFL, which was superior to the AFL and was recognized to have the better players, easily won the first two championships.

The two leagues hated each other; the NFL felt that the AFL was interfering in their league while the AFL was fed up with the business of the NFL and also resented the cockiness of the NFL, who thought they were the better league with the better teams. But in 1969, the AFL's New York Jets shocked the world by beating the Baltimore Colts in the Super Bowl. The Jets, a 17-point underdog, won 16-7 behind quarterback Joe Namath. And the following year, the AFL's Chiefs upset the NFL's Vikings, 23-7.

After these AFL wins, the two leagues decided to merge, and this is today's NFL. Two conferences were formed, along with three divisions in each conference. More teams would expand, including the Tampa Bay Buccaneers and Seattle Seahawks in 1976, the Jacksonville Jaguars and Carolina Panthers in 1995, and the Houston Texans in 2002.

MODERNIZING THE GAME

Obviously, the game today is nothing like it was in the 1800s and early 1900s. Many rule changes have transpired, with the biggest one being the forward pass.

When Walter Camp invented American football in 1880, the ball could only be moved by running it down the field. But for 14 years, the sport struggled to gain traction with just a running game. There was very little scoring and interest was waning.

The sport was also quite dangerous. Players didn't have facemasks, they wore little padding, and the game was very physical; there was a lot of rough-housing, eye-gouging, and kicking. Players ended up bloodied, hospitalized, and yes, even dead. In 1905, President Theodore Roosevelt demanded that Camp and the IFA make changes to the rules and equipment or else the game would be outlawed. One of the rule changes that proponents of a more open game pushed for was the forward pass.

In 1906, despite Camp's objection, a Rules Committee approved teams to move the ball by throwing it forward. One of the biggest proponents of the forward pass was John Heisman (for whom the Heisman Trophy is named). Teams could throw the ball down the field, but it had to be five yards past the line of scrimmage on both sides and could only be thrown to two players lined up on the end. As time passed, this rule would evolve. Within a couple of years, teams were allowed to throw it no more than 20 yards down the field.

Some teams struggled with the forward pass while others embraced it. But passing was different than the type we see today. Quarterbacks threw jump passes, underhand passes, or end-over-end passes.

Glenn "Pop" Warner used a unique style of offense that brought pass and run options into play. In 1907, he coached Carlisle Indian Industrial School and invented a system that allowed his far inferior players to compete against stronger college rosters. He developed the "Carlisle Formation," a type of offense that included wings on both sides of the line and gave players the option to pass, run, or kick the ball—basically a style of the wing option. Warner recruited Jim Thorpe to play on his team and help sell his style of offense, which other teams would buy into. In a game against the University of Pennsylvania, 20,000 fans showed up to watch Thorpe and Pop Warner's new style of offense pull off a massive upset. However, Princeton knew a way to limit the passing game—pass interference.

Princeton played Carlisle and pushed around wide receivers, grabbing them and knocking them over whenever the ball was in the air. At that time, there were no penalties against that and the NFL saw no reason to introduce them. Also, an incomplete pass was considered a fumble. The game was designed to be more of a ground and pound game, not an aerial attack like Warner wanted. The NFL realized they needed to continue to adapt the rules on passing.

In 1910, the following rule was put in place, which disallowed players from interfering with another from catching the ball:

"No player of either side while in the act of catching a forward pass shall be tackled, thrown, pushed or pulled, shouldered, or straight-armed until he shall have caught the ball and taken one or more step in any direction, provided that any such interference which is incidental to a bonafide attempt to catch or intercept the pass shall not come within this prohibition. Note: If a forward pass is merely touched or fumbled by a player, no player of either side may even interfere with an opponent until the ball is actually in the possession of the player except in a bonafide attempt to get at the ball." (Source: Pass Interference: The History of Rules on Pass Interference).

The rule was tweaked over the years as teams found loopholes around it. In 1928, the NCAA (National Collegiate Athletic Association) imposed a 15-yard penalty for such a foul and added the language that interferences are also for passes thrown beyond the line of scrimmage. Then in 1953, they made it an automatic first down. The NFL would follow the NCAA in both instances, but the NFL added a spot foul for defensive pass interference, meaning wherever the illegal contact occurred, that's where the offense would get the ball.

But the passing game was still only a small piece of the game. Teams used the run more than they did the passing attack to move the football. There were a few reasons for this. First, referees still allowed a lot of contact between the defender and receiver while the receiver was in route, though this changed in the 1970s. Defenders were still "mauling" the wide receiver as they went down the field. In 1974 and 1977, the NFL attempted to come down harder on their restrictions, giving the wide receiver the ability to catch the ball with less contact. Rule changes prevented defenders from contacting a wide receiver at any point during their route when the ball was in the air and heading in their direction.

Another reason teams focused more on the running game was that they didn't have dominant throwers and catchers. Outside of Sammy Baugh in the 1940s, teams preferred to run the ball because they didn't have a quarterback who could move the football consistently. Things started to change not just with the rule changes, but as teams developed better throwers. Joe Namath, a product of the University of Alabama, helped elevate the passing game in the NFL and helped lead the New York Jets to a Super Bowl Championship in 1969 through the use of an air attack, the first real NFL team to win a championship by throwing the ball more than running. In the late 1970s, Fran Tarkenton changed the game even more, becoming the first true dual threat quarterback—a great passer and runner of the ball. Tarkenton ran for more than 3,000 yards and threw for over 47,000, and more teams modeled their offense after him. More dual threat players came along, such as Randall Cunningham, Warren Moon, and John Elway. Today, more than half of the NFL starting quarterbacks are dual threat players and almost all teams in the NCAA have quarterbacks who can both throw and run the ball.

In 1996, the NFL implemented the illegal contact penalty, disallowing contact by a defender on a wide receiver after five yards. Even if a pass wasn't being thrown to the wide receiver, a defender couldn't interfere with a wide receiver's route or contact them down the field. They also increased holding calls on defensive backs, preventing a defender from grabbing the jersey of a receiver.

Additionally, the NFL revised a rule to allow a wide receiver who was forced out of bounds to come back in and make a play. The NCAA followed the NFL's rule changes in their game. Both the NFL and NCAA game have also brought in targeting rules and hits on defenseless receivers. These rules penalize any defender for leaning in with their head to hit an offensive player. Also, in an attempt to limit injuries on quarterbacks, defenders were penalized for any hit on a quarterback below the knees or above the shoulders, and late hits on the quarterback were more strictly enforced.

The implementation of all these rules changed the passing game forever. Offenses began throwing the ball more and scoring through the air increased. Teams started drafting quarterbacks and wide receivers more in the first round and relied less on running backs. In 1932, Jack McBride of the New York Giants led the NFL with 8 pass attempts per game. In 1960, Johnny Unitas led the league with 30 passing attempts per game. In 2022, Tom Brady had 45 passing attempts per game.

Up until 2008, Dan Marino was the only quarterback to throw for more than 5,000 yards in a season. Since then, that achievement has been reached an incredible 14 times. In fact, 10 of the top 11 career leaders in total passing yards played in the 2000s, with 8th ranked Marino being the exception, since he played his final game in 1999.

Marino's 420 touchdown passes were an all-time record before he retired just after the 1999 season. Since then, six players have topped that mark, with Tom Brady's 648 passes holding the all-time record.

In other words, football is now an aerial game. It's come a long way over the last 100 years, from when teams never even considered attempting a pass. Now, there are even teams that will play an entire game running the ball only a handful of times.

2

HOW THE GAME IS PLAYED

A standard football game is 60 minutes and is played by two opposing teams. Pop warner (named after Coach Pop Warner) games, or youth football, and high school games are both shorter). There are four quarters in college and professional football; each quarter is 15 minutes long with stoppages for incomplete passes, timeouts, and changes of possession. In college football, the clock is stopped temporarily for a first down so the officials can move the chains.

Each team is given three timeouts per half. Timeouts are mostly used late in the half or in the fourth quarter to stop the clock. A defense may use them to try and get the ball back quicker while the offense will want to use them to stop the clock and give themselves more time to try and score points.

The game begins with a coin toss, with the winner of the toss choosing whether to receive the opening kickoff or defer to receive the ball first in the second half. The two teams each send a player, usually the captain, (or players) to call the toss by the referee.

The game then officially opens with a kickoff. The receiving team has a returner who catches the kickoff and advances the ball as far as they can before their offense takes the field. The team that has the ball is given four downs to get 10 yards, at which point they will receive a new set of downs.

Teams can advance the ball using two methods—running it or passing it. A team can elect to punt on fourth down to hand over possession and avoid giving up the ball in favorable territory to the opposing team. They can also elect to kick a field goal or to risk keeping the offense on the field on fourth down to try to get a new set of downs.

The fields are marked and painted with out of bounds, yard lines and hash marks. A solid white line across the field is painted every five yards. Within those five yards are small white dashes or lines, called hash marks, to indicate the yard line inside those five yard lines.

SCORING

The ultimate goal for every team is to score a touchdown, which is worth six points. A touchdown is when you cross the other team's end zone with the football, either by running it or throwing it and having it caught. After a team scores, they may elect to kick for one extra point or attempt a two-point conversion from inside the five-yard line.

A team may also elect to make field goals during the game, which account for three points. These are usually kicked on fourth down, although a team can realistically kick the ball at any point during a game. Many times at the end of a game, a team will kick a field goal to tie or win it on any down. After each field goal or touchdown, the scoring team kicks off to the other team.

Teams can also receive two points for a safety, which is awarded to the defense when the team with possession of the ball is tackled in their own end zone by the defense. The defense can also score two points if the offense turns the ball over in their own end zone and it goes out of bounds. When a safety occurs, the team that scored the two points then receives the ball.

PENALTIES

Much like in most other sports, the game is run by referees. College and professional football use 7 referees who oversee different parts of the game play. Each referee carries a flag in their pocket and throws it when they see a penalty.

There are many things you can be penalized for as a player, including holding an opposing player, which is when you grab them by the jersey to keep them from advancing past you. Another popular penalty is a face mask, which is when one player grabs and twists the other player's helmet/mask. Then there are offsides, which is when the defense crosses past the line of scrimmage before the ball is snapped. When the offense does this, it's called a false start, and happens when an offensive player jumps or moves before the ball is snapped.

Penalties cost yards. If your team has first and 10 and makes a 20-yard pass but has a player who receives a penalty for holding at the line of scrimmage, the offense is pushed back to first and 20. A team can decline a penalty on their opponent if declining it gives them an advantage on the field. In most cases, accepting a penalty on the opponent means re-playing the down. Penalties on the defense like pass interference or holding automatically give the offense a first down.

THE POSITIONS

Each team is led by a **head coach** and usually includes position coaches. The head coach is in charge of managing the game and making the critical decisions that evolve throughout the course of the 60-minute contest. Many times the head coach will not call the plays, but instead defer that to the offensive and defensive coordinators.

A good head coach must make good decisions throughout the course of a game. They need to have a team philosophy that aligns with the make-up of their team. Some head coaches are aggressive and like to throw the ball a lot, like the Chiefs' Andy Reid, while others prefer to run it more and play more defensive, like Georgia's Kirby Smart.

Head coaches motivate their players and are true leaders who everyone respects, including the other coaches. They are able to pull the maximum potential out of their players.

Quarterback

Many call the quarterback position the most important one in football, and the toughest. The position has produced some of the greatest athletes in the game's history, including Tom Brady, Joe Montana, John Elway, Dan Marino, and Peyton Manning.

Ironically, the name came from being in a running back position between two fullbacks or halfbacks. Remember, when American football was first invented, a quarterback was a runner, not a passer. It wasn't until many years after its invention that the quarterback was in charge of throwing the football.

The quarterback is the captain of the huddle and calls the plays, usually relayed to him by the coach. He then calls out verbal signals at the line of scrimmage and receives the snap from the center. A quarterback can also call an audible at the line of scrimmage; this is when he decides to change the play because he sees an area of the defense they can exploit.

He will either call out a verbal signal or use a hand signal to his teammates. The quarterback and the center are the only two positions on a football team that touch the ball on every play.

Quarterbacks can do three things with the football once they receive it —run it, hand it off to another player, or throw it to a receiver. In the early 1900s, their main function was to run it or pitch it to the halfback. As the years have passed, the quarterback has taken on a greater importance because teams are throwing the ball forward so much more than they used to. Today, NFL teams are desperate for a great quarterback because of their ability to help a team score points.

The quarterback position requires the most homework and arguably has the most pressure. They must not only study and memorize the playbook, they must watch a lot of film and know the opposing defense. They must be able to read a defense and make the appropriate throws, as well as call an audible when it's warranted (a head coach can also do this).

Many times, being a great quarterback requires just as many mental skills as it does physical, like having confidence, poise, determination, and patience. They must also be smart because they have to learn a lot of information. A quarterback must also be a good leader, gain his team's trust and motivate his offense to score points.

This position has also been referred to as the signal caller, field general, gunslinger, or just simply the qb. Most teams like tall quarterbacks because of their ability to see over the offensive line and keep the ball from being blocked, but recently, smaller quarterbacks have succeeded because of their ability to run the football.

From a physical standpoint, coaches like quarterbacks who possess great arm strength and are able to throw the ball deep down the field. While mobility isn't a necessity, having one who can throw and run like Lamar Jackson or Kyler Murray makes it more difficult for a defense because of the uncertainty of what the quarterback might do. A great quarterback must also be incredibly accurate with the ball, and be able to throw it in between defenders.

Running Back

Most of us call this position a running back, but it can also be referred to as a halfback, tailback, fullback, or a wing back, depending on the offensive formation. Tailbacks are two runners on the field lined up between the quarterback, forming a T. Most teams today use an I-formation or spread offense with just one running back on the field.

A running back takes the handoff or pitch from the quarterback and looks for a hole in front of them to run as many yards for the offense as they can. They rely on blockers, chiefly the fullback, who usually lines up between the quarterback and running back. Many players love the position because of the ability to run away from the defense and score. Some of the best running backs in the game today include Derrick Henry, Christian McCaffrey, and Saquan Barkley.

The fullback often blocks for the running back. They can also run the ball if a team only needs to gain a couple yards. Fullbacks are usually bigger backs and more difficult to tackle.

To be a good running back, you must have great vision and awareness. You aren't only looking in front of you, you are looking for openings in the defense on your right and left. A good runner must also be able to make good cut backs and have skillful juke moves (fake-outs used to evade a tackle by means of deception) to try and confuse and race past the defender.

Speed is crucial; after all, you have to try and hit the hole fast and race past the defender to get first downs and touchdowns. A good running back must also have both a strong upper body and lower body because they have to take a lot of defensive hits. The best running backs get hit but keep moving forward.

Today, because of the evolution of the passing game, running backs are also required to be good blockers and pass catchers. They must block for the quarterback, so he doesn't get sacked. They are also asked to run routes like a wide receiver and catch the ball in order to gain yards.

Wide Receiver

If you love to catch the ball, this position is for you. The wide receiver's primary job is to catch the football when it's thrown by the quarterback. Some of the greatest pass catchers we've seen over the years include Jerry Rice and Calvin Johnson, and more recently Tyreek Hill, Justin Jefferson, and Cooper Kupp.

To be a good wide receiver, you must have good hands. You have to make some difficult catches throughout the course of the game to help your team advance the ball. But catching isn't the only job a wide receiver has; they also go down field and help block for the running back. They must run good routes to get open and help the quarterback. They must also possess decent speed so they can outrun the defender.

Good wide receivers are also strong; they can catch the ball and take a hit without losing the ball. They tend to be high jumpers, leaping into the air and going over the defender to catch a football.

Offensive Lineman

The last major position on offense is an offensive lineman. These are traditionally players with big bodies who block for the quarterback and the runner. Their primary goal is to prevent the other team from getting to the person with the football.

The center is in the middle of the offensive line and snaps the football to the quarterback. This is a difficult position because as soon as they snap it, they must block the rusher. Obviously, the center must be aware of when to snap the ball.

On either side of the center are two guards. The three of them help prevent rushes from up the middle and create holes up the gut (through the middle) for the runner. On the ends of the offensive line are the tackles. They must prevent defensive end rushers and linebackers from getting to the quarterback. They also help the guards and tight ends create holes.

A tight end is also a part of the offensive line. Sometimes tight ends will stay in and help the offensive linemen block; other times they become a wide receiver and go out to catch a pass. Tight ends are tall and physical, like Travis Kelce and Rob Gronkowski.

Defensive Lineman

A defensive line consists of three or four players, depending on the team's scheme. Some coaches like to run a 3-4 defense, which includes three defensive lineman and four linebackers. One linebacker in that scheme is a rusher.

Defensive linemen are responsible for trying to tackle the person with the football. They line up opposite of the offensive lineman. On a passing play, they are trying to get past the offensive lineman and tackle the quarterback. On a running play, they are doing everything they can to avoid a block and to tackle the runner.

Defensive lineman can frustrate a quarterback. Their goal is to give the passer as little time as possible to throw the ball, even tackle them while they're holding the ball. A good defensive line is able to get to the quarterback quickly and stop the runner from advancing past the line of scrimmage.

Linebacker

Some may say that linebackers have the biggest responsibility on defense. They are run-stoppers and pass-defenders, lining up three to five yards behind the defensive line. If a running back breaks through the first wave, linebackers almost act like goalkeepers in soccer, trying to prevent the offense from getting past them and scoring. (Safeties are also the final lines of defense.)

Linebackers are similar to quarterbacks in that they call the plays and make the audibles for the defense. They are the captains on that side of the ball. Linebackers must be physical and athletic and have to be powerful tacklers. When a blitz is called, it's usually the linebacker who is responsible for rushing past the offensive line to try and sack the quarterback.

Lawrence Taylor, Ray Lewis, Von Miller, Micah Parsons, and Mike Singletary are among the greatest past and present linebackers in the game. Linebackers are hard hitters. If you get hit by one, have the ice handy later on.

Defensive Back

There are two types of defensive backs—cornerbacks and safeties. Cornerbacks line up opposite the wide receivers while safeties protect the deep pass and line up approximately five yards behind the linebackers in the middle back.

Communication with defensive backs is imperative. As wide receivers move down the field, they must know who to cover and what territory to occupy. Defensive backs' main goal is not only to defend against a completion, but to intercept the football and change possession. Defensive backs also must defend against the run and tackle the opposing ball carrier.

Playing defensive back has become more difficult in recent years because of rule changes. They cannot make contact with wide receivers before a pass is thrown. This is known as illegal contact. If they make contact with the receiver while the ball is in the air before it reaches the hands of the receiver, it's pass interference, and results in a penalty.

Another new rule that has affected defensive backs, linebackers, and defensive lineman are targeting penalties and personal fouls. Defenders may only tackle an opposing player between their knees and their shoulders (quarterbacks are not allowed to be tackled in the backfield below the knees). If they hit or tackle a player with their head and make contact with the opposing player's helmet first, they are given a 15-yard personal foul penalty. Sometimes, this can even result in being disqualified from a game.

Special Teams

Special teams players are those on the field for kickoffs, field goals, and punts. They include place kickers, holders, punters, lineman, returners, punt protectors, gunners, jammers, and snappers.

The most noteworthy positions are the place kicker and the punter. The place kicker has two major duties; they kick off the ball to the opposing team and they attempt field goals or extra points. It's a critical position because field goals and extra points can win or lose a game. They also rely on a good snap and catch and placement from the holder. The holder is responsible for keeping the laces out (so the kicker can kick the smooth part of the ball) and setting up the ball quickly for the kicker on a field goal attempt. On windy days, they can also hold the ball for the kicker on the kickoff.

Justin Tucker of the Baltimore Ravens is considered one of the greatest kickers in modern history. He holds the record for the longest field goal, a 66-yarder against the Detroit Lions to win the game in 2021.

A punter comes onto the field on fourth downs to kick the ball to the opposing team. The punter's primary goal is to kick the ball as deep as they possibly can but to keep it from going in the end zone. If they do kick it into the end zone, it is a touchback, meaning the ball will then be placed on the 20 or 25-yard line. A good punter places the ball well and aims for a decent landing spot inside the 20 yard line. This affects field position and helps the defense coming out onto the field.

3

THE GREATEST OF ALL TIME

What constitutes the greatest? Most touchdowns? Most yards? Most sacks? It's really a combination of things, and is an all-around achievement. When choosing the greatest, we can't look only at statistics. We need to consider leadership, championships, respect, and how they contributed to the game.

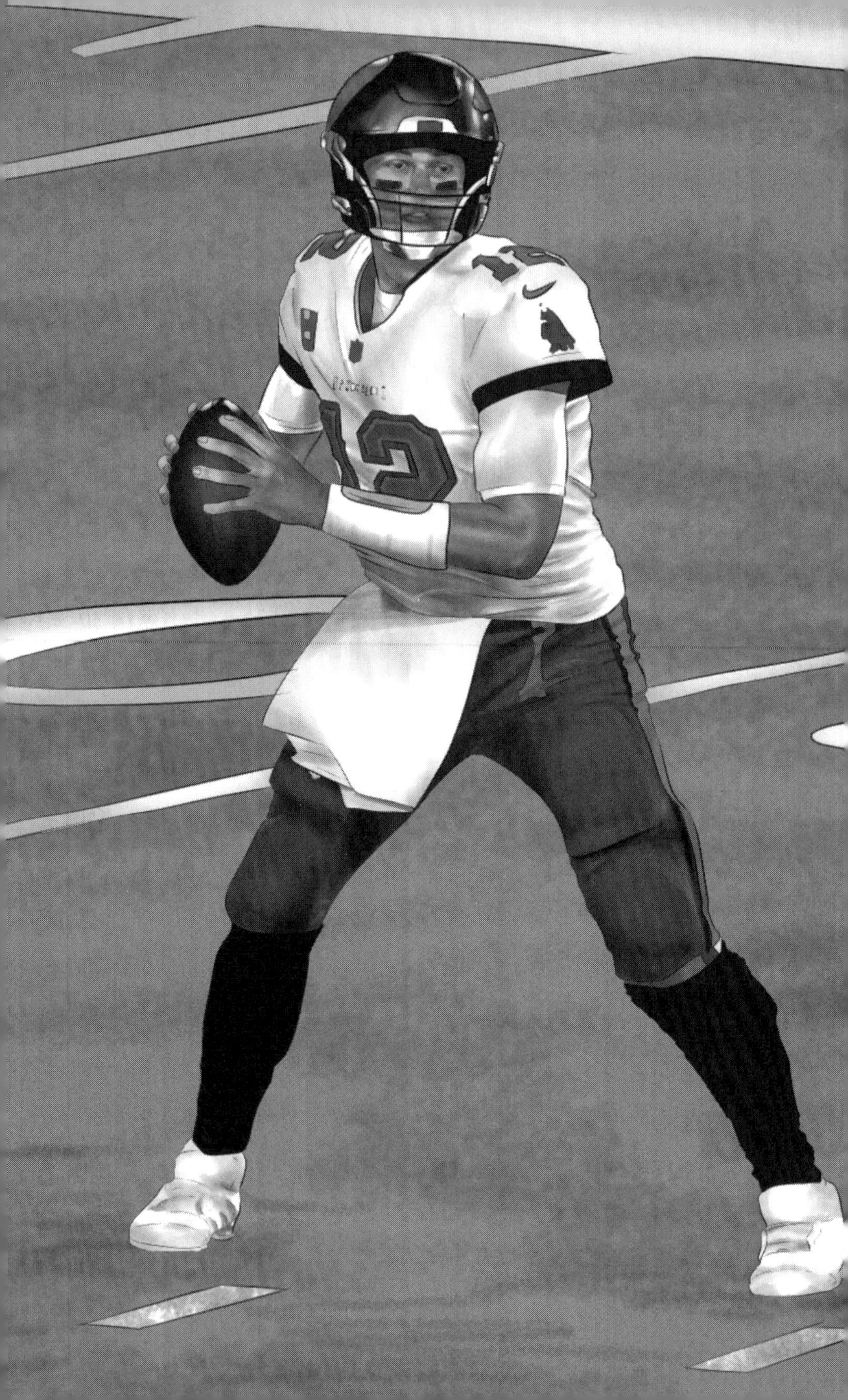
12

QUARTERBACK: TOM BRADY

- Seven Super Bowl rings (#1 all-time)
- 10 Super Bowl appearances (#1 all-time)
- 87,751 yards (#1 All-Time)
- 638 touchdown passes (#1 all-time)
- 7,754 completions (#1 all-time)
- 243 wins (#1 all-time)
- Five Super Bowl MVPs (#1 all-time)
- 15 Pro Bowls (#1 all-time)
- 624 Touchdown passes (#1 all-time)
- 39 Games with four TD passes (#1 all-time)

Biography

Full name: Thomas Edward Patrick Brady, Jr.

Nicknames: "The GOAT," "TB12," "Tom Terrific," "California Cool"

Uniform: #12

Teams played for: New England Patriots and Tampa Bay Buccaneers

Years Pro: 21 years (Retired 2023)

College: Michigan

Height/Weight: 6'4, 225 lbs.

Born: Aug. 3, 1977

Hometown: San Mateo, CA

Best quote: "Don't rely on others. You'll have great support from a lot of people, still. But, no one's going to hand you anything."

There's a reason people call Tom Brady the GOAT (Greatest Of All Time). And we're not just talking about the greatest quarterback…we're talking about Brady being among the greatest sports athletes that ever lived. What he's accomplished over the course of his career is nothing short of incredible.

But Brady's story didn't start out so promising in the football arena. As a boy, he loved football but was told by his family and friends that he'd have a better chance to make it as a professional athlete in baseball. In fact, the Montreal Expos (now the Washington Nationals) drafted Brady in the 18th round of the 1995 Major League Baseball Draft while he was still in high school. But Brady turned them down because he was convinced he would make it as a football player.

Growing up in Northern California, Brady loved the San Francisco 49ers and always envisioned himself as Joe Montana. No matter what people told him, he was convinced he would become an NFL player. That dream seemed to fade when he was demoted to backup quarterback during his first two seasons in high school. People around him scoffed at his chances of ever playing college football.

Brady started working harder than ever, convinced he could make his dream come true. He worked his way to the starting role in high school and was offered a scholarship by the University of Michigan. But things did not go so smoothly for him there either.

Brady found himself in danger of losing his scholarship and being forced off the Michigan Wolverines football team. At one point, **he was the eighth-string quarterback** on their roster. Eighth string! He had to work harder than ever before, and he did, moving up the depth chart week by week, impressing coaches with his arm. He finally started his junior season but then had to split time with Drew Henson as starter during his final year.

He wasn't sought after very seriously by any NFL teams. Most quarterbacks entering the draft receive dozens of calls from interested coaches and teams; Brady received one. In fact, the Patriots didn't select him until the sixth round of the 2000 NFL Draft, 199th overall. He was selected after quarterbacks Chad Pennington, Giovanni Carmazzi, Chris Redman, Tee Martin, Marc Bulger, and Spergon Wynn. Of that group, only Pennington and Bulger made anything out of their careers.

Brady has 35 playoff wins. That group of six quarterbacks taken ahead of him has three between them.

Nobody, and I mean nobody, gave Tom Brady any chance of being a successful NFL starting quarterback. Brady was expected to be a career backup or 3rd string player when he entered the NFL. In fact, he spent his 2000 rookie season as No. 4 on the quarterback depth chart. He worked mostly with the practice squad and was in danger of never making it as an NFL quarterback.

Things changed in 2001 when Brady had an impressive training camp and preseason and vaulted up to No. 2 on the Patriots depth chart. Still, with Drew Bledsoe solidly planted as the team's No. 1 quarterback, Brady had no chance of overtaking him as the team's starting quarterback. That was until Week 2 of the 2001 season, when Bledsoe left a game against the Jets after linebacker Mo Lewis leveled him, knocking him out of the game in the fourth quarter.

Brady came in trailing 10-3 and went 5-for-10 for 46 yards. It wasn't a great stat line, but with Bledsoe hurting and unable to play in Week 3, Bill Belichick turned to Tom Brady to lead the team Week 3 against the Colts. Brady would never see the bench again. The 0-2 Patriots led by Brady beat the Colts 44-13. Brady helped the Patriots win 11 of their final 14 games that season. He went seven straight games throwing a touchdown pass starting in Week 5, including a 4-touchdown performance against the Saints.

That postseason, Brady helped the Patriots beat the Oakland Raiders in a blizzard in Foxborough, Massachusetts, in what would be dubbed "The Tuck Rule Game," a reference to the overturning of a call from a fumble to an incomplete pass, which resulted in the Patriots getting the ball back. After that they beat the Steelers for the AFC Championship and went on to upset the St. Louis Rams 20-17 to win Super Bowl XXXVI. It was the first of Tom Brady's seven Super Bowl rings.

Brady played 18 seasons for the Patriots, winning six Super Bowl rings, but perhaps his best season was the one where he didn't win the Super

Bowl; he led the Patriots to a 17-0 perfect season in 2007 but lost to the New York Giants in Super Bowl XLII.

Brady is considered ageless. Very few quarterbacks have started in the NFL after the age of 40, but Brady is 45. In 2000, he signed with the Tampa Bay Buccaneers. Just when everyone thought he was over the hill, the 43-year old quarterback led the Bucs to an 11-win season. He then helped lead his team to a 31-9 win over the Chiefs in Super Bowl LV for his seventh Super Bowl ring. He threw three touchdowns in the game, two of those to his favorite target during his playing career, Rob Gronkowski. Brady would be named Super Bowl LV MVP.

Brady is considered one of the best leaders the game has ever seen. He's earned the utmost respect of his teammates.

"He's the greatest player to ever play the game," said Bucs wide receiver Mike Evans. "You add him on any roster, and I'm sure the outcome would be somewhat like this. He always gets his team to the playoffs. He's a winner. He's a natural-born winner, leader, all that. At this point in his career, he's just playing chess, and we're definitely very happy he's on our side."

Off the field, Tom Brady is just as big of an MVP. He founded the TB12 Organization, which helps low-income families and ailing individuals who can't afford health care. Brady's also helped those with disabilities, donating to Best Buddies International. He's raised more than $46.5 million for that charity since 2000. He is also an active participant in the Make-a-Wish Foundation, a charity that helps sick children. In addition to all this, he travels to Africa to help raise money for the impoverished in that nation.

Tom Brady and Michael Jordan have a lot in common. Not only are they among the greatest athletes in sports history, they are both great comeback stories. Michael Jordan became the greatest after being cut from his high school basketball team. Tom Brady became the greatest after being buried as the 8th string quarterback on the Michigan depth chart and 4th on the Patriots. At one point, no team wanted either of them.

Brady reminds us all to never give up hope and continue to work hard. If you do, good things will happen. Hard work always pays off in the end.

"I think sometimes in life the biggest challenges end up being the best things that happen in your life." - Tom Brady

Honorable Mention

Joe Montana

Joe Montana is often compared to Tom Brady. Like Brady, Montana was a winner and a champion. He achieved four Super Bowl rings, winning MVP three times. He was one of the first quarterbacks to run the West Coast Offense, and ran it to perfection. Today, teams use pieces of the West Coast Offense in their schemes, which is an offense that relies on short passes, slant patterns, and ball control. Montana ended his career with 273 touchdowns and 40,551 passing yards. He had maybe the greatest postseason ever in 1989, throwing 11 touchdowns, zero interceptions, and a postseason passer rating of 146.4 (only Josh Allen of the Buffalo Bills has topped that since).

Johnny Unitas

When we talk about guys who helped transcend the game—Unitas was it for the quarterback position. Other teams tried to model their quarterbacks after him. The game officially began its transition to a more passing style offense because of Johnny Unitas. He led the NFL in passing touchdowns four straight years from 1957 to 1960. He also threw a touchdown pass in 47 straight games, a record that held together until Drew Brees came along and topped that in 2012. But Unitas did it by throwing the ball 29 fewer times per game!

34

RUNNING BACK: WALTER PAYTON

- One Super Bowl ring
- 16,726 yards (#2 all-time)
- 275 rushing yards in one game (#5 all-time)
- 77 games with more than 100 yards rushing (#2 all-time)
- 110 rushing touchdowns (#5 all-time)
- Two-time NFC Offensive Player of the Year (#2 all-time for RB)
- Nine Pro Bowls (#2 all-time for RB)

Biography

Full name: Walter Jerry Payton

Nicknames: "Sweetness"

Uniform: #34

Teams played for: Chicago Bears

Years Pro: 13 years

College: Jackson State

Height/Weight: 5'10 200 lbs.

Born: July 25, 1954

Hometown: Columbia, MS

Best quote: "When you're good at something, you'll tell everyone. When you're great at something, they'll tell you."

Some may argue that Jim Brown, Barry Sanders, Emmit Smith, or Walter Payton could all hold the honor of greatest running back on the field. Even recent stars like Adrian Peterson and LaDainian Tomlinson could enter the conversation. It's a debate that could go on for days, and all would have compelling cases. But when we consider the overall impact a player had, not just on the field but off the field, Payton vaults to the top of the charts.

There's a reason why "The Walter Payton NFL Man of the Year Award" is named after Walter Payton. The award is given annually to the player who exhibits excellence both on and off the field, giving back to the community and helping others while also being the most respected athlete on the field. Nobody was as involved and helped others as much as Walter Payton did, and it goes back to when he was a boy.

Payton was an active participant in the community right from his childhood days. He participated in activities at his local church and was a local boy scout. In school, he played basketball, baseball, and ran track. He also regularly volunteered and helped out in his hometown of Columbia, Mississippi. However, he didn't start out playing football right away. One reason was because he wanted to focus on playing music and singing; being in the marching band conflicted with being on the football team. Another reason was because his brother, Eddie, was a star football player on the team and he didn't want to play against him in practice. He also feared the impact it would have on his mother if both of them got hurt.

Once Eddie graduated from high school, Walter signed on to play and was an immediate star. He would score a touchdown in every game and was almost impossible to catch. He had a unique running style, palming the ball when he ran, and had electric speed combined with power that made him the envy of every running back in the Midwest. He also had incredible juke moves which left defenders awestruck.

Payton believed in education first. As good an athlete as he was, he was equally as good a student, getting As and Bs in school and making the honor roll.

Payton faced a lot of trials early in his childhood. He grew up in racially divided Mississippi in the 1960s and he and his family battled segregation. Football helped him overcome that, though. Much like the movie *Remember the Titans*, his school was dealing with blacks and whites trying to integrate, which in the South was extremely difficult. However, Payton's play on the field helped bring the school together as blacks and whites bonded watching him rack up records at Columbia High School.

As talented as Payton was, though, he wasn't receiving offers from the universities he wanted to play for, mainly because of his color. He wanted to play in the SEC (Southeastern Conference), but didn't receive any offers from those schools, primarily because those schools were trying to avoid bringing in black athletes. Jerry Rice, also from Mississippi, faced similar challenges.

Payton would end up choosing Jackson State University, a Division II school. There, he produced more than 6,500 yards on the ground and averaged 6.1 yards per carry. His 65 touchdowns shattered the school record and he was recognized as one of the best running backs in college football. His numbers would normally equate to a Heisman Trophy Award, but because he went to a non-Division I school, he was ineligible. Still, he won multiple Player of the Year honors in college and was a first-team All-American.

Payton's smooth running style earned him the nickname "Sweetness," which would become his trademark for the rest of his playing career. He vaulted up draft charts and was projected to be a high first round pick in the 1975 NFL Draft. With the fourth overall pick, the Chicago Bears selected him.

Payton played a huge role in helping transform the image of the team. The Bears were "The Bad News Bears," a perennial NFL loser. They hadn't had a winning season in nearly 10 years and won just a total of 28 games between 1969 and 1975. That's an average of four wins per season.

The Bears stopped that trend with the arrival of Payton. They finished 7-7 in 1976 and 9-5 in 1977. In 1977, Payton won the Most Valuable Player Award, the youngest player in the history of the NFL to achieve such a feat. That season he had a game where he rushed for 275 yards against the Minnesota Vikings, at the time an NFL record (Adrian Peterson would break it). Payton averaged 5.5 yards per carry and rushed for 1,852 yards. The next closest rusher in the NFL that season had just 1,273 yards. Payton also led all rushers with 14 touchdowns.

Payton helped the Bears to their first division title and playoff appearance in nearly 15 years. They went 10-6 in 1979 and were clearly moving in the right direction. Despite some up and down years in the early 1980s, Payton and the Bears came together to produce one of the greatest teams in NFL history in 1985, going 15-1 and dominating teams in the postseason.

The '85 Bears were notorious for their defense, known by some to be the greatest of all time, but Payton helped balance the team out. They were gashing teams on offense with an unrelenting rushing attack led by Payton. He ran for 1,551 yards, third most in the NFL. He rushed for 96.9 yards per game and averaged 5.6 yards per carry. He was named 1985 NFC Offensive Player of the Year.

The Bears won their first round playoff game over the New York Giants 17-0, then shut out the Rams 24-0 in the NFC Championship. They continued their overwhelming dominance in the Super Bowl, beating the Patriots 46-10 for their first ever Lombardi Trophy.

Walter Payton retired in 1987 as the all-time NFL leading rusher. Only Emmitt Smith has come along to rush for more yards since. Payton was inducted into the NFL Hall of Fame in 1993 and the College Football Hall of Fame in 1996. Sadly, Payton suffered from a rare liver disease that took his life in November 1999, at the age of only 46. The Bears retired his jersey number 34.

In 1988, Payton and his wife started a charity called the Walter & Connie Payton Foundation, originally intended to help needy children in Chicago. The Foundation would soon spread beyond the Windy City. According to its website, its mission is to help "those less fortunate to find stability while providing positive opportunities needed to live their lives with dignity and pride."

Payton proved himself to be a class act on and off the field, and his overall impact on the game makes him one of the greatest players to have ever put on a uniform. He will always be remembered not just for his incredible talent on the field, but for his humanitarian work off of it.

Honorable Mention

Jim Brown

Jim Brown didn't have as long a career as some other backs, playing nine seasons and just 118 games, but he was one of the most dominant backs to ever play. Brown ran for over 12,000 yards and ran for 5.2 yards per carry. In 1963, Brown ran for 133 yards per game, ranking number two in history. He was inducted into the Hall of Fame in 1961.

Barry Sanders

Like Brown, Sanders didn't have a long NFL career, but he was the best running back by far in the 1990s. Sanders ran for more than 15,000 yards and achieved more than 5 yards per carry. He was most notorious for his ability to break the long run; he had 15 touchdown runs of more than 50 yards. Only Adrian Peterson topped that number with 16, but Peterson had 200 more rushes than Sanders. Sanders was also renowned for his class and sportsmanship, a true role model for other backs to follow who came during and after his time.

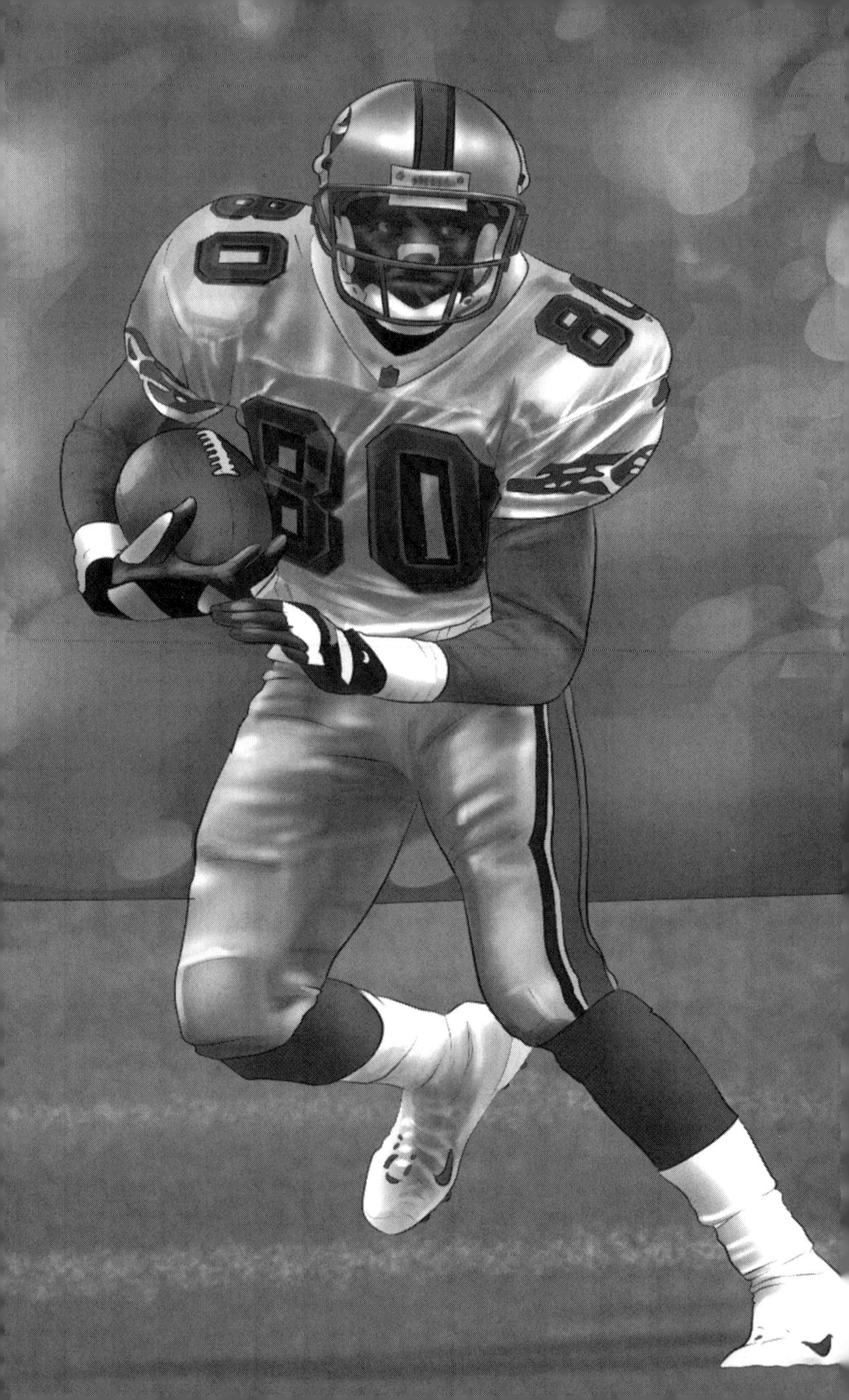

WIDE RECEIVER: JERRY RICE

- Three Super Bowl rings
- 1,549 receptions (#1 all-time)
- 22,895 receiving yards (#1 all-time)
- 76 100-yard receiving games (#1 all-time)
- 16 receptions in one game (#5 all-time)
- 13 Pro Bowls (#5 all-time)
- 1987 Most Valuable Player
- Super Bowl XXIII MVP

Biography

Full name: Jerry Lee Rice

Nicknames: "Flash 80," "Gentleman Jerry"

Uniform: #80

Teams played for: San Francisco 49ers (1985-2000), Oakland Raiders (2001-2003), Seattle Seahawks (2004)

Years Pro: 20 years

College: Mississippi Valley State

Height/Weight: 6'2, 200 lbs

Born: Oct. 13, 1962

Hometown: Starkville, MS

Best quote: "I will do today what others won't, so I can do tomorrow what others can't."

There is no debate on who the greatest wide receiver is. Jerry Rice dominated the position and helped lead the San Francisco 49ers to three Super Bowl championships between 1988 and 1994.

Jerry Rice's childhood wasn't easy. He grew up in a blue collar town in Crawford, Mississippi, helping his father lay bricks during the hot and humid summers so his family could make ends meet. He had seven brothers and sisters and used sports as a way to escape the stress of living in a difficult neighborhood.

Rice would admit that the hard work and difficult living was the best part about growing up because it taught him the meaning of perseverance. If everything had been easy, he may not have been as tough in football as he turned out to be. He worked harder than any other wide receiver in the game, and it helped him become a three-time champion, a Super Bowl MVP and Hall of Famer.

Rice grew up running back and forth on dirt roads and developed speed. Growing up, he thought track and field would be his primary sport. When he entered high school, he had no aspirations of playing football. His mother didn't want him to play and his dad needed him at home after school. So, Rice went his first year of high school never touching a football.

All that changed when he tried to sneak out of school one day. When the vice principal saw him and chased after him, he couldn't catch the speedy Rice. The vice principal was angry but amazed at the same time. He would finally catch and discipline him. It wasn't a detention or suspension; instead, he talked Rice up to the football coach and punished him by making him play football.

Rice's parents had no choice but to accept the vice principal's decision, and the rest is history. Rice went on to impress the football coaches so much that they made him a permanent player at B.L. Moor High School. Soon he would be starting, and before long, he was catching touchdown passes and helping his team win games.

Like Payton, Rice's aspirations were to play for the SEC, ideally at Mississippi State or Mississippi. However, very few blacks were recruited because of racial bias and fear of riots breaking out around and inside the football program. So, Rice, again like Payton, went to a Division II school in his home state, Mississippi Valley State.

Rice was fast, but not electric, and that lack of speed also played a role in him not getting more college offers. But he had the best hands of anyone in school. In his first season at Mississippi Valley State, he caught 66 passes for 1,133 yards and seven touchdowns. Those numbers would only improve during his junior and senior seasons.

In Rice's junior season, he caught a record 102 passes for 1,450 yards and 14 touchdowns. His final year, he helped his school to their best ever school record, 9-2. That year, Rice caught an incredible 103 passes for 1,682 yards and a record 27 touchdowns. In comparison, the highest ranked Division I receiver was David Williams, who'd caught 101 passes for 1,278 yards, and in the touchdowns category, the highest was Doug Allen's 14. No one was even close to Rice.

But again, like Walter Payton, because Rice went to a Division II school, he wasn't considered for the Heisman Trophy. While rules were lifted to allow a Division II player to be eligible for the award, he finished 9th. But he still was highly sought after in the NFL Draft.

With the 16th pick in the first round, the San Francisco 49ers traded up to select Rice. He was the third wide receiver selected, taken after Eddie Brown and Al Toon. The 49ers didn't need to go after a wide receiver; they were the Super Bowl champions and had Joe Montana at quarterback and Freddie Solomon at wide receiver. But they saw a superstar in Rice.

Rice started his career slowly with the Niners, catching just 28 passes through his first 13 games. But he broke out in a Monday night game against the Los Angeles Rams, where he exploded with 10 catches for a team record 241 yards and a touchdown. It was Rice's coming out. He caught 21 passes those last three games, nearly as many as he caught in the first 13. It set the tone for his incredible 1986 season.

Rice had a record-setting sophomore season, catching 86 passes for 1,570 yards and 15 touchdowns. He was accepted into his first Pro Bowl, finished sixth in the MVP race and third for Offensive Player of the Year. He led the league in total yards, touchdowns, and yards per game (98.1). The next season, he shattered his previous season touchdown total, racking up 22 scores and winning Offensive Player of the Year.

In 1988, Rice's best game came in the biggest moment, Super Bowl XXIII. He set a Super Bowl record for receptions and yards, catching 11 passes for 215 yards and a touchdown. He caught a critical pass from Joe Montana on the final drive that helped up the game-winning score under a minute and led the 49ers to a Super Bowl win. Rice would win Super Bowl XXIII MVP. He was the third-ever receiver to win Super Bowl MVP, and one of only seven today.

The 49ers would prove to be a dynasty during the late 80s and 90s, and Rice was a primary reason for that. He shined with Montana and Steve Young, helping lead the 49ers to another Super Bowl in 1989 and again in 1994. He would score touchdowns in both those Super Bowls.

Rice continued to rack up Pro Bowls and record-setting seasons. He led the league in total yards five times in seven seasons between 1989 and 1995. In 1995, Rice shattered the NFL record for most receiving yards in a season with 1,848 yards. The NFL's rule changes and transition to a more passing league has led to three other wide receivers breaking that record since, a record currently held by Calvin Johnson.

Rice signed with the Oakland Raiders towards the end of his career and helped lead them to a Super Bowl appearance against the Tampa Bay Buccaneers. In 2002, Rice led the Raiders with 1,211 yards and made his 13th Pro Bowl appearance, one shy of the overall record. The Raiders would lose the Super Bowl to the defensive dominant Buccaneers.

Rice finished his career with Seattle in 2004. When all was said and done, he finished with 1,549 catches for 22,895 yards, both all-time NFL records. He had 14 seasons with 1,000 or more yards, also an all-time NFL record.

In terms of position players, Rice is second only to Tom Brady for the most postseason appearances—29. His 22 postseason touchdowns are the most of any wide receiver or tight end by far (Rob Gronkowski has second place, with 15).

Rice currently works for ESPN as an analyst and gives back to the community on his own, starting the Jerry Rice 127 Foundation, which provides financial support to underprivileged children and their families in the San Francisco Bay Area. He has also teamed up with Steve Young to create the 8 to 80 Zones organization, which provides youth in underserved communities the skills and resources to pursue careers in technology.

While wide receivers will continue to produce league-shattering numbers because of changes made to benefit the passing game, Rice will always go down as forever changing the wide receiver position. He was as dominant a player at his position as there ever has been in the history of the league, and in our generation, we may never see another superstar like Jerry Rice.

Honorable Mention

Randy Moss

At 6'4, 210 pounds, there wasn't a more physical wide receiver in the game than Randy Moss. He was perhaps the most gifted athlete to ever come along in terms of hands, size, and speed. Moss concluded his career with 982 receptions for 15,292 yards and 156 touchdowns while playing mostly for the Minnesota Vikings and New England Patriots. His dominance in 2007 with Tom Brady helped lead the Patriots to their second-ever perfect regular season. The rule changes to aid the passing game put him further down the list in terms of records, but he is one of three players in history to rank in the top five in receiving yards, touchdowns, and 100-yard games (Rice and Terrell Owens are the other two).

Don Hutson

Passing wasn't a big part of the game in the 1940s, but when the ball did go in the air, you didn't want to cover Don Hutson. He dominated the wide receiver position. He is considered the NFL's first-ever elite wide receiver. Hutson finished his career with 7,991 yards and 99 receiving touchdowns; it was four decades in an era when passing became more prevalent before someone finally topped Hutson's touchdown total. When he retired, Hutson held 18 NFL records, including 488 receptions. He was inducted into the Hall of Fame in 1963.

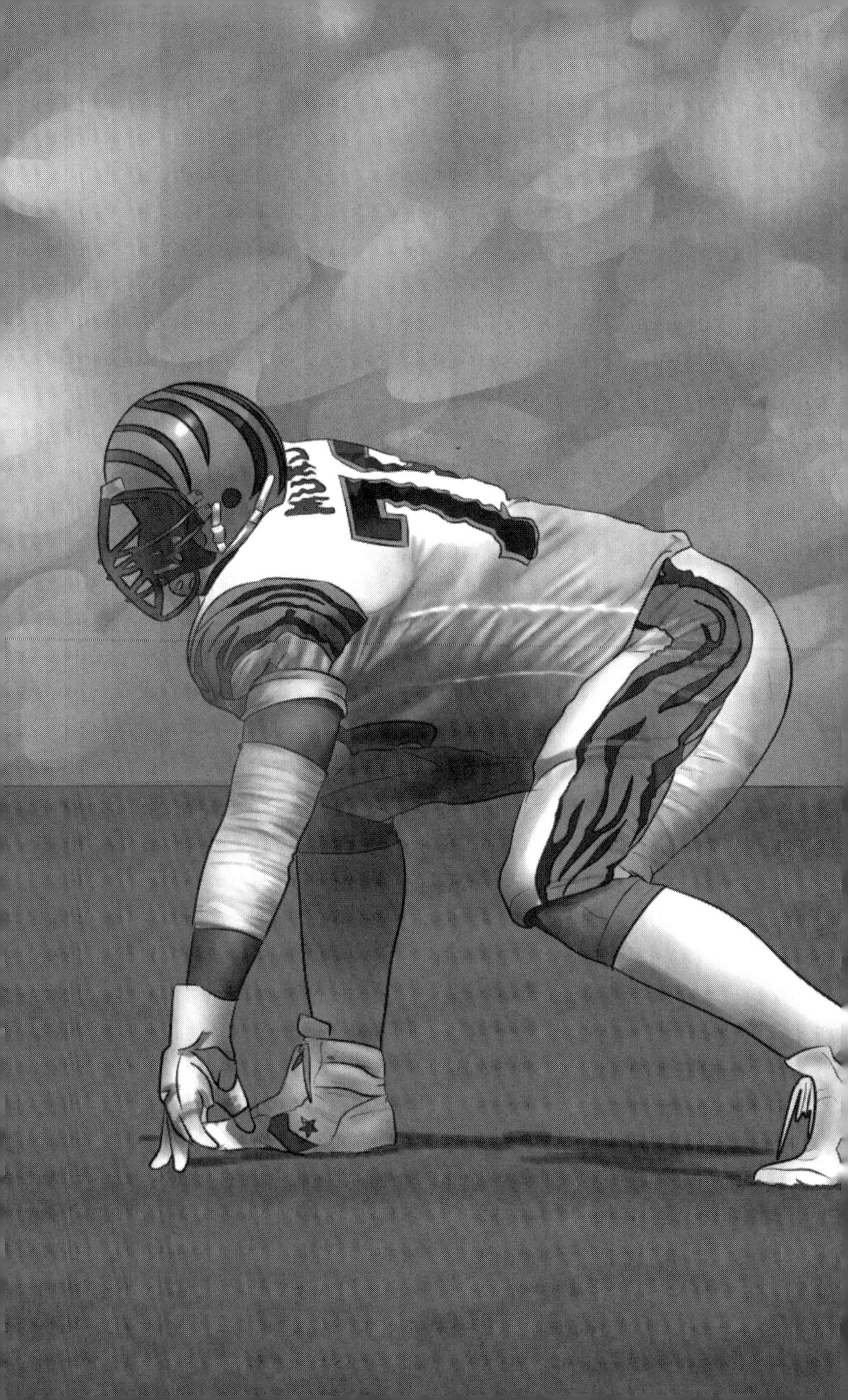

OFFENSIVE LINEMAN: ANTHONY MUÑOZ

- 11 Pro Bowls
- 11 All-Pro selections
- Four touchdown receptions (Tied #1 all-time for offensive lineman)
- Started 182 of 185 games
- 1991 Walter Payton Man of the Year
- Two Super Bowl Appearances
- Inducted into Hall of Fame in 1998

Biography

Full name: Michael Anthony Muñoz

Nicknames: N/A

Uniform: #78

Teams played for: Cincinnati Bengals (1980-1992)

Years Pro: 13 Years

College: University of Southern California

Height/Weight: 6'6, 278 pounds

Born: Aug. 19, 1958

Hometown: Ontario, CA

Best quote: "I was always a lead by example type of person, said very few words," Muñoz said. "You can talk all you want, but unless you roll up your sleeves and you're out there with law enforcement, you're out there with the community trying to be the solution. It's about getting out and being the solution to the problem and not just verbalizing. Talk is cheap, man."

When we talk about underrated positions, most would agree that the offensive linemen don't get the recognition they deserve. On offense, everyone wants to talk about the quarterback, running back, and wide receiver. But it's the offensive lineman who makes all the scoring possible.

Anthony Muñoz dominated his position like no one else and helped elevate the Cincinnati Bengals offense from practically a laughing stock to a Super Bowl contender. During the 1970s, the Cincinnati Bengals offense ranked in the top 10 in points just twice. From 1981-1990, the heart of Muñoz's tenure in Cincinnati, they ranked in the top 10 seven times, including No. 1 in 1988, their Super Bowl season. While Muñoz wasn't throwing the passes or carrying the ball, his blocking helped open big holes for "Ickey" Woods and gave quarterbacks Ken Anderson and Boomer Esiason extra time to throw the ball. In 1988, Woods and Esiason ranked No. 2 at their position in total touchdowns.

But he wasn't just a hero on the field; he was a hero off of it as well. Muñoz has given back to the community like very few ever have and has been a positive influence in Cincinnati. He's helped give children and individuals hope through the Anthony Muñoz Foundation. His contributions and determination to help those in need helped him win the Walter Payton Man of the Year Award in 1991. Muñoz helped those with physical and mental ailments and encouraged others to get involved and take action rather than just talking about it.

But life wasn't always easy for Muñoz. He grew up in a difficult situation in his hometown of Ontario, California. His mother raised four children by herself after their father deserted them. Muñoz would see his father only twice despite him living nearby. He wanted nothing to do with his family.

The Muñoz family were dirt poor; Anthony and his brother helped out their mother as much as they could, working at a local farm and packing eggs for dollars and cents. Fortunately, Muñoz had relatives who helped keep his family going. They gave him rides to and from school and helped support them whenever possible.

Muñoz's mother pushed Anthony to get involved in sports. Muñoz wanted to try baseball, but he needed equipment to play, and that was something his family couldn't afford. Thankfully, he met people who were willing to help, and this was something he would forever be grateful for. Someone donated a ball and glove for him to play baseball, and then when he couldn't afford a football, a friend stepped in and bought him one. In his Hall of Fame speech, Muñoz credited all those who helped him when he couldn't afford anything, and said it made him a better person.

"It's opportunities like that that motivate me now as an adult to put in the energy and time in charitable causes in the community of Cincinnati to provide those opportunities for those that have a dream, that want to accomplish something," Muñoz said. "To give those people that God has created help to make the most of the gift that he has given them. That's why I take the time because it's the people that have allowed me to reach the pinnacle of my career."

As his body grew as a teenager, he was encouraged to give football a try. On the field, his coaches put him at offensive tackle because of his enormous size. He was big and physical, and with the help of good coaching, he was an incredible blocker. He mauled his opponents. His athletic skills were superior, and he soon became a superstar in both baseball and football.

Muñoz was recruited by the University of Southern California to play both sports, but knee injuries on the football field prevented him from playing four full years. He would only end up playing one season of baseball and two years of football at USC. However, in his one year of playing baseball, he pitched and helped USC win the National Championship.

In the two years that he played football for USC, Muñoz dominated at the left tackle position, even starting as a freshman. But NFL scouts worried about his knee problems. He played just 16 total games at USC during his four years there, and tore knee ligaments his senior year that forced him to miss most of the season. Because of his size and talent, he was projected to be the best NFL offensive tackle in the Draft, but a lot of teams considered him a major risk because of his knees and didn't even list him on their draft board.

The Bengals chose not to pass, though. Owner Paul Brown visited Muñoz at USC and was mesmerized by not just the talent he saw in him, but how humble and charismatic the big man was. Muñoz was a class act and a leader, and Brown knew right away he had to draft him.

With the third pick in the 1980 NFL Draft, the Bengals stunned teams by selecting Muñoz so early. The Bengals were criticized by the media, who said they'd wasted their first round pick. They said Muñoz's career would be hindered by knee problems, but they soon ate their words; Muñoz missed just three games his first 12 seasons in the NFL. His knees eventually gave out in his 13th year, and when he tried to play with the Tampa Bay Buccaneers in 1993, he realized in preseason that he couldn't endure it. He would retire before the 1993 season began, but he had already left a legacy.

Muñoz won Offensive Lineman of the Year in 1981 and 1988, and also won NFLPA Lineman of the Year in 1981, 1985, 1988, and 1989. He had at least one major award as offensive lineman in six of his 13 seasons. Muñoz was also an All-Pro selection in nine of his first 11 seasons, an honor given to the player seen as the best at their position in the league. He would be named to the 1980s All-Decade Team and to the 75th Anniversary All-NFL Team.

At the time of his retirement, he was tied all-time for the most Pro Bowls by an offensive lineman, a record which has since been surpassed. Prior to the 2000 season, *The Sporting News* ranked him No. 17 on the All-time Greatest Players in History and best overall offensive lineman.

Muñoz was notorious for his work ethic. He worked tirelessly in the weight room and on the football field, continually trying to improve. Perhaps the greatest moment in his career happened when he was inducted into the Pro Football Hall of Fame in 1998, the first-ever inductee from the Cincinnati Bengals. He is also tied for most touchdown catches by an offensive lineman - 4.

Once Muñoz's career was over, he began fighting for positive change. He wants others to get out there and make a difference in the world, not just through words, but actions, to help those in need and be the difference.

Honorable Mention

Larry Allen

Larry Allen was a major contributor to the Dallas Cowboys 1990s dynasty, helping the team win a Super Bowl in 1995. While Muñoz is considered the best tackle of all time, many list Allen as the greatest guard of all time. Allen stood out for his size, strength, and speed; he was 6'3, 325 pounds, and ran a 4.8 40-yard dash. He also bench-pressed up to 700 pounds! He was named to the 1990s and 2000s All-Decade Team and is in the Pro Football Hall of Fame. Allen started in 197 of his 203 games and was named Offensive Lineman of the Year in 1996 and 1997.

Bruce Matthews

A 19-year NFL standout, Bruce Matthews holds the NFL record for going to 14 consecutive Pro Bowls. He started 293 games for the Houston Oilers/Tennessee Titans in his long career and had the versatility to not just dominate at the offensive tackle position, but also play interior guard and center. He even did long-snapping for a while. Matthews was named First-Team All-Pro nine times and is part of the 1990s All-Decade Team.

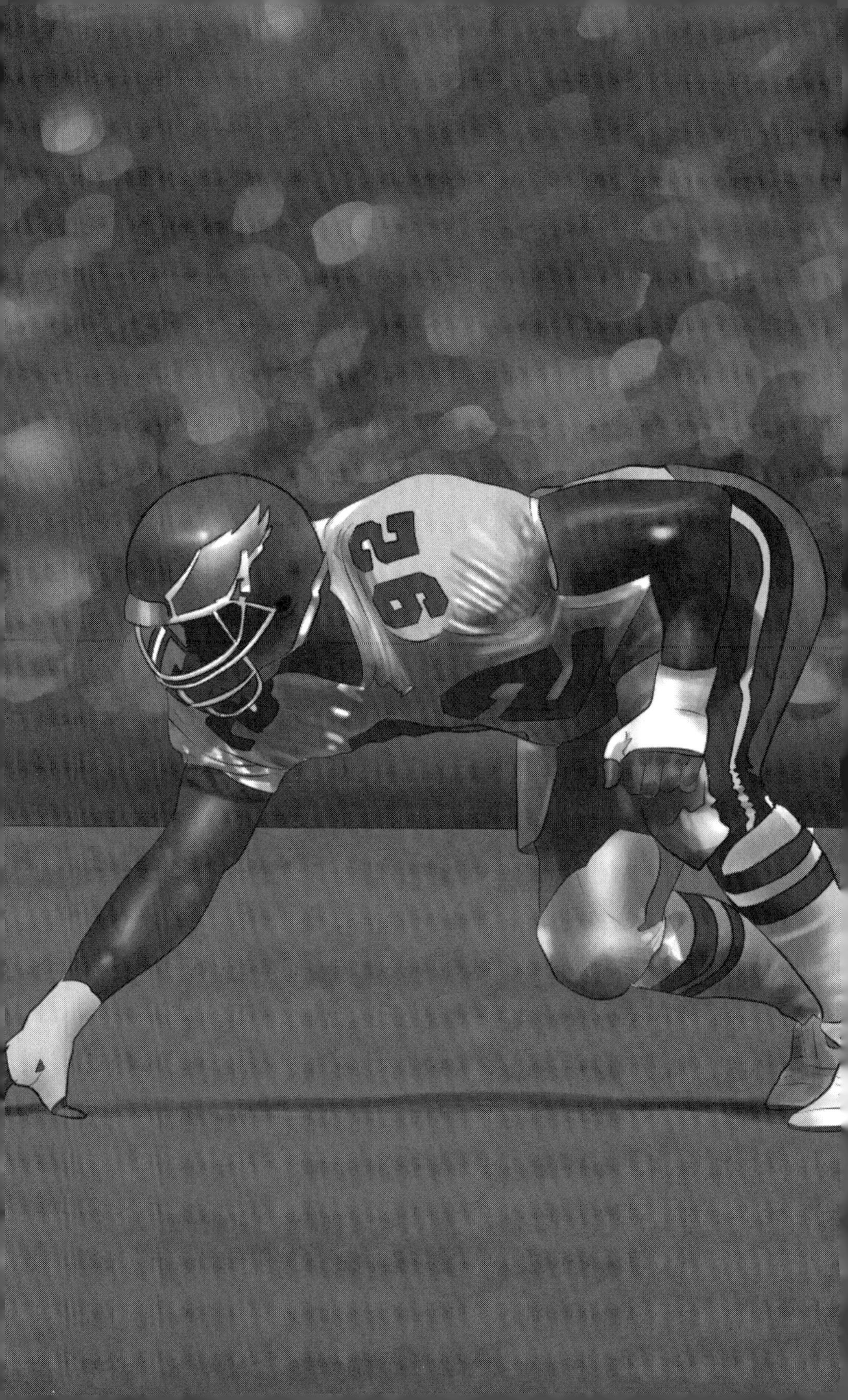
26

DEFENSIVE LINEMAN: REGGIE WHITE

- Played Defensive End
- 13 Pro Bowls (all consecutive)
- 13 All-Pro Selections (#1 All-time)
- 198 career sacks (#2 All-time)
- 0.85 Sacks Per Game (#1 All-time min. 100 games played)
- One Super Bowl Ring
- Two Defensive Player of the Year Awards

Biography

Full name: Reginald Howard White

Nicknames: "The Minister of Defense"

Uniform: #92

Teams played for: Philadelphia Eagles (1985-1992), Green Bay Packers (1993-1998), Carolina Panthers (2000)

Years Pro: 15 years

College: University of Tennessee

Height/Weight: 6'5", 300 pounds

Born: Dec. 19, 1961

Hometown: Chattanooga, TN

Best quote: "One thing I don't think my critics realize is that I've been trained to look adversity in the face."

Quarterbacks feared Reggie White. His ability to break through the offensive line and chase down the quarterback was unlike anyone who came before him. Over the course of his career, he played defensive end and sacked the opposing quarterback 198 times, the second-most by any defensive player in history. But while Bruce Smith has two more sacks than White during his career, he did it while playing in 47 more games. Thus, most people regard White as "the sack king."

White holds the all-time record for most sacks per game, 0.85, for players who have competed in at least 100 games. Furthermore, he is the only player in NFL history to record 20 or more sacks in just 12 games, a feat he accomplished in 1987. His 1.75 sacks per game that season is an NFL record. Only five players in history have more sacks in one season than White, but they did it while playing in a full course of games.

White won the NFL Defensive Player of the Year Award twice during his career and was named to 13 All-Pro teams. He was also voted to 13 consecutive Pro Bowls from 1986 to 1998. He helped transform the Philadelphia Eagles defense into one of the most dominant units of the early 1990s and helped the Green Bay Packers win their first Super Bowl in almost 30 years.

But as sweet as his career may seem, life didn't start out that way for Reggie. Growing up, he was the victim of bullying. His personality contrasted with others, and his appearance was different from children in his grade. He was a very large child, much taller than anyone else, and kids used his size and uniqueness to tease him.

White, who had always been a person of faith, didn't retaliate with his fists. He wanted to find another way to unleash his anger. He was always one to abide by the rules and behave. His mother suggested he try football, and he listened.

"When I was a child, I was always bigger than the other kids," White said in an interview with *Sports Illustrated*. "Kids used to call me 'Big Foot' or 'Land of the Giant'. They'd tease me and run away. Around seventh grade, I found something I was good at. I could play football, and I could use my size and achieve success by playing within the rules. I remember telling my mother that someday I'd be a professional football player and I'd take care of her."

White was also teased because of how much he practiced and preached religion, something he was a big advocate for even during and after his career. At just 17 years old, he was ordained as a Baptist minister, hence his nickname "The Minister of Defense."

Growing up in Chattanooga, Tennessee, football was a way of life. You couldn't help but walk around town and see orange; it turned White into a Tennessee Volunteer fan as a kid. He was the best player at his high school and was named High School All-American in both football and basketball. His dream came true when the University of Tennessee offered him a scholarship to play football for them.

White dominated at Tennessee, where he holds the all-time school record for most sacks in a game (4), most sacks in a season (15), and most sacks during a career (32). White opted to play in the USFL (U.S. Football League), which was a popular alternative to the NFL in the early 1980s. Jim Kelly, Steve Young, and Doug Williams also played in the USFL.

But with the league on the verge of folding, White entered the NFL Supplemental Draft in 1985 and was selected fourth by the Philadelphia Eagles. He would play eight seasons for them before being traded to the Green Bay Packers.

White made a huge difference for both teams while playing in his prime. From 1982 to 1986, before his prime, the Eagles had zero winning seasons and ranked near the bottom half in terms of defensive rankings. They were 26-45-2 during those years. From 1987 to 1992, which were White's best seasons in Philadelphia, they had five winning seasons, four playoff appearances, and a combined 59-36 record. From 1987 to 1992, the Eagles ranked in the top-10 in every season but one.

As an NFL rookie in 1985, White sacked the quarterback 13 times in 13 games and contributed on 100 tackles. The stellar season earned him the NFL Defensive Rookie of the Year Award. In 1991, he led the Eagles defense, regarded by some as one of the best units of all-time. They allowed an average of 3.0 yards per carry, ranking third best in the Super Bowl era. They ranked first in the NFL in pass defense, rush defense, and total yards allowed. Only five teams in the NFL since 1975 have accomplished that feat.

White was traded to the Packers prior to the 1993 season and gave that defense the boost they needed to get them over the top. Playing alongside Gilbert Brown and Santana Dotson, the Packers defense was the best in football in the mid-1990s. They won the Super Bowl in 1996, giving up the least amount of yards in the league. They were fourth in rush defense and first in pass defense. Couple that with an offense led by Brett Favre and the 1996 Packers team are regarded as one of the greatest in history.

White retired in 2000 and was inducted into the Hall of Fame in 2006. However, he never got to don the gold jacket given to inductees. Sadly, he suffered from cardiac arrhythmia and passed away in 2004. He was only 43 years old.

White was a face you could not forget in the 90s. He and his mom made the Chunky Soup Commercials famous and a fixture in the NFL at the time. As tough a competitor as he was, he was always seen with a smile on his face and was one of the most liked players in the game. He was a leader of faith, spreading the Word not just to those who practiced religion in the NFL, but beyond. He faced backlash for his stance on certain political matters that also garnered attention. But 17 years after his death, he is still regarded as not just one of the greatest defensive linemen in history, but one of the greatest defensive players to ever play football.

Honorable Mention

Aaron Donald

He may not be at the level of a Reggie White yet, but Aaron Donald is getting there. Drafted in 2014 by the St. Louis (now Los Angeles) Rams, he is one of two interior lineman in NFL history to post 100 sacks. Donald has been selected to the Pro Bowl every season since his rookie year, and has already won Defensive Player of the Year three times. He helped lead the Rams defense in 2022 to their second-ever Super Bowl trophy. In five years time, he may surpass Reggie White as the greatest defensive lineman in history, and is already arguably the greatest defensive tackle to play the game.

Bruce Smith

The Buffalo Bills Hall of Famer is the all-time leading sack master with 200 sacks. Perhaps Bruce Smith's greatest achievement was helping lead the Buffalo Bills defense to four straight Super Bowl appearances in the 1990s. Smith was named Defensive Player of the Year twice during his career and was selected to 11 Pro Bowls. He also ranks fifth all-time in forced fumbles, with 46.

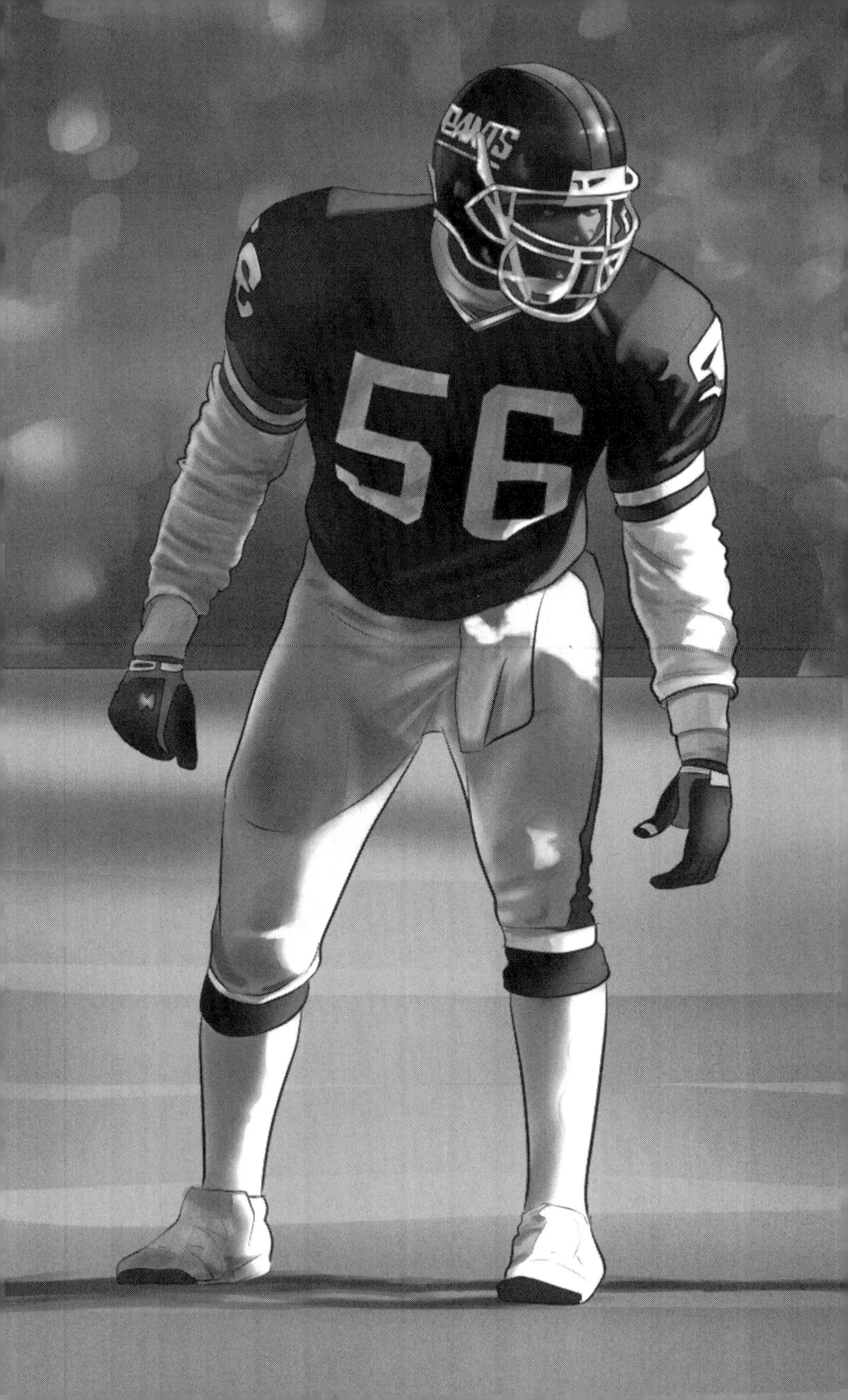
GIANTS
56

LINEBACKER: LAWRENCE TAYLOR

- Three-time Defensive Player of the Year (Tied for most All-time)
- Two Super Bowl rings
- One NFL MVP (one of two defensive players ever to receive honor)
- 10 Pro Bowls
- 132.5 career sacks (#2 all-time among linebackers)
- 10 All-Pro selections

Biography

Full name: Lawrence Julius Taylor

Nicknames: "LT," "Godzilla"

Uniform: #56

Teams played for: New York Giants (1981-1993)

Years Pro: 13 years

College: University of North Carolina

Height/Weight: 6'3", 240 pounds

Born: Feb. 4, 1959

Hometown: Williamsburg, VA

Best quote: "You always try to stay within the rules for the sake of the game, but you can always turn up the intensity."

Fearful. Wild. Reckless. Intense. Ferocious. Intimidating.

These are all words to describe the machine that was Lawrence Taylor, an incredible force that played with fury and batted quarterbacks around like they were pinatas. The former New York Giants linebacker was one of the most impactful defensive players in the Super Bowl era.

When we think of the dominant New York Giants teams of the 80s and early 90s that won two Super Bowls, Lawrence Taylor and that defense is the first thing that comes to mind.

Taylor's motto had always been play hard, wild, and on the edge, and he lived up to every bit of that during his career. Many people saw him as an adrenaline junkie who was afraid of nothing and destroyed everything in his path. His nicknames beyond simply "LT" were Superman and Godzilla.

Taylor lived like he played. His teammates used to tell stories about how he went to a bar and just "tore everything up—chairs, glasses, everything."

Taylor loved being the main attraction. He thrived off of being the leader and making the big tackle in a game. He wanted to make a difference and will his team to a Super Bowl, even if he had to do it alone.

"There comes a time in a game when you know a key play is coming up," Taylor said. "You can just feel it in the air. There are guys who shun those moments. It's like basketball. There are guys who want to shoot that last shot, and others who want to pass off. I want that last shot."

Perhaps Taylor's "nothing to lose" perspective came from his childhood. His family grew up poor in Williamsburg, Virginia. His father worked at the shipyards, while his mother was a schoolteacher. He grew up ill-tempered and regularly got into trouble in school. His parents scolded him a lot, and his mother called him "challenging." He went by the name Lonnie, and whenever a kid called him "Larry," he'd beat them up.

But sports changed Taylor. HIs mother encouraged him to play baseball and he became an All-Star catcher. But it was football where he really thrived. Initially, his mother refused to let him play because of how dangerous it was, but "danger" was Lonnie's way of life. It suited him. The football coach actually sought him out in his junior year of high school and convinced him and his family that he should play. It was the best decision he ever made. He would play both defensive line and linebacker for Lafayette High School.

Taylor loved playing linebacker because, as he said, "you control the game from there." It's why he loved playing catcher in baseball—because he called the pitches. In his two years of playing high school football, Taylor stunned coaches with the ferocity with which he hit players. They had never seen anything like it. He was powerful, and played with a type of viciousness. He was perfect for the game.

Football offered him better opportunities in terms of college scholarships as well, so he decided to put baseball in his rearview mirror and focus on football. He was recruited by the University of North Carolina, where he set a school record with 16 sacks in one season. He was named First-Team All-American and ACC Defensive Player of the Year.

Taylor was the most sought after defensive player in the 1981 NFL Draft. The New York Giants, with the second pick, selected Taylor. His first season, he recorded a career-high 133 tackles, defended eight passes, and sacked the quarterback 9.5 times. He also forced two fumbles and intercepted a pass. It's no surprise he was the 1981 NFL Defensive Rookie of the Year.

From 1984 to 1990, the heart of Taylor's career, he had at least 11.5 sacks each season. His best season came in 1986 when he recorded 20.5 sacks and 105 tackles. He was one of only two defensive players in NFL history to be named the NFL Most Valuable Player.

Taylor helped lead the Giants to a 14-2 season in 1986 and helped them cruise through the playoffs and stomp the Broncos in Super Bowl XXI. Four years later, he and his defense stunned Joe Montana and the San Francisco 49ers in the NFC Championship, holding them to 13 points and preventing them from winning their third straight Super Bowl. In the Super Bowl, they held the vaunted Bills defense to just 19 points, beating them to secure Taylor's second Super Bowl ring.

Taylor is second all-time for sacks amongst linebackers with 132.5, although he would have easily broken the mark if he'd played longer. Kevin Greene's 157 career-leading sacks by a linebacker came from playing 42 more games than Taylor. Taylor was inducted into the Hall of Fame in 1999.

Some have called Taylor the toughest football player to have ever lived. In 1988, he played with torn shoulder ligaments and a detached pectoral muscle, yet forced three sacks and two fumbles to help the Giants beat the Saints. He also played with a hairline fracture in his tibia and a broken bone in his foot. But as Taylor always said, "No pain, no gain."

"Lawrence Taylor, defensively, has had as big an impact as any player I've ever seen," John Madden once said. "He changed the way defense is played, the way pass-rushing is played, the way linebackers play and the way offenses block linebackers."

Honorable Mention

Ray Lewis

Like Taylor, Ray Lewis was fierce and intimidating. He is considered one of the hardest hitters to ever put on a uniform. Ray Lewis played 15 seasons for the Baltimore Ravens, winning two Super Bowl rings, and being awarded Super Bowl MVP in 2000. He helped lead one of the most dominant defenses in history, the 2000 Ravens defense. Under Lewis, the Ravens ranked in the top six in total defense 11 times. Lewis is the only player in NFL history with at least 40 sacks and 30 interceptions; he was selected to 12 Pro Bowls and is part of the 2000s All-Decade Team.

Mike Singletary

The 1985 Chicago Bears "Monsters of the Midway" defense is to this day recognized as the greatest unit of all time, and it was led by linebacker Mike Singletary. The Hall of Famer was a two-time Defensive Player of the Year, seven-time first-team All-Pro, and was selected to 10 Pro Bowls. He played solely for the Bears, ending his career with 1,488 tackles and 19 interceptions in 12 seasons.

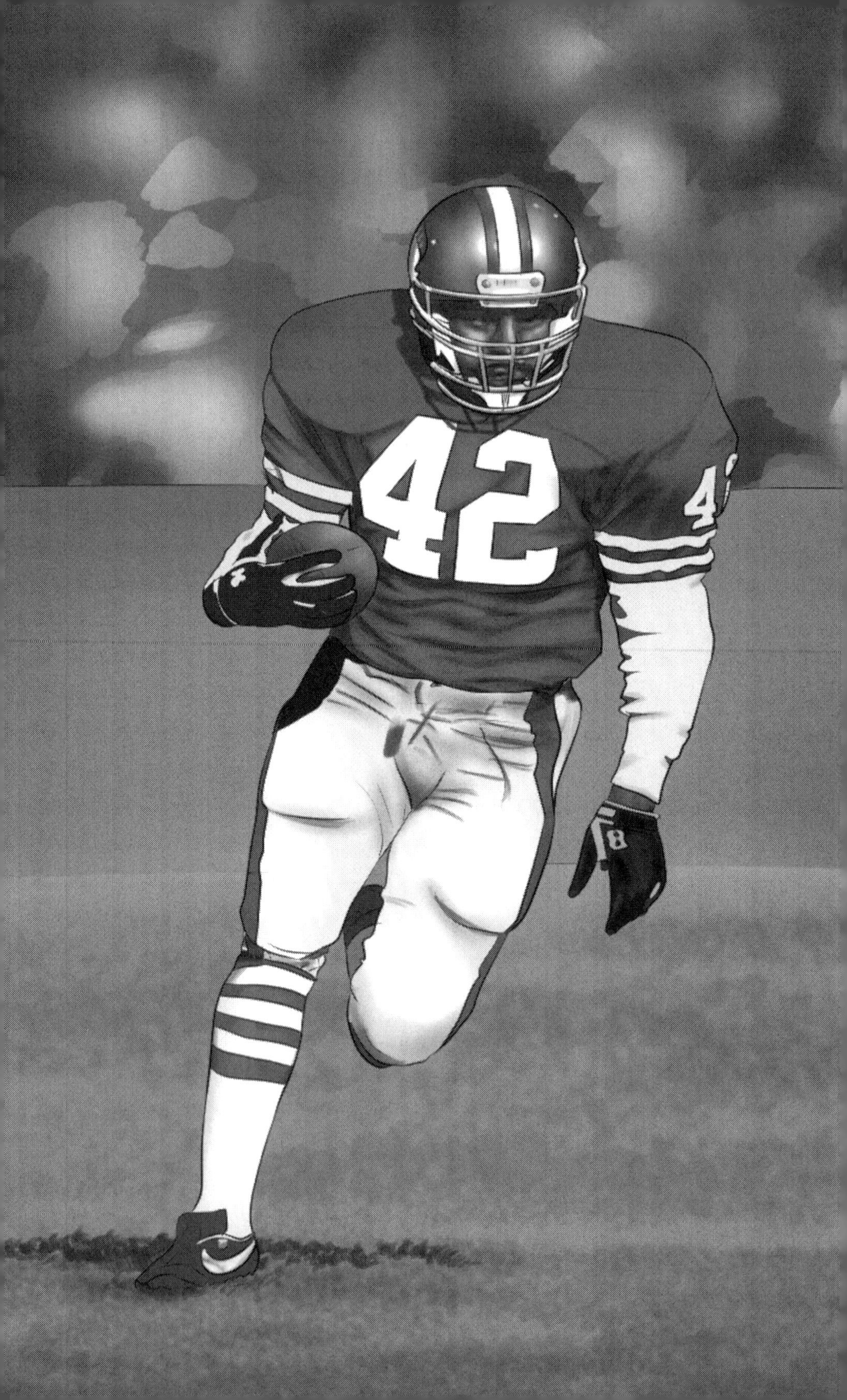
42

DEFENSIVE BACK: RONNIE LOTT

- 10 Pro Bowls
- Four Super Bowl rings
- Eight time All-Pro
- 63 career interceptions (Twice led the NFL)
- Nine Postseason Interceptions (Tied for #1)
- 1,146 tackles
- 10 interceptions in single season (Team high)

Biography

Full name: Ronald Mandel Lott

Nicknames: "Ronnie"

Uniform: #42

Teams played for: San Francisco 49ers (1981-1990), Los Angeles Raiders (1991-1992), New York Jets (1993-1994)

Years Pro: 14 years

College: University of Southern California

Height/Weight: 6'0", 203 pounds

Born: May 8, 1959

Hometown: Albuquerque, NM

Best quote: "If you can believe it, the mind can achieve it."

When we talk about the full package, Ronnie Lott was it. He was a high school and college All-American, a National Champion, an annual Pro Bowler, a Hall of Famer, a four-time Super Bowl champion, and arguably the greatest safety to ever live. But that's just part of his story. He is also recognized for his charismatic personality, his giving nature as evidenced by his charitable contributions, and his willingness to do whatever it took to help his team, including amputating part of his finger so he didn't have to miss any time on the field. He was a class act all around, and was one of the most well-liked players in the NFL.

While Lott was born in Albuquerque, New Mexico, he moved to Washington, D.C. shortly after his birth and lived there during one of the most turbulent times in American history. Lott's father, an Air Force officer, regularly moved his family around, thus Ronnie would bounce around a lot as a kid.

While in D.C., Lott, an African American, witnessed first-hand the rioting and protesting in the streets during the heart of the Civil Rights fight. Times were challenging, and this stayed with him.

"I take a lot of values from my mom and dad and my mom's mom, who was a domestic worker," Lott said. "I take a lot from them because of the things they had to do and things they had to live through. When I lived in DC, I witnessed people fighting for their liberties."

Football helped take Lott's mind off the chaos going on around him. Growing up in Washington, he became a big Washington Redskins fan. Watching them play motivated him to want to play football. When his father was transferred to California, he signed Ronnie up to play Pee Wee Football. Lott played defense and was known for his tackling and hitting power. He loved it so much he sometimes took tackling to a whole new level.

"I would drive my helmet into him, keep my feet moving, and lift him in the air before dumping him on his butt," Lott said.

Lott was a standout athlete in California, not just becoming a superstar football player, but also lettering in basketball and baseball, where he also received All-American honors. He could play any sport he desired because he was so good, but he settled on football. One of the stars Lott played against in high school in California was Anthony Muñoz, arguably the greatest offensive lineman to ever play (#1 on our list).

"Ronnie Lott and I competed for two years in high school," Muñoz said. "We were in the same conference. I competed against him in football, basketball, and baseball. I knew what kind of athlete he was. He was a

QB/DB, a point guard and a shortstop. I don't think I ever threw him a fastball because he couldn't hit a curve, but he could hit a fastball. I wasn't surprised with the type of player he became."

Lott and Muñoz both went on to play at USC, where Lott received a full scholarship. Lott also played with Hall of Fame legends such as Marcus Allen and Bruce Matthews. They had 12 future Pro Bowlers starting on their roster. It's no wonder that the 1978 Trojans went on to win the National Championship.

As a senior, Lott led the nation with eight interceptions in one season. He is perhaps most remembered for creating problems for Stanford's superstar quarterback John Elway, holding their vaunted offense to just nine points. Lott finished his USC career with 250 tackles, 14 interceptions, and 10 forced fumbles. He received All-American mentions in 1978 and 1979, and was a unanimous All-American choice in 1980.

Lott was selected with the eighth overall pick by the San Francisco 49ers in the 1981 NFL Draft. He was a key contributor in helping the 49ers become the "Team of the 80s," winning eight division championships and four Super Bowl championships from 1981 to 1989.

He started immediately as a rookie as a cornerback and was able to adapt and play different positions in the secondary, wherever the coaches needed him most. He had an impressive seven interceptions, three touchdowns (a league high), two fumble recoveries, and 89 total tackles during his rookie season. The only reason he didn't win Rookie of the Year was because he was edged out by the guy we just talked about, Lawrence Taylor.

Lott played primarily safety during his career. His best season was arguably 1986 when intercepted a league-high 10 balls, returning them for 134 yards and one score. Perhaps his most impressive statistic is intercepting opposing quarterbacks nine times in the playoffs. He was voted to the Pro Bowl 10 times. He finished off his career with both the Raiders and Jets before retiring in 1994.

Lott was inducted into the Hall of Fame in 2000. Since then, he has become a broadcaster for both the NFL and college football. He also has contributed to multiple charities, including founding All-Stars Helping Kids, a non-profit organization that has raised hundreds of thousands of dollars.

Honorable Mention

Rod Woodson

Like Ray Lewis, cornerback Rod Woodson was part of that dominant 2000 Ravens defense that won Super Bowl XXXV. But he was most known for his tenure with the Pittsburgh Steelers, who he played with for 10 seasons. Woodson played an incredible 17 seasons where he racked up 71 interceptions for 1,483 return yards. He was selected to 11 Pro Bowls and has one Defensive Player of the Year honor. He was inducted into the Pro Football Hall of Fame in 2009. He played for not just the Steelers and Ravens, but also the 49ers and Raiders.

Mel Blount

A 14-year pro, Blount helped the Steelers to four Super Bowls during the 1970s and was part of the dominant Steel Curtain defense. Blount won Defensive Player of the Year six times and was selected to five Pro Bowls. He finished with a career 57 interceptions, which could have been a lot higher if he hadn't retired early. Blount was inducted into the Hall of Fame in 1989.

4

AMAZING GAMES

Football has produced some incredible games in its history. Stories that have been told and will continue to be told from generation to generation.

Below, I've selected five of the greatest professional football games along with three of the greatest collegiate games ever to be played. These games were chosen based on not only their entertainment value, but also the stakes involved and the impact the game had on football.

"THE GRIM REAPER" BUFFALO BILLS AT KANSAS CITY CHIEFS

January 23, 2022

2021 AFC Division Round

Kansas City, MO

Importance of the Game

The Bills and Chiefs have developed a bit of a rivalry in recent years because of the breakout stars Josh Allen and Patrick Mahomes, considered the two best quarterbacks playing today. Many see them as this generation's Tom Brady and Peyton Manning.

To add to the stakes, the winner of this game would go on to host the Cincinnati Bengals in the AFC Championship Game the following week. The Chiefs were searching for their third straight trip to the Super Bowl while the Bills were trying to finally get past Kansas City. Allen had led them to the AFC Championship a season ago, but the Chiefs got the best of them.

With a 5:30 p.m. kickoff on a Sunday night, the final playoff game played that weekend would be played under the lights. Prior to the game start, the weekend had already produced massive drama, with the three other games coming down to the final play. The Bengals had upset the Titans in overtime, the 49ers stunned the Packers on a final second field goal in the snow at Lambeau Field, and the Rams avoided an incredible comeback by Tom Brady, kicking a last second field goal to beat the Bucs.

As good as those games were, little did America know they were nothing compared to what they were about to witness.

The Game

There was the game...and then there were the final two minutes.

The first 58 minutes were enough to keep the interest of the fans, but couldn't compare to the final two minutes. Both teams went back and forth throughout the entire game. Buffalo took an early 7-0 lead, but Kansas City responded with two touchdowns to take a 14-7 lead. Allen, though, connected with receiver Gabe Davis just before halftime to tie the game at 14.

Kansas City seemed to be taking control by scoring the first nine points of the third quarter to lead 23-14 with a couple minutes left in the quarter. But then Allen hit Davis again, this time on a 75-yard pass, to cut the Chiefs lead to 23-21.

Harrison Butker kicked a 28-yard field goal to give the Chiefs a 26-21 lead. With under two minutes to go in the game, the Bills were driving. They had made it to the Chiefs 27-yard line just inside the two-minute warning, setting up another dramatic finish for Divisional Round Weekend.

The final two minutes

The first play after the two-minute warning, Allen fake-pumped to the right and then looked back left. In the end zone stood Gabriel Davis, wide open. Allen fired a missile right into his chest for a touchdown. The Bills had re-taken the lead,

"Remarkable," screamed announcer Jim Nantz on CBS' telecast.

But Allen wasn't done. On the two-point conversion, he avoided the pressure, running backwards and around the Chiefs. He threw through heavy traffic, hitting Stefon Diggs for the circus catch and the score.

29-26 Bills. 1:54 to play.

Kansas City came right back. With 1:13 left, Kansas City had a second-and-ten on their own 36-yard line. Wide receiver Tyreek Hill ran a simple slant pattern across the field. Mahomes hit him in stride, and he caught it at the Chiefs logo midfield. And then he exploded. Hill, the fastest player on the field, looked like Usain Bolt as he turned on the jets. He was gone. Touchdown.

33-29 Chiefs. 1:02 to play.

That was plenty of time for Josh Allen. He hit Gabe Davis twice to work their way down to the Chiefs 35 with 32 seconds to go. Then he hit Isaiah McKenzie at the 19-yard line with 17 seconds left. Finally, he fired another missile to Gabe Davis, who was streaking down the middle of the field. Bullseye. Touchdown Bills.

36-33 Bills. 0:13 to play.

It was Davis' fourth touchdown of the game. The stadium had deflated. The Bills were celebrating on the sideline, anticipating the defense to do their job and send them to the AFC Championship. But never underestimate Mahomes, especially with all three timeouts remaining.

Starting at their own 25, Mahomes threw a quick pass to Hill who burst up 19 yards to the 44 yard line. Timeout. Seven seconds left.

With the Bills playing a prevent defense, Mahomes continued to look down the middle of the field. He found a streaking Travis Kelce open and hit him up the field. "Oh my goodness," yelled Nantz. Kelce plunged forward at the Bills 30-yard line with three seconds left. Another timeout.

Chiefs kicker Harrison Butker, one of the best in football, ran onto the field to try and tie the game to send it to overtime. As he had done all season, Butker calmly strode up to the ball and knocked it right through the goal posts.

Chiefs 36, Bills 36. End of regulation.

"It sounds impossible. 25 points in less than two minutes," Nantz told the audience.

"This is the most perfect quarterback play I've ever seen. Big plays. Smart plays," Tony Romo added.

Overtime

The Chiefs won the overtime toss. Per NFL overtime rules, if the team that gets the ball first scores a touchdown, the game is over. However, if the Bills force a turnover, a punt or a field goal, the next score wins the game, even if that's a safety or a field goal. In other words, the Bills had to stop them from scoring a touchdown.

But the way the Chiefs offense had been moving, and with Patrick Mahomes as quarterback, that was a tall task. Mahomes moved swiftly down the field, hitting Kelce, Hill, Jerrick McKinnon, and finally Mecole Hardman on a big play to maneuver the ball inside the Bills 10-yard line. He made it look like a Madden video game.

Everyone knew at this point what was coming. The Bills defense simply could not stop Mahomes, just as if the Bills had the ball, the fear would have been that they probably couldn't have stopped Allen.

On the first play from the 9-yard line, Mahomes found Travis Kelce in the corner end zone. Kelce made a great catch, tip-toeing his feet in bounds for a touchdown. Game over.

Chiefs 42, Bills 36.

Impact of the Game

After the game, reporters asked Chiefs coach Andy Reid what he said to Mahomes before the qb went out onto the field for those final 13 seconds.

He told him, "When it's grim, be the grim reaper."

It's hard to find a crazier final two minutes than this game, especially with everything that was on the line. Josh Allen just sat on the sidelines with a stunned look on his face after watching the Chiefs score twice in a row without him getting another chance to touch the ball.

The Chiefs went on to the AFC Championship Game against the Bengals and darted out to an early 21-3 lead, appearing to cruise to their third straight Super Bowl. But Joe Burrow coolly led the Bengals back, and Mahomes seemed to run out of his magic from a year ago.

The Bengals came back to take the lead late in the game before the Chiefs rallied to tie it and send it to overtime.

In overtime, Mahomes threw a costly interception, and the Bengals offense strode down the field to kick the game winning field goal, sending them to the Super Bowl to play the Rams.

Because of the Bills-Chiefs game, the NFL competition committee made changes to the overtime rule for the postseason only. The new rule states that even if the receiving team scores a touchdown, the other team will be given a chance to match them.

"THE ICE BOWL": DALLAS COWBOYS AT GREEN BAY PACKERS

December 31, 1967

NFL Championship Game

Green Bay, WI

Importance of Game

A number of different factors were in play. First of all, a trip to the Super Bowl was on the line. This was the NFL Championship Game (later named the NFC Championship Game when the AFL/NFL combined). Second, it was arguably two of the most historic franchises of all time that were playing each other. We had "America's Team of the Past," the Packers, against "America's Team of the Future," the Cowboys. Both teams combined to play in seven of the first 13 Super Bowls and currently have a combined nine Super Bowls titles between them.

The Packers were the team of the 1960s. They had won league championships in 1961, 1962, 1965, 1966, and 1967. They had revered names like quarterback Bart Starr, linebacker Ray Nitschke, running back Jim Taylor, and defensive lineman Henry Jordan, all Hall of Famers. No team had ever won three straight championships, and they were going for number four in this game. Meanwhile, the Cowboys had won the NFL Eastern Championship two years in a row but kept losing the NFL

Championship to the Packers. They hoped the third time would be the charm.

Add in the weather. This was the coldest game in NFL history (to this day). The game-time temperature was -13 degrees with a wind chill of -36. Lambeau Field officially got the name "The Frozen Tundra" because of this game. The heating system malfunctioned because of how cold it was and the field was literally frozen. Whenever they showed shots of players or fans, all you saw was a blast of smoke coming out of their mouths because it was so cold. In fact, some players and coaches even suffered frostbite during the game, including Packers quarterback Bart Starr.

The Game

The game started out poorly for Dallas. Bart Starr threw two touchdown passes to Boyd Dowler in the first half to capture an early 14-0 lead. Then Green Bay had the ball midway through the second quarter looking to put a dagger in the Cowboys, but Green Bay fumbled and George Andrie picked it up and returned it for a touchdown, reversing the momentum of the game. Dallas would maintain that momentum until late in the game. They added a field goal before halftime to cut the Packers lead to 14-10, and then scored on a 50-yard touchdown pass from Dan Reeves to Lance Rentzel.

17-14 Cowboys. Less than five minutes to go in the game.

It looked like the Cowboys had finally gotten the best of the Packers, especially when Green Bay was pushed back to their own 32-yard line. Their offense had been stalled for most of the second half. Given the icy conditions, it was hard to move the football. The field was frozen, so trying to run down the field was difficult, and throwing an icy football was even harder.

But Green Bay stayed cool (pun intended). Starr marched them down the field with a series of short passes to fullback Donny Anderson, running back Chuck Mercein, and wide receiver Boyd Dowler. One first down. Then another. As the clock ticked down under a minute, Green Bay had marched inside the Cowboys 10-yard line. Mercein then ripped off an 8-yard run to put the Packers 1st and goal at the Cowboys 2-yard line.

It looked as if the Packers had the game won, but getting those last two yards would not be easy. First, Anderson took the handoff and pushed ahead just short of the goal line, but couldn't get in. On second down, Starr again handed it to Anderson. He buried his head down into the pile but couldn't cross the line.

The Packers called their final timeout with 16 seconds left. They had a decision to make. They could kick the field goal and send it to overtime, or they could go for it on third down. However, having no timeouts, if they were stuffed on a running play (or sacked), the clock would run out. Head coach Vince Lombardi decided to gamble and go for the touchdown.

Starr called for another running play to Mercein in the huddle. But as he got to the line of scrimmage and barked out the signals, Starr saw a brief opening in the Cowboys defensive line. When the football was snapped, instead of handing it off, Starr went straight forward with the football and tried to sneak it over the goal line himself.

It worked. Touchdown Packers.

Lambeau Field erupted. The Packers had won the game 21-17; it was their fourth straight NFL Championship, and they were headed to their second straight Super Bowl.

Impact of the Game

This game was so good, it was given a place in the Hall of Fame. All the drama was there. The Cowboys-Packers rivalry, the history of the franchises, the icy weather, Lambeau Field, and a Super Bowl berth on the line. It lived up to all the hype going into the game and more. To this day, it's regarded as one of the greatest games of all time.

The NFL 100 Greatest Games ranked "The Ice Bowl" as the 3rd best game of all-time.

The Packers were knocked down in this game. But as their head coach Vince Lombardi said, "It's not about whether you got knocked down, it's whether you get back up."

The Packers went on to beat the Oakland Raiders the following week in Super Bowl II. The Cowboys kept building their franchise and soon would be a regular Super Bowl participant. They went on to compete in five of the next 11 Super Bowls, winning two of them.

If you're looking for a gem to watch on YouTube, just do a search for "The Ice Bowl." Just bring a blanket and some hot chocolate to get into the spirit of the game!

"GREATEST GAME EVER PLAYED": BALTIMORE COLTS AT NEW YORK GIANTS

December 28, 1958

NFL Championship Game

New York, NY

Importance of the Game

The game's impact is discussed below, but before the game, there was nervousness and fear. The NFL was still struggling to garner attention. Interest in the product was extremely apathetic and the thought was that professional football wasn't going to survive. It was overshadowed by baseball, college football, and even boxing. In fact, New York Giants rookie Frank Gifford recalled the NFL Commissioner telling him, "You're not going to make a living playing pro football, so don't quit your day job."

So when the Baltimore Colts played the New York Giants for the 1958 NFL Championship, there wasn't much optimism that the game would help professional football's image. That was until NBC decided to nationally broadcast the game, the first time in NFL history that a game would reach television sets all across America. This was a big deal, given that television was new and growing, so the chance to advertise their product could be boom or bust.

The game had star power; 12 future Hall of Famers played in this game. The Colts were led by Johnny Unitas, a blue-collar quarterback who had been cut by the Pittsburgh Steelers but had helped give the NFL some momentum with the forward pass, which had gone over well in Baltimore. He had developed into the league's top passer.

More than 70,000 fans packed Yankees Stadium to witness what would be dubbed, "The Greatest Game Ever Played."

The Game

Johnny Unitas' and the Colts' passing game put the Giants on their heels in the first half. After kicker (and future Hall of Fame announcer) Pat Summerall gave the Giants an early field goal, Unitas put together two big drives, the second one ending in a 15-yard touchdown pass from Unitas to wide receiver Raymond Berry. The Colts led 14-3 at halftime.

But the Giants came back in the second half. Mel Triplett got the Giants within four with a one-yard touchdown run in the third quarter, and it was 14-10. Then, with just a few minutes to go, Charlie Conerly connected with Frank Gifford for a 15-yard touchdown, bringing the score to 17-14 in favor of the Giants.

Yankee Stadium erupted. It looked even better when they pinned the Colts back at their own 14-yard line on the kickoff. But Johnny Unitas and the Colts offense was one of the best in football, and fans became frustrated as they watched Unitas calmly lead his team down the field with a series of short passes. Unitas worked the Colts all the way down to the Giants 13-yard line with seven seconds left. Steve Myrha kicked a game-tying field goal to end regulation with the score 17-17.

Now up until this game, it would have ended in a tie. No game in the history of football had ever gone beyond the 60 minutes of regulation play. But the league adopted a new overtime rule for the NFL Championship. Thus, for the first time in history, the game would be decided in sudden-death overtime and fans all across the country got to witness it first-hand.

Between the screaming fans, the mix of passes and runs in the game, and the drama, the Championship game delivered quite a show for fans across the country.

The Giants received the overtime kick but couldn't muster any offense, so they punted the ball to Baltimore. Again, just like in regulation, the Colts were pinned back deep in Giants territory. But again, Unitas put together a heartbreaking drive, mixing in runs and passes. The Colts swiftly moved their way down the field and found themselves deep in Giants territory.

Finally, after 12 plays totaling 79 yards, Unitas handed the ball off to Alan Ameche, who plunged into the end zone from one yard out to give the Colts the 23-17 win. Unitas and the Colts players threw their arms in the air in celebration, as they had just won the NFL Championship in an epic overtime game.

Despite the letdown of watching their team lose at home, fans could not help but feel good about the game they had just seen and left appreciating the game of football much more. But the game had even more of an impact on the nation than it did on the fans who'd come to the stadium to watch it.

Impact of the Game

After the game, Frank Gifford said it best: "December 28, 1958 was the day the NFL grew up."

Even famous *Game of Thrones* author George R.R. Martin, who wrote a story about the game, said, "It transformed the NFL into a national passion."

Many modern-day fans ask themselves why this game was given the title "Greatest Game Ever Played." Yes, it had a dramatic finish and was great football played on a big stage, but what separates this game from the Cowboys-49ers games or the Bills-Chiefs Divisional playoff game?

Well, it has everything to do with what this game meant for football moving forward—it saved the game. Football was a different product after this. People all across America watched this game on television and were enthralled with what they saw and wanted to see more. Ticket sales for future games increased and professional football began getting more attention than college football.

Everyone wanted to throw the ball like Johnny Unitas. They loved his story, a blue-collar kid who was cut and had to work hard to find his way onto the Colts roster and become a superstar. In fact, the Colts made an 80-cent long-distance call to sign Unitas. They also loved the story of the Giants' Sam Huff, another blue-collar player who was not wanted by anyone and soon became a star. By 1960, Huff was on the cover of *Time* magazine. Famous newscaster Walter Kronkite also helped sell the sport after this game, doing a documentary on Huff, which only further generated interest.

Who knows if professional football would have survived if it wasn't for the Colts-Giants NFL Championship Game? But we're sure glad it did.

"THE CATCH" DALLAS COWBOYS AT SAN FRANCISCO 49ERS

January 10, 1982

NFC Championship Game

San Francisco, CA

Importance of the Game

The Cowboys and 49ers are seen as rivals today, but it truly began with this game. This was the 1981 NFC Championship; the winner of this game would go to Super Bowl XVI to play the Cincinnati Bengals.

It was the makeup of the two teams that made this game so intriguing. Simply put, the Cowboys were legends. In the 16 years of the Super Bowl era, they had 16 winnings seasons with 16 playoff appearances. They had already won two Super Bowls in five appearances and had won the NFC East 12 of 16 times. In other words, they were the previous generation's New England Patriots, who had a similar run with Tom Brady. They had veterans with Super Bowl experience, such as Drew Pearson, Tony Dorsett, Tony Hill, Pat Donovan, Randy White, and Harvey Martin.

Then there was the 49ers. They had zero playoff wins in their team's history. They'd had just one winning season over the previous eight years. Their previous three seasons, they had gone 2-14, 2-14, and 6-10. They had players and coaches with virtually zero experience in the postseason, led by rookie safety Ronnie Lott, third-year quarterback Joe Montana, and third-year wide receiver Dwight Clark.

Even the coaches' experience was a mismatch. Tom Landry had been head coach of the Cowboys since 1960, while Bill Walsh of the 49ers had only been a head coach since 1979. But yet, these two teams came together in San Francisco for the NFC Championship.

It was the game that would forever define Joe Montana.

The Game

This game was all about the final five minutes. Up until that point, it had gone back and forth. The 49ers took an early 7-0 lead, but the Cowboys scored the next 10 points to take a 10-7 lead. Montana threw his second touchdown pass to pull the 49ers ahead, but the Cowboys struck just before halftime to re-take the lead, 17-14.

The 49ers took back the lead in the third quarter with a Johnny Davis 2-yard run. The Cowboys kicked a field goal early in the fourth quarter to cut the 49ers lead to 21-20.

Midway through the fourth quarter, 49ers running back Walt Easley fumbled and the Cowboys' Everson Walls recovered in 49ers territory. Just four plays later, quarterback Danny White hit Doug Cosbie from 21 yards out to give the Cowboys a 27-21 lead.

The 49ers began to move back down the field, but Montana was picked off by Everson Walls, his second interception of the game. The Cowboys had the ball at midfield and had a chance to put the game away with just a field goal, but the 49ers kept them from pushing the ball any further.

They punted and pinned the 49ers back at their own 11-yard line with just under five minutes left.

It was then Joe Montana's moment in the spotlight. He had been in this position before, helping bring Notre Dame back from a 34-12 deficit in the Cotton Bowl a few years earlier, becoming legendary for remaining cool under pressure. He also propelled the 49ers from a 28-point deficit a season earlier against the Saints in an overtime win.

"Joe does so many intelligent things you can't coach," former coach Sam Wyche once said. "He has so much poise and savvy. He just has the right stuff."

Montana calmly led his team down the field. Lenvil Elliot ran for a couple first downs, and then Montana hit wide receivers Freddie Solomon and Dwight Clark for a couple more first downs. They had worked their way down to the Cowboys 13-yard line with just over a minute left.

Montana had the opportunity to put the 49ers ahead, but uncharacteristically missed an open Freddie Solomon in the end zone. On second down, Elliot ran a sweep play for seven yards to set up a critical 3rd and 3 from the Cowboys 6 with 58 seconds left. The 49ers called timeout to set up the play.

On third down, Montana rolled out to his right. He was looking for an open wide receiver as he approached the sideline. He cocked his arm but held it in. Then he let it go. Everyone thought he was throwing it away. It was high and the average fan figured that no one could jump that high and catch it. But lo and behold, as the ball reached the back of the end zone, Dwight Clark leapt high into the air and grabbed it with his fingertips before hauling it in.

Touchdown 49ers. 28-27.

"I thought of throwing it away," Montana said. "I cocked my arm to do that when I saw Dwight covered. I didn't want to take a loss in that situation. But just then I saw Dwight getting away from the coverage."

"I thought it was too high," the 6'3" Clark added, "because I don't jump that well. And I was really tired. I had the flu last week and I had trouble getting my breath on that last drive. I don't know how I caught the ball. How does a lady pick up a car when it's on top of her baby? You get it from somewhere."

Candlestick Park became hysterical. That throw from Montana to Clark would be dubbed, "The Catch." The Cowboys still had 50 seconds to work with and were able to work it down to midfield. A field goal would have won it, but defensive tackle Lawrence Pillars sacked Danny White and stripped him of the ball, and the 49ers recovered.

Final score: 49ers 28, Cowboys 27

Impact of the Game

The game was almost seen as a passing of the torch, with the 49ers as the new kings of the NFC. It set up an improbable run by the 49ers over the course of the decade, earning them the name "Team of the 80s." They won Super Bowl XVI against Cincinnati the following week, and then followed it up by winning Super Bowls XIX, XXIII, XXIV. They added another Super Bowl five years later but with a different group and head coach.

Montana continued his reputation as clutch, winning Super Bowl XXIII in similar fashion as this game, hitting John Taylor in the back of the end zone with under a minute to go. Montana would finish his career with four Super Bowl rings and three Super Bowl MVPs.

In 1992, the teams faced off again in the NFC Championship, where the torch was passed back to the Cowboys. That year, Troy Aikman, Emmitt Smith, and Michael Irvin went to Candlestick Park and won a classic game to set up the first of three Super Bowls in four years for the Cowboys, earning them the moniker, "Team of the 90s."

"28-3": ATLANTA FALCONS VS. NEW ENGLAND PATRIOTS

February 5, 2017

Super Bowl LI

Houston, TX

Importance of the Game

It was the Super Bowl, the biggest game in the world. But it was also a matchup of experience vs. inexperience. The Falcons had never won a Super Bowl and had only appeared in the game once in 50 years. The Patriots, on the other hand, were a proven dynasty, going for their fifth Super Bowl ring in 16 years. Tom Brady and Bill Bellichick had already been on this stage six times.

Both teams were led by veteran quarterbacks. Matt Ryan was the league's reigning MVP and helped lead the Falcons to a league-high 540 points, 71 points more than the second-highest team. The ever-famous Tom Brady led the Patriots, finishing their second-best season in history, 14-2, and cruising through the postseason. Brady was going for his fifth ring.

The Game

If we didn't know that the Patriots were a 3-point favorite entering the game, we wouldn't have known it from watching the first 2½ quarters. It was all Atlanta.

Midway through the third quarter, the Patriots offense was stuck in neutral. They couldn't do anything except muster up a Stephen Gostkowski field goal. Meanwhile, Matt Ryan was moving the Falcons offense up and down the field like they were playing a high school team. Prior to this point, the Falcons had blitzed out to a 21-0 lead after Robert Alford picked off Brady to return it 82 yards the other way. When Tevin Coleman caught a six-yard touchdown from Matt Ryan at the halfway point of the third quarter, the Falcons were in complete command.

28-3.

It felt like the Super Bowl blowouts of the past, except we didn't expect it to come against one of the great dynasties in NFL history. 28-3. Sadly, that score would become one of the most famous scores in NFL history, and not for good reason for Atlanta.

Tom Brady began to move the Patriots forward. He orchestrated a six-minute, 13-play, 75-yard drive that ended in a five-yard pass to James White for a touchdown. The two-point conversion failed; the Falcons still led 28-9.

The Patriots long drive did more than chew up the clock and gain some momentum. It started to wear out the Falcons defense, especially when the Falcons offense began being the ones stuck in neutral. They would give the ball right back to the Patriots who then put together a 12-play, 72-yard drive that ended in a field goal. It was 28-12. The Patriots had Atlanta on the field for nearly an entire quarter straight.

"I think for sure we ran out of gas some," Falcons head coach Dan Quinn said. "They executed terrifically. That was one of the things that we don't talk about with them a lot, is the way they can execute."

The Falcons got the ball, but Ryan was sacked and fumbled. The Patriots recovered at the Falcons 25-yard line. At this point, fans began to wonder whether the Falcons were going to crumble.

It only took a few plays for the Patriots to drive down and score from a Brady pass to Danny Amendola. James White ran in the two-point conversion.

28-20 Falcons. 5:56 left.

The Falcons seemed to be avoiding a colossal collapse when they drove down inside the Patriots 30-yard line with under four minutes to go. A field goal would essentially put the game away. However, a costly penalty pinned the Falcons back, and they were forced to punt the ball back to New England. The Falcons defense, gassed from being on the field for most of the second half, now had to go out there and find a way to make a play to win the Super Bowl.

Brady was pinned back on his own 9-yard line with 3:30 to go. The scene was reminiscent of Brady's icon, Joe Montana, 28 years earlier, who had been in a similar position, down three to the Cincinnati

Bengals. All he did was march his team right down the field for the Super Bowl-winning touchdown.

As expected, Brady moved his team down the field. The key play came on a 1st and 10 from their own 36 with 2:26 to go. Brady's ball was tipped in the air but wide receiver Julian Edelman somehow made a miraculous catch at the Falcons 41 while on the ground and between three Falcons defenders. To this day, it is regarded as one of the greatest catches in Super Bowl history. It kept the drive alive.

The Patriots kept moving. Brady to Amendola for 20 yards. Brady to White for 13 yards. Brady to White for 7 yards. From the 1-yard line with 58 seconds left, White plunged the ball across the goal line to cut the lead to two. Brady then hit Danny Amendola for the two-point conversion.

28-28.

The game would go into overtime, marking the first time in history a Super Bowl has ever gone past 60 minutes. The Patriots won the coin toss and would never surrender the ball. The Falcons defense, completely out of gas, watched as Brady moved the ball with incredible ease down the field. Completion after completion went to several different receivers. Finally, after working it down to the 2-yard line, James White took a pitch and ran towards the goal line. He reached and barely crossed the end zone as his knee hit.

Touchdown Patriots. 34-28. Game over.

Impact of the Game

If there was any question that Tom Brady was the greatest football player to ever live, this game answered it. While statistically it may not have been the largest comeback in history, it may have been the greatest, considering a championship was on the line. Down 28-3, Brady and the Patriots never panicked and instead calmly picked away at the Falcons' lead.

It was Brady's fifth Super Bowl ring. Incredibly, he wasn't done. He went on to appear in three more Super Bowls, winning one more with the Patriots and another one with the Tampa Bay Buccaneers before retiring for the first time.

Of Brady's seven Super Bowl rings, this one had to feel the sweetest.

"CATHOLICS VS. CONVICTS": #1 MIAMI AT #4 NOTRE DAME

October 15, 1988

Regular Season Game

South Bend, IN

Importance of the Game

This wasn't just No. 1 vs. No. 4. These were two schools who hated each other…and I mean HATED. In fact, Notre Dame had T-shirts printed up before the game and handed them out to fans. The green shirts said, "Catholics vs. Convicts." Notre Dame had given Miami the nickname because of the number of players who had been in trouble with the law in recent years, and the label stuck with the media.

Miami embraced the title, though. These were two totally different cultures. Miami were the "bad boys" of college football. They liked to crush you and then crush you some more. Notre Dame's seniors in 1988 were witness to that. In 1985, Miami beat Notre Dame 58-7 and intentionally ran up the score, throwing the ball and calling a fake punt late in the game. A season earlier, they kept the foot on the gas as well, throttling the Irish 24-0.

Miami was a dominant force. They hadn't lost a game in two seasons, had won the national championship twice since 1983, and had been ranked No. 1 at some point in every one of the previous six seasons. This was a school that had produced quarterbacks such as Bernie Kosar, Jim Kelly, and Vinny Testaverde in the 1980s, all future NFL stars. It had been nearly a decade since Notre Dame had been No. 1.

Notre Dame was a classic brand with mystique and tradition. Miami was all about flash. They liked the reputation of being non-classy showboaters and thrived on "the bad boy" label. Notre Dame defensive back

Pat Terrell said, "I've never been involved in a game with so much crazy hype in all my years of playing college and pro football." Backup quarterback Steve Belles added, "I couldn't stand Miami. There was a deep-rooted dislike for them and we didn't mind saying it, either. They were kind of the bullies on the block."

The Game

This one was ugly from the start. Before even entering the field, a massive brawl broke out in the locker rooms. The stadium was under renovation, so both teams had to walk the same route to their locker rooms. In an effort to frustrate Notre Dame, Miami intentionally crossed into their path as they came onto the field. A massive fight ensued.

"[The game] was already on the verge of exploding with intensity," Terrell said. "We had just had it pounded into our heads the entire season not to flinch. It started as a shoving match, but then it was an all-out brawl. I mean, security couldn't break us up."

Finally, after the brawl broke up, both teams went back to their locker rooms. Notre Dame players were nervous that Coach Lou Holtz would scold them. After all, Holtz wasn't one to hold back his fury. He was one of the most fiery coaches in college football. If you thought it was just *the players* who didn't like each other, think again.

"His face was red," Terrell said. "He was mad and we had no idea what was going to come next. You assumed he was going to go off on us for fighting, but he said, 'We've got an hour to play and a lifetime to remember.' He said, 'If we want to fight in the parking lot after the game, that's fine. You represent our school properly in the game. **But do me one favor: After we kick their butts, you leave Jimmy Johnson for me.'**

Holtz's speech was recognized as one of the most motivating speeches a Notre Dame coach has ever given. He was fired up, and the team went out and played with that same kind of fire in their belly.

Notre Dame jumped out to a big 21-7 lead in the first half and played like they wanted to crush the Hurricanes. But Miami was too good to be blown out. Quarterback Steve Walsh connected with his receivers on two touchdown passes just before halftime to tie the game at 21.

In the third quarter, Miami fumbled right out of the gate deep in their own territory. Notre Dame was able to get three points out of it. Then later in the quarter, Irish quarterback Tony Rice hit running back Ricky Watters on a huge 44-yard play, getting them inside Miami's 6-yard line. Running back Pat Eilers pounded it in from there to give Notre Dame a 31-21 lead after three quarters.

In the fourth, though, Walsh and Miami dominated. Walsh found huge gaps in the Notre Dame defense and made several big plays. However, two huge fumbles deep in Notre Dame territory would cost Miami. One was extremely controversial, as running back Cleveland Gary appeared to score a touchdown by stretching the ball over the goal line before he fumbled, but referees ruled otherwise, saying it was a legitimate fumble, and Notre Dame recovered.

Miami still kept coming back. Down 31-24 late in the fourth quarter, Walsh moved Miami right down the field. Facing a 4th and 7 from the Notre Dame 20, Walsh laced a beautiful pass for wide receiver Andre Brown, who dove for the ball and caught it to cut the score to 31-30.

Now back in those days, there was no overtime. An extra point likely would have ended the game in a tie, in which case Miami would retain their edge over Notre Dame in the rankings. But Jimmy Johnson didn't want the tie—he wanted the win. So, he went for two. Walsh floated a lob pass towards the back of the end zone but it was underthrown. Terrell deflected the ball away to keep Notre Dame ahead 31-30.

When the onside kick failed, the game was over. The Irish beat Miami and went on to claim the No. 1 ranking in the country.

Impact of the Game

This win dethroned Miami from their championship status. As a result of the Irish victory, they would not play for the championship for the first time in three years. Notre Dame went on to complete an undefeated season, beating No. 2 USC and then West Virginia in the Fiesta Bowl for the National Championship.

The game was great, of course, but it became greater over the years as people re-told the story. ESPN even did a special 30-30 two-hour episode specifically on this game. The "Catholics vs. Convicts" label spread with time.

The Miami-Notre Dame rivalry has lost some luster over the years, since they stopped annually playing each other after 1990. Miami got revenge in 1989 on their home turf, beating then No. 1 Notre Dame and going on to win another National Championship. The Irish won in 1990, and then the two teams didn't play again for over two decades.

While Miami and Notre Dame have had brief championship runs over the years, neither has been able to maintain the winning consistency they had back in the late 80s and early 90s. Their rivalry was one of the best in football at the time.

"THE 2006 ROSE BOWL": #2 TEXAS VS. #1 USC

January 4, 2006

2005 National Championship Game

Pasadena, CA

Importance of the Game

This wasn't just the national championship, these were two of the greatest offenses of the decade going up against each other. Texas were the new kids on the block; they hadn't played for a national championship in decades.

USC, on the other hand, had just won two consecutive national championships (they shared one with LSU in 2003). They had won 34 consecutive games, and nine of their 12 wins leading up to the National Championship were by 17 points or more. They were seen as a machine, perhaps the greatest college football team ever assembled. They had two players who had just won back-to-back Heisman

Trophies on their roster, quarterback Matt Leinart and running back Reggie Bush.

This is why Texas wasn't given much of a chance, even though they had their own superstar quarterback, Vince Young. He was seen as the present-day Michael Vick, able to make plays with his lightning speed and his arm.

Even more significant, this game was played at "The Granddaddy of Them All," otherwise known as The Rose Bowl. Legendary announcer Keith Jackson had come out of retirement to call one more game in his career, and he couldn't have ended it any better.

The Game

This game was the definition of "back and forth." All game long, both offenses traded blows. USC looked like the force we all expected early, jumping out to a 7-0 lead thanks to a Reggie Bush touchdown run. But a key turning point happened late in the first quarter, when Leinart hit Bush. Bush took the pass and darted up the field towards the Texas goal line. But inexplicably, trying to keep the play alive, he tried to lateral it as he was being tackled. The lateral failed, the ball fell on the grass, and Texas recovered. This resulted in a huge momentum swing.

Next thing you know, Texas had scored three times in a row, two of those touchdowns. They had opened up a 16-7 lead. USC added a field goal before the half to cut it to 16-10.

More problematic for USC going into the half was Vince Young, who was piling up big runs against the Trojans' defense. USC had never seen a quarterback with that much electricity in his legs. And it would only continue in the second half.

USC regained command of the game in the third quarter. Leinart worked the Trojans down the field, and LenDale White plunged it in from a couple of yards out to give USC the 17-16 lead. But Young used his legs to bring the Longhorns back. After a series of long runs, Young pulled a perfect read option play, keeping it 14 yards for a touchdown. Texas moved ahead 23-17.

But as I said, this game was the definition of "back and forth." USC went right back down the field on the next drive with a series of passes and runs. LenDale White finished off the drive with another touchdown run, and USC moved back in front 24-23.

Back came Texas. Young dropped back from his own 35 before taking off, finding a huge gap in the USC defense. He ran it 35 yards deep into USC territory. But a missed field goal swung the momentum back in USC's direction. They went right down the field yet again for another touchdown and took control of the game, 31-23.

After a Texas field goal, USC's offense went back to work. For the fourth drive in a row, they found paydirt. This time, Leinart hit wide receiver Dwayne Jarrett from 21 yards out and USC seemingly had full command of the game, at 38-26. Only six minutes were left on the clock.

That's when the Vince Young legend grew. He willed his team down the field, working Texas down to the USC 17-yard line with just over four minutes to go. Young scrambled, found a hole, and then took off, weaving his way through the USC defense and walking in for a touchdown. The extra point cut the USC lead to 38-33.

USC, though, took the kickoff and worked their way into Texas territory, and with just over two minutes left, they were a first down away from icing the game and winning the national championship. Texas was out of timeouts. But the Texas defense forced USC into a 4th and 2 situation with 2:13 left from the Texas 44. USC could have pinned Texas deep, making it almost impossible to go down and score with two minutes left and no timeouts. But with a big back like White, they felt like they could pound their way for yards, so they went for it.

White, who had gashed Texas' defense for most of the night, was hit in the backfield and dropped, and the ball went back to Texas with 2:09 left. Just like he had the previous drive, Young worked the ball down the field with his arm and legs. A critical facemask penalty moved the ball deeper into USC territory.

But USC's defense stepped up and forced Texas into a 4th-and-5 from the USC 9-yard line. As Keith Jackson famously said on air, "Fourth down...for the national championship."

Young dropped back to pass. Just like he had all game, he saw a hole in front of him to the right and took off. "Young going for the corner...he's got it!" Jackson screamed. "Touchdown!"

After a successful two-point conversion, Texas was ahead 41-38 with just 20 seconds left. USC failed to work their way into field goal range in those last 20 seconds, and Texas had pulled off the stunning win, ending USC's 34-game winning streak and winning the Longhorns their first national championship since 1970.

Impact of the Game

Many called this "The greatest college football game they ever saw." It had everything you wanted. Both offenses traded punches all game long, and Vince Young's ability to run the ball on USC's defense only added to the excitement. Young eclipsed 200 yards rushing and was named the Rose Bowl MVP.

"Nobody ever saw No. 1 and No. 2 go at it like we did," Young would say years later. "I've probably watched it 100 times or more. But it feels like your first time seeing it."

It was deflating for USC. Shortly after this loss, Pete Carroll left to become the head coach of the Seattle Seahawks. USC's program failed to garner the same success they had from 2003 to 2005 and are still searching for it today. Texas has also seen its share of struggles over the years, bouncing from head coach to head coach.

But for one night, these were the two best schools in the country and they proved it. Some call them the two greatest teams to ever put on a college uniform. The talent they illustrated and the show they put on could not be matched.

"THE IRON BOWL": #1 ALABAMA AT #4 AUBURN

November 13, 2013

Regular Season Game

Auburn, AL

Importance of the Game

When we talk about football rivalries, Alabama vs. Auburn is right up there as one of the greatest in the country. These are two Alabama schools that flat out do not like each other. The game has been referred to as "The Iron Bowl" for many years.

Leading up to this game, however, Alabama had controlled the rivalry in recent years. They'd won four of the last five meetings. Worse yet for Auburn, the last two seasons they had been beaten 42-14 and 49-0. This was a one-sided rivalry.

Alabama was also the two-time defending national champion (and three of the last four) and were the No. 1 team in the country, searching for a three-peat. They were 10-point favorites in this game.

The only other team to win a national championship since 2009 stood in their way, however. Auburn entered the game 10-1, their only loss coming to LSU early in the season, which dropped them from the national rankings. They worked their way back up with a series of wins, including over No. 7 Texas A&M and No. 25 Georgia.

Having the game in Auburn was huge. Auburn had the crowd behind them, and it would mean a lot as this game went down the stretch. But trying to take down the champs would prove a difficult task.

The Game

While Auburn rushed out to an early 7-0 lead after quarterback Nick Marshall gashed Alabama's defense on a 45-yard run, it didn't take long for Alabama to flex their muscles. Alabama scored three times in a row to start the second quarter, two of them touchdown passes by quarterback A.J. McCarron. As the game approached halftime, Alabama had blitzed out to a 21-7 lead and were in firm control.

But with just under three minutes to go in the first half, Auburn put together an important drive deep into Alabama territory. With 1:40 remaining, running back Tre Mason plunged the ball over the goal line for a touchdown, and the lead was cut to 21-14.

Auburn came out in the third quarter running the football. Running backs Cameron Artis-Payne and Mason worked their way inside the Alabama red zone just a few minutes into the half. Then from the 13-yard line, Marshall connected with tight end C.J. Uzomah for a touchdown and tied the game at 21.

Alabama bounced back and worked their way down the field, but couldn't get a first down in Auburn territory. That's when Alabama's one true weakness reared its ugly head—the kicking game. Having already missed a kick in the first quarter, Cade Foster badly hooked a field goal attempt that would have put Alabama ahead. The game remained tied at 21.

Early in the fourth quarter, Auburn pinned Alabama back to their own one-yard line on a beautiful punt. From their own end zone, McCarron dropped back to pass and heaved up a bomb to wide receiver Amari Cooper. Cooper outran the first defender, and the ball fell perfectly into his chest. When the second defender missed the tackle, Cooper was off and running for a touchdown. A 99-yard pass, the longest-ever touchdown throw in Iron Bowl history. Just like that, Alabama was ahead 28-21.

Alabama got the ball back and was seemingly on the verge of putting the game away. They worked their way into Auburn's red zone with under six minutes left. With a field goal, the game would be all but over. But Auburn's defense forced Alabama into a 4th-and-1 situation with 5:42 to go. Normally, Coach Nick Saban would kick the field goal for a 10-point lead. But he was nervous about the way they were missing field goals, so he bypassed the three points and went for the first down. Auburn's defense stuffed Alabama and got the ball back.

But Auburn couldn't do anything with the ball, and again Alabama worked their way deep into Auburn territory. Just as they had been in their previous drive, Alabama was faced with a fourth down with 2:41 left, this time from the Auburn 25-yard line. Saban went for the field goal to again try to put the game away. But Auburn blocked the kick, and Alabama came up empty again in kicking a field goal. The game remained 28-21 Alabama.

Auburn was running out of time, though, and timeouts. They worked their way down to the Alabama 39-yard line, but only 42 seconds remained on the clock. Marshall faked the handoff and looked like he was going to keep it himself and run. But all of a sudden, he saw Sammie Coates wide open down the field. Marshall quickly put the ball into his right hand and threw it. Coates caught it and took off down the field, no one around him. Touchdown Auburn.

28-28. 33 seconds left.

Alabama was seemingly content to take the game into overtime. But with just seven seconds left, running back T.J. Yeldon took a draw play and ran it 20 yards to the Auburn 39-yard line. One second was left on the clock when he crossed out of bounds.

If Alabama tried the field goal, they were unsure how it would go. They were already 0-for-3, and it was unknown if Foster could get it there from 57 yards out. But Saban felt the chances of them making a 57-yarder were better than trying a Hail Mary, so he went for the field goal.

Auburn coach Gus Malzahn sent Chris Davis, Jr. to the end zone in case Foster's kick came up short. Foster's kick was away and started drifting right. It didn't have the distance. Some of the Alabama players started walking off the sideline to prepare for overtime. Unexpectedly, however, Davis caught the ball just in front of the end zone's out-of-bounds and started running down the left sideline. The few Alabama players on the field paying attention tried to tackle him but missed. The hysteria in the crowd grew and grew. The 50…the 40…the 30…Davis had stayed in bounds, and cut towards the middle of the field.

Touchdown Auburn! No time left.

Final score: Auburn 34, Alabama 28.

Impact of the Game

Picking the greatest games in college football is a difficult task. This, like hundreds of other games, was exciting. But when you talk about finishes, it's really hard to top this one. Never have we seen a game end the way this did and with the excitement from the crowd.

Alabama's kicking woes were their kryptonite. After winning two straight national championships, special teams were what finally got the best of them. The king had finally been taken down.

Auburn went on to play in the SEC Championship game and beat No. 5 Missouri to advance to the National Championship Game against Florida State. In another classic game, the two teams went down to the wire. But Florida State scored in the final minutes to knock off Auburn, becoming the first non-SEC school to win a national championship since Texas in 2005.

Honorable Mention

#1 Alabama vs. #2 Clemson, 2017 National Championship

For years, no one could crack the Alabama wall. National champions in 2009, 2011, 2012, and 2015, they were going for yet another national championship under Coach Nick Saban. Clemson entered as the underdog, losers to Alabama in the national championship a year earlier in Arizona. This time around, though, Clemson had put themselves in a better position to win.

It looked as if Alabama had done it again. When quarterback Jalen Hurts hit tight end O.J. Howard from 68 yards out, Alabama had taken a 24-14 lead after three quarters. In the fourth quarter, though, Clemson scored twice to regain the lead, 28-24. With 2:17 left and from the 30-yard line, Jalen Hurts dropped back and then took off. Just like Vince Young had done 11 years earlier, Hurts dodged tackles and broke free. He crossed into the end zone and propelled Alabama to a 31-28 lead.

Everyone thought it was over because this was Alabama. But Clemson worked their way quickly down the field. With 17 seconds left, quarterback Deshaun Watson hit wide receiver Leggett on a huge pass play, getting it down to the Alabama 9-yard line. With nine seconds left, Alabama committed a pass-interference penalty in the end zone, putting the ball at the two-yard line with just five seconds to go.

With everything on the line and just five seconds left, Watson rolled right and found a wide open Hunter Renfrow for the touchdown.

Clemson knocked out Alabama 35-31 to win the national championship.

#10 Boston College at #12 Miami, The "Hail Flutie" Game

Quarterback Doug Flutie is remembered for a lot of things, but none more than what he did in 1984 against the Miami Hurricanes.

This game went back and forth all day long. Trailing 34-31, Miami's Melvin Bratton scored from 52 yards out on a run to give his team a 38-34 lead in the fourth quarter. Boston College responded, though. Flutie worked his Eagles down the field and running back Stephen Strachan scored from one yard out to put the Eagles back in front 41-38.

Quarterback Bernie Kosar then put together an epic 79-yard drive late in the fourth quarter and ate up almost every second of the clock. With just 28 seconds left, Bratton scored again from one yard out and Miami had seemingly won the game, 45-41.

Flutie needed a miracle. He completed two passes and worked the ball down to the Miami 48-yard line with six seconds left. He had to try a Hail Mary pass. He rolled out, backtracking as he avoided Miami defenders. He let the ball go from his own 35-yard line, traveling 65 yards to the Miami end zone. Everybody went up for the ball, but it went through their hands undeflected and right into the hands of Gerard Phelan just over the goal line. As Brent Musberger famously announced on air, "Flutie…throws it down…..caught by Boston College! I don't believe it! It's a touchdown!"

Final score: Boston College 47, Miami 45.

5

FUN FACTS ABOUT FOOTBALL

We've shared a lot of information with you in this book—the history of football, the evolution of the teams, the greatest players, the greatest games. But there may still be things you do not know that will interest you. Here are 10 cool facts about football, along with some other random facts that even many of the game's greatest experts may not know.

Did You Know?

Fact #1: The first two Super Bowls weren't "The Super Bowl."

We call it the Super Bowl today, but when this ultimate football contest was first introduced, it was called the AFL-NFL World Championship Game. The NFL didn't adopt the name "Super Bowl" until 1969, in time for Super Bowl III. The game did not generate much interest at first. In fact, the first Super Bowl was played at the Los Angeles Memorial Coliseum, but of the 94,000 seats, 33,000 went unsold! Can you imagine a Super Bowl today having a single empty seat?

Fact #2: The Tampa Bay Buccaneers lost their first 26 games.

The Bucs began playing football in 1976 and finished the first season 0-14. They started the 1977 season 0-12. That's 26 consecutive losses! Today, they are two-time Super Bowl champions, and have made three straight postseasons. But the Bucs used to be derisively called "The Yucs." They wore orange creamsicle jerseys that many called ugly and, well, that aligned with their play on the field. They had a hard time fielding an NFL roster and brought in guys off the street to play for their team. They didn't score a single point until their third game. They lost games in 1976 by scores of 42-17, 48-13, 49-16, 42-0, and 34-0. Their closest loss in 1976 was 14-9, and this was at the hands of the second-worst team in football, the Buffalo Bills. The Bucs were the NFL's Bad News Bears.

When a reporter asked head coach John McKay after a game, "What do you think of the team's execution?", McKay quipped, "I'm all in favor of it."

Fact #3: The Georgia Bulldogs were once The Georgia Goats.

When Georgia played its first football game in 1892, they introduced a goat as their mascot. This seems strange to us now, given that the Georgia Bulldog is one of the most iconic mascots in sports today. How they got to the bulldog, though, is even more intriguing. It wasn't suggested by the school, but by a writer named Morgan Blake. He wrote in *The Atlanta Constitution* that the name "Georgia Bulldogs" would sound intimidating and ferocious. The article gained some traction among fans, and even other writers used "Georgia Bulldogs" in their stories. Eventually the university president caught the Bulldogs craze, and in 1926, the team officially changed its name to the Georgia Bulldogs.

Fact #4: The 1958 NFL Championship Game was disrupted by...a television guy.

We learned earlier about "The Greatest Game Ever Played" and how it was the first-ever game nationally broadcast. Well, just as Johnny Unitas was leading his team on the game-tying drive, NBC lost coverage when a cable was accidentally unplugged because of the raucous crowd at Yankee Stadium. So NBC devised a plan to have a statistician named Stan Rotkiewicz run out onto the field pretending to be drunk to disrupt the game. While the crowd laughed and officials stopped the game to catch the "drunk" guy, producers at NBC re-connected the cable and got the game back on television. Thankfully for NBC, viewers at home got to watch the incredible finish.

Fact #5: The Baltimore Colts actually moved to Indianapolis in the middle of the night!

When we say a team's relocation came out of nowhere, we mean this one really came out of nowhere. The Baltimore Colts were established in 1947 and were seemingly content there for 37 years. But like a thief in the night, owner Bob Irsay hired a moving company to come to Baltimore Colts headquarters and move the team to Indianapolis. It all transpired in the middle of the night. Irsay had been in secret talks with Indianapolis for a couple of months about moving the team, but news on it was scarce. No public announcement was ever made. When fans in Baltimore woke up on the morning of March 28, 1984, they had no football team!

In today's media circus, it'd be a little tougher to fly under the radar like that, but in 1984, Irsay succeeded. They have been the Indianapolis

Colts ever since. Ironically, in late 1995, then Cleveland Browns owner Art Modell stunned fans by announcing he was moving the Browns to Baltimore. Today, that franchise is known as the Baltimore Ravens, and *today's* Cleveland Browns is part of an expansion team established in 1999.

Fact #6: Not all college mascots match with their team name.

When we watch the Clemson Tigers, we see a tiger mascot. And when we watch the Penn State Nittany Lions, we see a lion mascot. Of course we love watching the Oregon Ducks because we see a mascot that looks like Donald Duck on the sideline. For most teams we get the team's mascot…but not all. Alabama's team name is the Crimson Tide, but its mascot is an elephant. The Stanford Cardinal mascot is a tree. Then there's Texas A&M. They are known as the Aggies, but their mascot is a collie dog.

Fact #7: Sammy Baugh was an animal!

Okay, not literally. But during a football game, Baugh was like Los Angeles Angels baseball pitcher Shohei Ohtani, producing on both offense and defense. During a game in 1943, Baugh threw four touchdown passes! You may say "Big deal," but back then throwing the ball wasn't done very often. But wait, there's more. Baugh also played defense and was a defensive back. In that same game, he picked the quarterback off four times! That's a heck of a game. And there's still more. To top it off, Baugh was the team's punter, and he booted an 81-yard punt during that same game. He was basically Offensive Player of the Week, Defensive Player of the Week, and Special Teams Player of the Week. That season, he led the league in touchdown passes, tackles, and punting average. Good luck ever seeing a player do that again.

Fact #8: Two teams actually finished an NFL season undefeated.

Football fans recognize the 1972 Miami Dolphins coached by Don Shula as the "perfect team," finishing the regular season with a perfect 14-0 and going on to win the Super Bowl. Thus, a 17-0 season. But Tom Brady and the New England Patriots also finished the 2007 regular season 17-0, and with two playoff wins, were 19-0 going into Super

Bowl XLII in 2008. Everyone was already crowning the Patriots the greatest team ever assembled, since they were playing the Super Bowl against the 10-6 New York Giants, who hadn't even earned a home playoff game. The Giants barely made the postseason and the Patriots were favored to win by 14 points. But as the saying goes, "That's why they play the game." The Giants stunned the Patriots 17-14 to win the Super Bowl and spoil the Patriots perfect season.

Fact #9: Some college football rivalries are, well, unique.

We love college football rivalries. Most of them have names, too. For example, we love to watch "The Game" between Ohio State vs. Michigan; it makes our Thanksgiving weekend. Or "The Iron Bowl," an in-state rivalry between Alabama vs. Auburn. There's the "Holy War" between two Utah Mormon schools, BYU and Utah. But some of the rivalry names and what they play for can be pretty interesting. For example, Mississippi and Mississippi State play "The Egg Bowl" every year. The winner gets a golden egg. There's the "Battle for the Milk Can" between Fresno State and Boise State. And then we have "The Battle for the Bones" between Memphis and Alabama-Birmingham. Others include "Bedlam" (Oklahoma-Oklahoma State), "The Crab Bowl Classic" (Maryland-Navy), "The Battle for the Paul Bunyan Axe" (Minnesota-Wisconsin), and "The Beehive Bowl" (Southern Utah-Weber State).

Fact #10: The meaning behind the "Hail Mary" play.

When we hear the name "Hail Mary" pass we often wonder about the origin of the name. You may recall Doug Flutie used it in his miraculous touchdown pass against Miami. Well, in a 1975 playoff game in Minnesota, quarterback Roger Staubach and the Cowboys were about to lose and were given no chance to come back and win. That's when Staubach, a devoted Catholic, heaved the ball up and hit Drew Pearson on a 50-yard pass with 24 seconds left. The Cowboys had beaten the Vikings. After the game, someone asked how Staubach did it and he responded, "I just closed my eyes and said a Hail Mary." Since then, a long throw at the end of the half or game is referred to as "A Hail Mary."

Other Random Facts

- The Pittsburgh Steelers and New England Patriots are tied for most Super Bowl wins, with six each.
- The Patriots have the most appearances in the Super Bowl—11
- Four active teams have never been to a Super Bowl—the Detroit Lions, the Cleveland Browns, the Jacksonville Jaguars, and the Houston Texans.
- The University of Michigan has the most wins in college football—989.
- The University of Oklahoma once won 47 straight games between 1953 and 1957. It is the longest winning streak in college football history.
- If you love the story of "The Ice Bowl" and bad weather games, check out some of these other "bad weather" games. There's the "Fog Bowl" (Eagles at Bears, 1988), "The Snow Bowl" (Ohio State at Michigan, 1950), "The Tuck Rule Game/Snow Bowl (Raiders at Patriots, 2002), "The Mud Bowl" (Vikings at Rams, 1977), "The Freezer Bowl" (Chargers at Bengals, 1982), and "The Monsoon Game" (Chiefs at Bucs, 1979).
- Yale has won 18 national championships, the most in college football.
- Tom Brady is NOT the oldest player to play in a football game. That honor belongs to George Blanda, who played until he was 48 years old! Amobi Okoye was the youngest player to ever play in an NFL game at 19 years old.

CONCLUSION

As we look back at history, it's amazing to think how close we were to not having professional football. Several times the sport was practically on life support. Thanks to the perseverance of some men and the evolution of several star athletes, the game gained momentum and was saved.

What would the weekends be like without football? Imagine a February without Super Bowl Sunday. Iconic figures like Tom Brady, Jerry Rice, and Patrick Mahomes would be doing something entirely different, maybe not even in sports, instead of throwing a football.

The game has undergone so many changes from its birth, and it continues to see change every year. Many of the changes have to do with protecting the players' health; referees have begun handing out strong penalties for severe hits, particularly to the helmet. Concussions are a growing concern because too many of them can cause serious damage to the brain.

The style of play has changed as well. We've seen the NFL go from wing-backs to I-formations to West Coast offenses to "Run and Shoot" offenses to Pro Style offenses. In college football, the spread offense has overtaken the game, with quarterbacks operating out of the shotgun and being in control of whether to hand the ball off, keep it themselves and run, or throw it. Some NFL teams are now even adopting that strategy.

It's an ever-changing game, but the changes they've made have produced the most exciting sport in the United States. So when you go to a stadium or turn on the TV and watch your favorite football team going head to head with a rival team, be thankful. We almost didn't have it.

THE BASEBALL BOOK FOR BOYS 9-12

THE HISTORY OF THE GAME, BIOGRAPHIES OF THE GREATEST PLAYERS OF ALL TIME, STORIES OF AMAZING GAMES, AND INCREDIBLE FACTS

JIMMY MCCALL

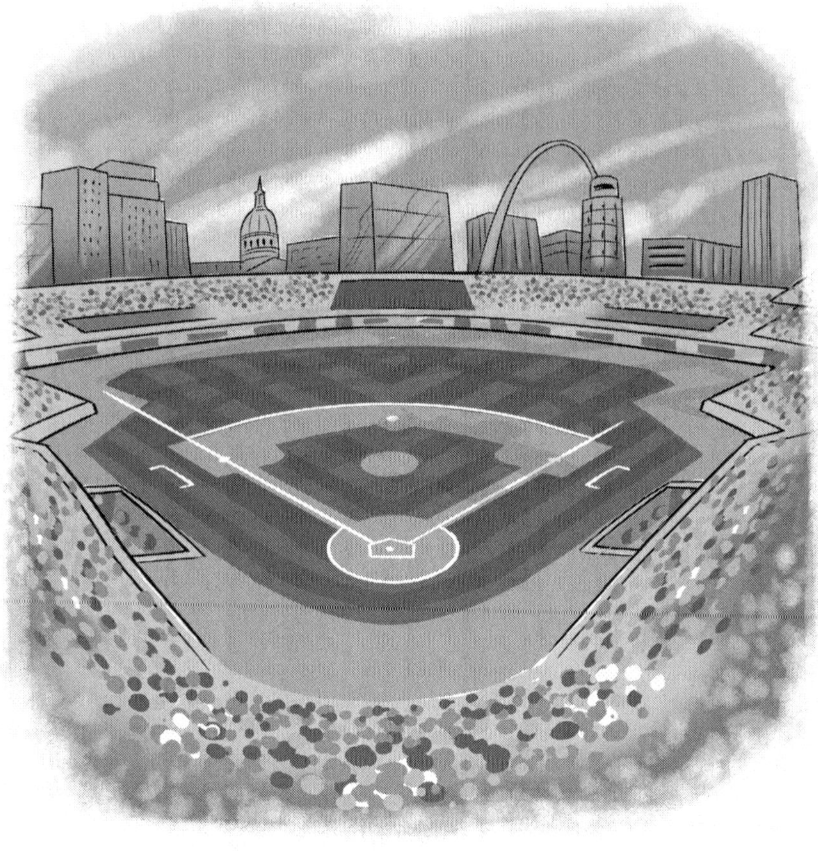

INTRODUCTION

I remember it like it was yesterday. I was seven years old and visiting New York City. On a beautiful July Saturday afternoon, my dad took me and my brother to one of the most iconic places in America–Yankee Stadium.

We got there early and visited Monument Park, a museum in the back of the stadium honoring the greatest Yankees of all-time. We saw the retired jerseys, plaques, monuments, and feature stories on legends like Gehrig, Mantle, DiMaggio, and The Babe. I was in awe of the history that surrounded me.

The Yankees played the Kansas City Royals that day but I honestly couldn't tell you what the final score was. I just remember there was something special about going to a baseball game with my dad that felt incredible. It's a memory I'll always cherish. It was relaxing and fun and I've loved baseball ever since. I've also noticed that the players all seem to smile more than they do in other sports, which is funny since they fail to get a hit seven or eight times out of every 10 at-bats!

I had a hot dog and my dad reached for his wallet when he heard someone yell "Cold beer here!" in that typical Tony Soprano accent where you couldn't hear the "r's" in the words.

Oddly enough, I can't remember my first football or basketball game, but that Yankees game stands out so vividly. It's because there's a mystique about baseball that other sports just can't capture. Sure, football, basketball, and hockey are exciting and keep you on the edge of your seat for the whole game, but with baseball, you can just sit back, relax, enjoy the game and soak in the atmosphere.

In fact, my favorite sporting event I ever attended was a baseball game and was at the *new* Yankees Stadium. I was there in 2009 when the Tampa Bay Rays played the New York Yankees and Derek Jeter needed three hits to tie Lou Gehrig's all-time Yankees hit record. I didn't think I'd see history that day, but I did. I'd never in my life seen an atmosphere like that one, especially when Jeter got his third hit of the game, a deep shot off the centerfield wall, tying Gehrig's record. It was the loudest I ever remember a stadium being, and the chants of "Derek Jeter" went on for minutes and still ring in my head today.

Memories. That's what baseball gives you. Photographs are in my head of the Yankees games I've been to, as well as all the other stadiums I've visited in my life. I've been to a lot of football and hockey games, but the memories aren't the same as they are for baseball.

I loved to play it, too, and am grateful my dad got me into it. I started in t-ball and worked my way up. When I was 10, I played Little League baseball and was actually teammates with the current Florida governor, who went on to play in the Little League World Series that season. Baseball was probably my best sport, and I even made the All-Star team in Junior League and then started for my high school team.

Of all the sports I played growing up (and I played them all), baseball ranks right up there with golf as the most challenging. It's not easy to play, but if you love a good test, it's worth trying. As I mentioned earlier, when you're up at the plate, you're struck out a lot. Even the best hitters to ever play failed more than they succeeded. But the game is just as much mental as it is physical; you have to be mentally strong to be good at it.

The history of the game is unlike any other as well. Today, many may think of football as America's pastime, but baseball was America's favorite sport for well over a century and is still going strong. It dominated the headlines while everything else was a distant second. The strike in '94 undoubtedly hurt the game, and the steroid scandal added a black mark to its name, but it nevertheless has a history that no other sport in the world can match.

Some of the best stories in sports today come from baseball. Babe Ruth's called shot against the Cubs in the World Series, a story that still sparks great conversation and debate today. Hank Aaron's record-breaking home run in Atlanta. Kirk Gibson's iconic game-winning home run in the World Series in '88 and Jack Buck's famous call, "I don't believe what I just saw." Nolan Ryan's sixth no-hitter in his career, a feat that we will probably never see again.

I wish more people knew of baseball's history. My goal is to show you the best parts of the game, the game I remember growing up, when athletes cared more about the fans than they did about money. That said, there are still plenty of good guys in the game today; guys like Anthony Rizzo, who visits cancer patients throughout the year. Or Yu Darvish who stood in the rain to sign autographs for kids. There still are plenty of stories that make you smile and encourage you to want to become a baseball player just like them.

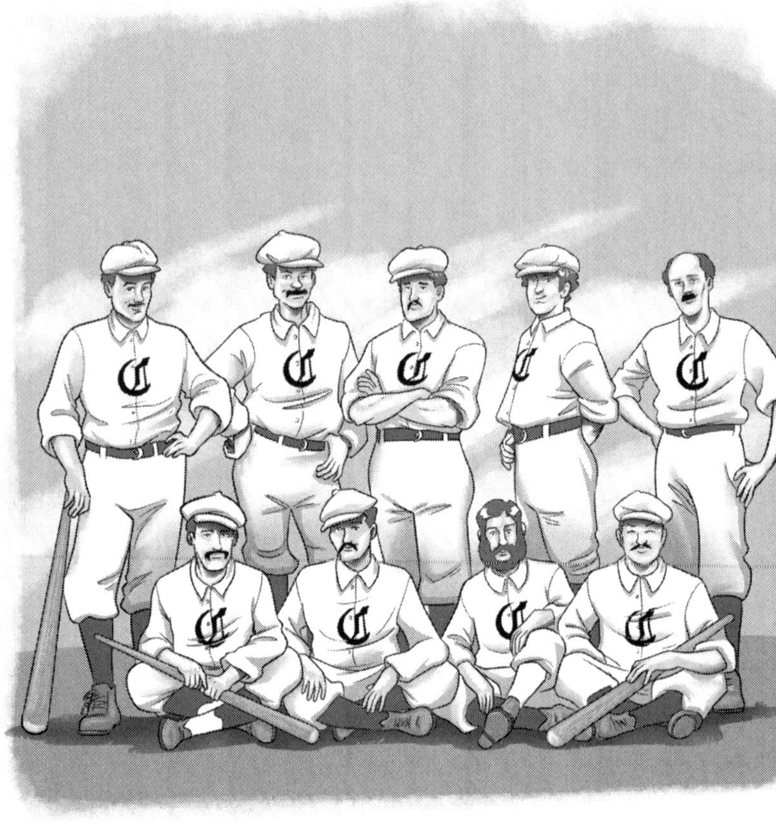

1

THE HISTORY OF THE GAME

WHO REALLY INVENTED BASEBALL?

The question of who invented baseball is one of the biggest mysteries in baseball. The official records state that war hero Abner Doubleday invented baseball. However, many say the true "Father of Baseball" was Alexander Cartwright. In 1845, Cartwright led the establishment of baseball's first club, the Knickerbocker Base Ball Club, later simply called the New York Knickerbockers. He has also been credited with designing the modern-day baseball field and helping institute many of the rules that we use today.

Others claim the "Father of Baseball" was Henry Chadwick, who developed the first rule book and invented the box score after playing rounders and cricket (both bat-and-ball games played in England). Chadwick would become the first chairman of rules for the first organized baseball association.

However, while all that may be true, there is evidence the game goes back even farther than that.

But before we look back into where the game started, one question needs to be answered: Why do so many people think Abner Doubleday invented baseball? There are no records of Doubleday claiming he started it, nor are there records of him organizing any game or sport. Well, the main reason is that the Mills Commission, a group specifically formed in 1905 to determine the origins of baseball, told us so and everyone simply accepted it. In their report, the Commission stated, "The first scheme for playing baseball, according to the best evidence obtainable to date, was devised by Abner Doubleday at Cooperstown, NY, in 1839."

But historians have claimed that's a myth, and they have good reason to say so. You see, back in the late 1800s, shortly after the Civil War, "Where did baseball come from?" was a growing question because the sport was starting to increase in popularity. Chicago Cubs president Albert Spalding and National League President Abraham Mills (yes, that Mills) didn't like the story of Alexander Cartwright inventing baseball because he was British, and they wanted people to recognize baseball as "an American game," built on American principles.

When people began spreading stories of Cartwright's invention, Mills and Spalding decided to put together a commission investigating the question of who invented baseball and then share the results with the public. Historians claim they conspired to arrive at an answer they wanted; someone who bled red, white, and blue.

Unfortunately, their investigation included letters from all different types of people relating different stories about how baseball had started. Finally, they came to a letter from a man named Albert Graves, who wrote that he'd gone to school with Abner Doubleday and claimed Doubleday had shown him a baseball diamond in 1839 and set up the first game in Cooperstown, New York. Spalding considered this as eyewitness testimony and thought the idea of Doubleday inventing baseball made a great story. He was a West Point graduate and Civil War hero, so it would be an inspiring story of how baseball had been founded by a patriot.

Of course, there were a lot of holes in Graves' story that people still scratch their heads at. For one, he was the only eyewitness. Second, in 1839, he would have been just five years old; it's unclear how a five-year old would know about Doubleday's diagram-drawing when Doubleday was at West Point at the time and per Army records, had never even gone to Cooperstown. To top it off, shortly after Graves' recollection, he was sent to an insane asylum after committing a violent crime.

Even more head-scratching was that Mills was close friends with Doubleday, but in all those years of knowing him, Doubleday never told him he'd invented this cool game played on a diamond with bats and balls. Unfortunately, Doubleday passed away in 1893, long before the investigation. Those who knew him best had no recollection of him ever saying anything about inventing baseball.

Needing to give the public an answer, in 1908 the Mills Commission used Graves' story as the basis for their claim that Doubleday had invented baseball, and even touted Cooperstown as the home of baseball, which is why it later became the site of baseball's Hall of Fame. The story (or myth) grew and we have what we have today.

Of course, we're talking about events from over 100 years ago, when there was no press, no Google, and no television. We can only go by what we have in writing and from what people have claimed. But perhaps the best testament came from revered and respected Major League Baseball historian John Thorn, who researched the matter thoroughly and came up with the following conclusion on Doubleday's inventing baseball:

This would have been a surprise to Doubleday. The late Civil War hero "never knew that he had invented baseball. [But] 15 years [after his death], he was anointed as "the father of the game."

SO HOW DID BASEBALL *REALLY* START?

Whether it was Doubleday, Cartwright, Chadwick, or someone else who invented baseball, the truth of the matter is that pieces of baseball were around well before any of their times. In fact, around the time of the American Revolution, people were playing a game similar to baseball with rules like we see today. Back then, it was known simply as stick ball, or rounders. There was also a game called cricket, which originated in England, and was brought to America and used in colleges, just like soccer was.

New York, Massachusetts, and Philadelphia all had variations they were playing that were similar to baseball. According to the historian John Thorn, some were playing this game as early as 1735. The games started on farms and later moved to the cities. A picture was published in 1760 with people playing rounders and children standing on bases similar to those we see today in baseball. Obviously, there were some differences, one of which was that to throw people out, you had to peg them with the ball.

Eventually, someone had to step into the picture and put together a product that would be universally accepted. Just like Walter Camp used rugby and soccer to form football, Alexander Cartwright (so records say) used cricket and rounders to create baseball. He designed a set of rules that included a diamond-shaped infield, foul lines, and a batter getting three strikes before they were officially out. Players also had to tag a runner or throw it to their teammate on the base to get the runner out.

Baseball quickly grew in popularity. When The Knickerbockers and the New York Baseball Club, also known as the New York Nine, played the first "officially recorded" game, the sport spread around the country. There was no organized league yet; kids played the game on farms or local fields and local clubs were established. New equipment was produced and sold to clubs everywhere.

Then in 1857, a group got together for a convention to discuss forming a baseball league. With the help of Henry Chadwick, they adopted an official set of rules, very similar to the ones established in 1845, and interested participants set out to form teams. In 1858, the first ever amateur baseball league was formed, called The National Association of Base Ball Players (NABBP). *(Important note: in the 1800s, baseball was two words).*

Colleges also picked up the game in the late 1850s. The first collegiate game took place between Williams and Amherst on July 1, 1859, in

Pittsfield, Mass. However, they used a different set of rules than those adopted by the NABBP.

In 1860, baseball was considered the most popular sport in America, replacing the British game of cricket as the nation's new pastime. People went to watch college games and the amateur league, but no professional league had yet been formed. If not for the start of the Civil War, one would almost certainly have been put together early in the 1860s. In fact, many teams in the amateur league had to fold because men went off to fight in the war and the country split apart.

During the war, however, the game was popular. Soldiers would play baseball while camped out in different towns and cities. Pictures exist of them throwing the ball and rounding the bases in the fields. It was a way to escape the horror that was destroying our nation. Soldiers actually helped spread the game to other parts of the country as they marched along.

After the war ended and the nation reunited, another convention was established to discuss forming a professional baseball league in which players would be paid for competing. Over 100 interested teams were present. In 1869, the Cincinnati Red Stockings became the first organized professional baseball team. For the first time in history, players would be paid to play baseball.

The team was led by Harry Wright, a professional cricket player who was recruited by Cincinnati's amateur club to play baseball. Wright joined and helped recruit many other cricket players to join the team. Soon, Cincinnati was filled with talent, and fans everywhere wanted to see them play. Cincinnati was beating some of the best clubs in the country by scores of 45-9 and 86-8. They were that good.

The Red Stockings toured the country, playing amateur teams from the NABBP. But while the game continued to grow in popularity, Cincinnati struggled to hold up financially. In 1871, Cincinnati's board couldn't pay its bills and the team folded. Players spread out to other amateur clubs. Meanwhile, Harry Wright moved to Massachusetts and started another club, the Boston Red Stockings, taking some of the Cincinnati players with him.

Side note: At this point you're probably thinking, "Wait, I thought the Cincinnati Red Stockings would become the Cincinnati Reds." Wrong. And now maybe you're thinking, "Oh, so the Red Stockings became the Boston Red Sox!" Well, that's also wrong. Crazliy enough, the original Cincinnati Red Stockings are the present-day Atlanta Braves, and considered baseball's oldest franchise because the Red Stockings changed their name to the Boston Braves, then moved to Milwaukee in 1953 and Atlanta in 1966.

But let's return to our story. At the same time Wright formed the Boston franchise, a new professional league was formed, the National Association (NA). The Boston Red Stockings joined the Chicago White Stockings as the first professional teams in the NA. (*Of course, now you're probably thinking the Chicago White Stockings became the White Sox, but once again, no! While Chicago would go through a few name changes over time, they finally settled on the Chicago Cubs in 1903.*)

Seven other clubs joined from the NABBP; the Philadelphia Athletics, the Washington Olympics, the New York Mutuals, the Troy Haymakers, the Fort Wayne Kekiongas, the Cleveland Forest Citys, and the Rockford Forest Citys. These teams all made up the NA.

Wright's Red Stockings were the best team, however, winning four straight league championships from 1872 to 1875. Then professional baseball went through another big change.

MAJOR LEAGUE BASEBALL

In 1876, Chicago businessman William Hulbert formed a convention in Cincinnati, Ohio to eliminate the NA, which he and others complained was poorly organized and becoming too corrupt. Money was also a growing problem. So Hulbert and others established the National League of Professional Base Ball Clubs (also simply known as the National League, or NL).

Albert (A.G.) Spalding played a big role in popularizing the new professional baseball league. In 1876, then a pitcher for the Chicago White Stockings, Spalding proposed a new baseball for the league that included a core rubber inside of tightly wound yarn. He also was one of the first players to regularly use a glove; most players didn't use one back then.

Then in 1882, Spalding opened a sporting equipment store, selling all kinds of baseball equipment to anyone who wanted to play the game, including his newly designed balls and gloves. Spalding's store was extremely popular and helped sell the sport to the public. From then on, gloves became more permanent in baseball and the new balls were regularly used. Soon, Spalding opened up more stores and became one of the first major baseball manufacturers nationwide. This is why many of the balls and gloves today are Spalding brand. He also helped Hulbert organize the league and spread the game to other parts of the country.

But the NL went through some difficult times. Just like the NFL had to deal with the AFL, the NL had to deal with their own rival league, the American League of Professional Base Ball Clubs (also known as the American League, or AL). The AL was led by Bancroft Johnson, commissioner of the Western League, a minor league for professional baseball.

According to Johnson and his supporters, the National League was becoming too much of a monopoly, and didn't want expansion. In fact, after the NL expanded to 12 teams, it eliminated four teams and went back down to eight, forcing more players into the Minor Leagues. Included in those franchises kicked out were the Philadelphia Athletics and Chicago White Stockings.

Johnson felt the talent in his Western League was strong enough to challenge the NL's league, so in 1901, a separate convention was held and the American League was formed. The American League was composed of eight teams, just like the current National League, and included teams like the Milwaukee Brewers, Detroit Tigers, and Baltimore Orioles. The White Stockings and Athletics also joined.

"The National League is forcing this war on us," Johnson said. "All we ask is a chance for good, healthy rivalry and competition, but if the National League insists on fighting we shall be able to take care of ourselves."

In 1903, the two leagues came to an understanding that both leagues were part of professional baseball and that they relied on each other to keep the game going. While they remained separate and only played against teams in their respective league, they decided upon a championship matchup, in which the winner of each league at the end of the year would play the other for one 'world' championship (even though it was only in America). This would become known as "The World Series."

The World Series would be composed of a "best-of-nine" series, with the first team to win five games winning the championship. It would be changed the following season to a best-of-seven series, although the best-of-nine format would be used again in 1919, 1920, and 1921, as an experiment to increase popularity of the sport and to generate moe revenue.

With this merger, the name "Major League Baseball" was officially coined. In 1903, the first World Series was played between the American League's Boston Americans and the National League's Pittsburgh Pirates. The Americans would beat the Pirates five games to three to win Major League Baseball's first ever World Series.

Unlike other sports, though, baseball never went through a major expansion during the first half of the century. The American and National Leagues remained at eight teams each, and while some teams changed their name, no relocations took place. Other leagues tried to form to challenge the Major League, like the Federal League in 1914, but failed.

Baseball thrived off its Minor League system, which is why it stayed at 16 total teams for so long. They were worried expanding would water down the league. Another reason was that baseball was more of an East Coast game; it didn't have the popularity out West until after World War II. Fourteen of the 16 teams were located east of the Mississippi

River; the exception was St. Louis, with two teams, the Browns and the Cardinals. But after the war, more people began to migrate West and baseball became more nationwide; in 1952, baseball finally began to grow in popularity.

Major relocations started in 1953. The Boston Braves relocated to Milwaukee (and then eventually Atlanta), the Philadelphia Athletics relocated to Kansas City (and eventually Oakland), the Brooklyn Dodgers went to Los Angeles, and the New York Giants moved to San Francisco.

Finally, in 1961, Major League Baseball began to expand. First, Los Angeles got its second team, the Angels. The Washington Senators then relocated to Minnesota and became the Twins, but baseball added a new expansion team in Washington to replace the Senators (they would also be named the Senators). That Senators team would move too, though, and become the Texas Rangers in 1975.

The next year, New York found itself with another team, the Mets, and the Houston Colt .45s were formed, later changing their name to the Astros. The league continued to see expansions and relocations over the next several decades. The most recent teams added are the Tampa Bay Devil Rays (now just the Rays) and the Arizona Diamondbacks in 1998. The last team to relocate was the Montreal Expos, which went to Washington to become the Nationals.

Baseball also eliminated the two-league system in 1997 when it began playing interleague games. At first, these games would only be played for a couple weeks out of the season, with one division from each league playing the other during a specified time over the summer. For example, the Yankees would play the National League East during two weeks out of the year in June. But interleague baseball's popularity, combined with the fact that there are now an odd number of teams in both leagues (15 each) has led to interleague games being played regularly throughout the season. While teams from the American League still predominantly play other teams from the American League, the landscape is more mixed than it used to be.

EVOLUTION OF THE GAME

While baseball was extremely popular when it first arrived in the 1800s, it began to lose some luster in the early 1900s. Part of that was because it was a pitcher's game; there was no power in the hitting. In 1908, the home run per game rate was a dismal 0.11 (today, it's 1.16), and the average runs per game by a team was 3.38 (today, it's 4.5). Baseball had great hitters, like Ty Cobb, Honus Wagner, and Rogers Hornsby, but they were few and far between, and they were strictly base hit players.

Things were done to try and bring about more offense, like tweaking the baseballs and not winding the yarn so tight, and changing the way bats were made. Of course, pitchers wanted the game to stay "a pitcher's game" so they found ways around it, like putting tar on baseballs so they could grip it better and spitting on the ball. Eventually, these kinds of actions would be outlawed. But despite some of these changes, baseball's growth had halted.

Scandals also damaged the sport's image. In 1919, eight Chicago White Sox players were banned from Major League Baseball for accepting money to intentionally lose the World Series. The scandal left the team with the moniker "The Black Sox" and fans left the game. (If you ever want to learn more about this story, *Eight Men Out* is a great movie.)

But all that changed when Babe Ruth came along. Ruth's build was different from other players; he was bigger and more filled out compared to the average ball player. He played for the Boston Red Sox early on, but eventually made his way to New York, where he built his reputation as part of the Yankees. Prior to 1919, the Major League record for most home runs in a season was 16 by Socks Seybold. In 1919, Ruth blasted 29! In 1920, he hit 54. In 1921, he hit 59! The game had changed, and Ruth was the architect behind it all.

The evolution of the home run in baseball excited fans like nothing ever had before; people flocked to ballparks to watch Babe Ruth hit home runs. The Yankees played at the Polo Grounds in the early 1920s, but had to build a bigger stadium in the Bronx because of Ruth's towering home runs. That's why it was eventually dubbed "The House that Ruth

Built." He even hit the first home run at that park on the first day the stadium opened.

Ruth inspired players, and shortly after his entrance into baseball, more home run hitters came along, such as Lou Gehrig, Jimmie Foxx, and Hank Greenberg. All of a sudden, hitting 30 and 40 home runs in a season was normal. Before Ruth came along, it was unheard of.

Another major influencer on the game was Jackie Robinson (see story below). Robinson brought a new faction of players into baseball. Before Robinson, baseball was a white man's sport. But Robinson broke the color barrier in 1947, and more African Americans followed. They were fast and could hit, and their entrance only made the game more exciting and more competitive.

Baseball was thriving in the 1950s and 1960s. Other greats like Joe DiMaggio, Mickey Mantle, and Willie McCovey came along. Then in the 70s, just when you thought the sport couldn't get any more popular, it was Hank Aaron, Tom Seaver, and Pete Rose who stole the headlines.

Baseball's evolution has had its ups and downs, though. Technology and medicine have had major impacts on the game. In the 1980s and on through the 2000s, players sought ways to gain a competitive advantage and hit more home runs. In 2007, George Mitchell, a former senator and federal prosecutor, was appointed by the commissioner of baseball, Bud Selig, to investigate the use of performance-enhancing drugs in Major League Baseball. Mitchell released a report that found that 89 players had used illegal drugs to boost their performance. Some of these included players who had broken home run records, such as Mark McGwire, Sammy Sosa, Roger Clemens, and Barry Bonds. These players have never been awarded entry into the Baseball Hall of Fame and many fans now consider home run records tarnished and have turned away from the game itself.

As for technology's influence, it has brought instant replay into baseball. Since 2008, managers have been able to challenge home runs and safe/out calls. There has even been debate about when computers should be used to call balls and strikes.

Baseballs have also been continually tweaked. With home run numbers still high in recent years, some have called for an adjustment of the baseball to try and better equalize the sport between offense and defense. Critics have claimed the balls are juiced while others believe that players are simply stronger than they used to be. In 2022, Commissioner Rob Manfred announced the adoption of a new, lighter baseball, taking away some of the power from the hitter, since lighter balls carry a shorter distance. While home run numbers dramatically dropped in 2022, fan favorite Aaron Judge still enthralled fans by hitting an American League single-season record (and some claim Major League record) 62 home runs.

Baseball will see another huge rule change in 2023; for the first time, an actual pitch clock will be used during games. Pitchers will have to throw the ball to home plate before the clock reaches zero, and batters will have to have entered the batter's box by a specific time as well. Penalties, such as awarded balls and strikes, will be enforced if players commit time infractions. The purpose of this clock is to try and speed up the game.

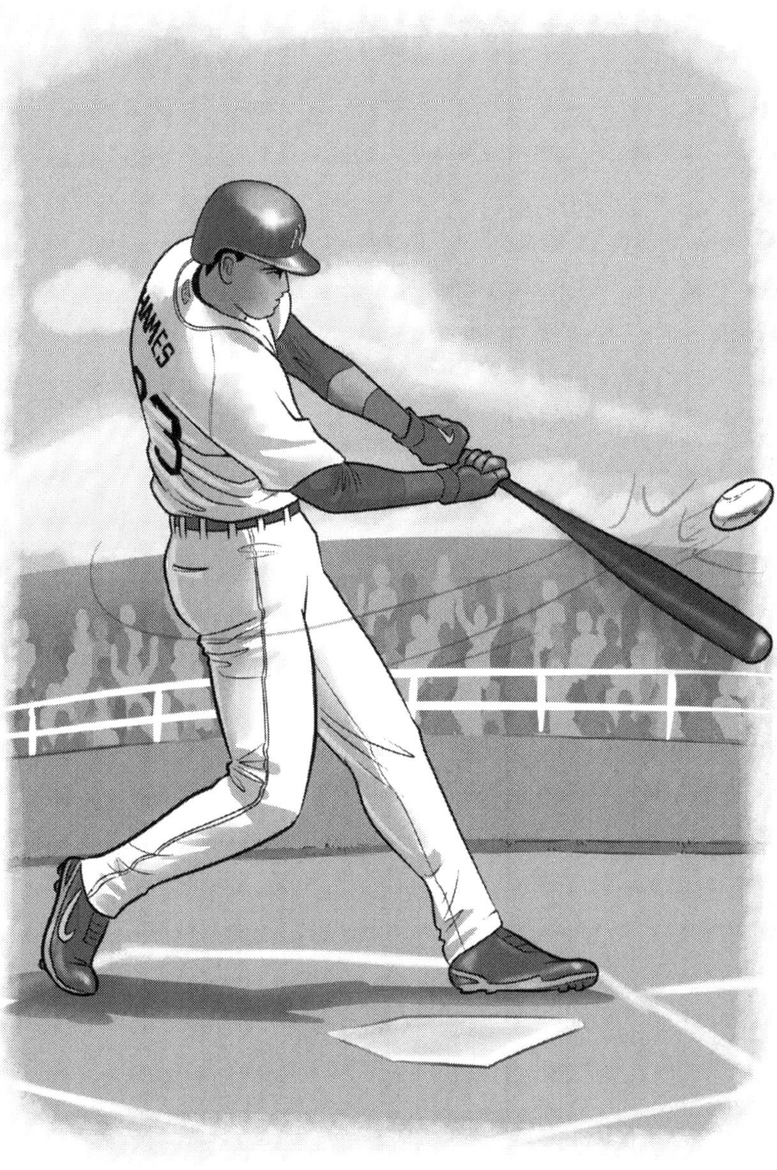

2

HOW THE GAME IS PLAYED

THE BASIC RULES

Baseball is a nine-inning game played between two teams, with each inning divided by halves. The teams play on a diamond-shaped field with four bases placed in each corner of the diamond; those bases, in order, are called first base, second base, third base, and home plate. Within those bases is the infield.

The diamond shape of the infield is made up mostly of dirt and grass. In the middle of the infield is the pitcher's mound, which is where the person throwing the ball (the pitcher) stands. They throw the ball to the catcher, who is crouched behind home plate. Behind the catcher is the umpire, who calls the balls and strikes and determines if players are safe or out.

The goal for each team on offense is to score a run by going around each of the bases and making it safely to home plate. In order to score runs, the offense needs to get hits and keep away from the defense. The team with the most runs wins the game.

Each team is composed of nine players, with replacements on the bench. One team is on offense in the top half of the inning and tries to score, while the other team is on defense out in the field, and does all they can to prevent the offense from scoring. To do this, they need to have a good pitcher who can make it difficult for the hitter to put the ball in play. They also need a good defense that can work together to get the player out. The game has nine different positions, each with its own responsibility.

The hitter stands beside home plate and awaits the ball from the pitcher. The hitter's goal is to make contact with the ball to put it in play and keep it away from members of the team in the field. Once they hit the ball, they run to first base. If the defense in the field gets ahold of the ball and throws it to first base before the runner makes it there, it's an out. Three outs make up a half-inning. If a batter can get to first base and then round all the bases without being called out, they score a run.

A hitter has three chances to put the ball in play. Each time they swing and miss is a strike. A strike is also called when the ball crosses home plate between the hitter's knees and shoulders, whether they swing or not. Every time the batter makes contact and the ball is hit outside the foul lines, it is a foul ball and also counts as a strike. Three strikes is an out, but a player can't be called out on a foul ball. Three strikes is called a strikeout.

If a hitter doesn't swing at a ball and it is outside of the strike zone, it is called a ball. If a hitter receives four balls before they're called for three strikes, they get a walk (or a base on balls) and automatically proceed to first base without hitting again.

On each side of the infield and outfield are the foul lines, and batters must try to keep the ball between these lines. These lines go all the way up the field to the outfield fences, which enclose the field of play.

OTHER BASEBALL TERMINOLOGY

Double/Triple: A double is when a hitter is able to put the ball far enough away from the fielders that they round first base and make it to second base in the same at-bat. If they manage to pass second base and get to third base, they get a triple.

Home Run: Sometimes a hitter puts the ball over the outfield fence within the foul lines. This is a home run and the batter rounds all four bases. A player can also record a home run when they hit the ball away from the defense and can round all the bases and reach home plate before the other team can get them out.

Stolen Base: After a player gets a hit, they become a runner and stand on the base they reached. As soon as the pitcher delivers the ball to the next hitter, the runner can take off and try to get to the next base before they can be tagged out. If the catcher cannot get the ball to the defender on base in time to tag out the runner, that's recorded as a stolen base.

Run Batted in (or RBI): This is a common statistic we hear all the time. When a hitter is able to put the ball in play and a runner scores as a result, that hitter gets an RBI. A runner can get multiple RBIs in one at-bat, depending on how many of their teammates are on bases.

Batting Average: The higher the batting average, the better. This is calculated as the percentage of hits a player gets per the number of at-bats. For example, if a player gets one hit in four attempts, they are hitting .250, which translates numerically to a quarter of the time. Any batting average over .300 is considered excellent.

Sacrifice: Sometimes a player will get an out but advance the runner who is on base. This is referred to as a sacrifice. A hitter might record a sacrifice run when there is a player on third base who can score as a result of an out.

Shift: Many hitters are really good at pulling the baseball to one side. For example, a good right-handed hitter may hit the ball to the left side in 90 percent of their at-bats. In this case, the manager or catcher on the other team may call a shift, in which the defensive team moves all their players to the left side. The second baseman will even move to the other side of second base. A good hitter will recognize this and be able to push the ball to the other side of the field where there is a gap.

Double-Play: This is when a defense is able to get two outs in one play. The most common double play is when a player is on first base and the batter hits a ground ball to an infielder or the pitcher or shortstop. The fielder can then throw the ball to second base to get one out and then the second baseman throws it to first base to get the hitter out. If a defense records three outs in one play, it is a triple play, but those are extremely rare.

Around the Horn: If no players are on base and a pitcher strikes a batter out, the pitcher will usually throw the ball to third base. The third baseman then throws the ball to second, who then throws it to first, who throws it to the pitcher. This is called throwing it around the horn.

Balk: When a runner is on base, a pitcher must act within the rules. One of these rules requires a pitcher to throw the ball to home plate once they start a motion. This tells the runner on the base it is okay to move or even steal. However, if a pitcher stops the delivery to home and then tries to turn and throw out the runner on the base, it is an illegal move and considered a balk. The runner on base is automatically allowed to move forward to the next base.

Choke up: An embarrassing story…when a coach first told me to do this, I started coughing. But seriously, choking up means to move your hands up on the bat. This makes the bat feel lighter because there is less weight above the hands and a little more below them. This gives hitters the ability to swing the bat faster than if they gripped it on the bottom of the handle.

Cycle: These are extremely rare; only very good hitters can do this. Players who hit for the cycle get a base hit, a double, a triple, and a home run all in the same game.

Earned Run Average (ERA): This is the number of earned runs a pitcher gives up per nine innings. For example, if a pitcher gives up six runs over 18 innings pitched, he would have a 3.00 E.R.A. Any E.R.A. under three is excellent. The lower the number, the better.

Error: When you see a line score, you'll see the amount of runs a team scores, the number of hits each team gets, and the amount of errors they committed. Errors are simply mistakes made by position players. They are determined to be plays that would have been outs if the player had properly fielded the ball. These can be simple drops of the ball in the outfield, errant throws to first base, or mishandled balls in the infield or outfield.

Grand Slam: When there is a player on all the bases, the bases are said to be loaded. When the hitter then hits a home run and drives all those runners in on top of themselves, they have hit a grand slam home run.

Force Out: When a ball is hit in the infield and there is a player on first base, it's best to try and get the ball to second base first and get out the lead runner. An infielder can simply step on the second base bag without tagging out the runner. This is called a force out. This only works if players are on consecutive bases. For example, if a runner is on second base but no one is on first, the only way to get that player out is to tag them out.

Intentional Walk: When a pitcher purposely puts a batter on base, it's called an intentional walk. There are usually two reasons for this: Either the hitter is very good and the pitcher worries they won't be able to keep them from getting a good hit or there is a player on second and first base is open. This sets up a potential force out.

Perfect Game: Another rarity; when a pitcher is able to get every single batter out in a game without a walk or an error involved, they have pitched a perfect game. The opposing team had no hits or base runners. If the other team was able to get someone on base through a walk or an error, this is simply called a no-hitter.

Pickoff: If a runner has moved off a base, a pitcher is allowed to throw to that base before the pitch to try and catch them before they make it back to the base. They do this if the runner has a big lead off the bag and looks like they're considering stealing the next base. This is called a pickoff play. But again, once the pitcher begins their throw to home plate, they cannot turn around and try a pickoff, since this would result in a balk.

Bunt: Instead of swinging a bat, a hitter may simply make a full turn towards the pitcher and stick their bat straight out, putting their right hand behind the barrel of the bat. They are trying to bunt the baseball. A bunt is a short hit that goes just a few feet. If successfully executed, it makes it hard for the players to get to the ball before the runner reaches first base. Teams do this if they have a fast player up at bat or if they want to sacrifice and move a player successfully from one base to another.

Save: If a defensive team has a lead of one to three runs with one or two innings left to play, they will often bring in a relief pitcher to try and close the game out. If they are successful, they are awarded the save, while the pitcher who left the game with the lead is awarded the win.

Squeeze Play: If a runner is on third base, some teams will try to have the batter bunt the ball. Once the bunt is made, the runner from third base darts home and tries to score. This is called a squeeze play. A suicide squeeze play is when the runner from third starts running toward home as soon as the pitch is delivered but before the hitter even performs the bunt. This is a bigger gamble, but if the bunt is successful, it's almost a guaranteed run.

Tag: This can mean two things. One is basic–it's when a fielder tags a player out. The other "tag" is when a runner is on base and a fly ball is hit. Once the ball is caught, the runner will try to advance to the next base. This is a tag play.

POSITIONS ON THE FIELD

Pitcher

This is the player who delivers the baseball to the catcher. A pitcher's primary goal is to strike out batters and prevent the other team from getting hits that can turn into runs. As a pitcher grows and improves, they develop different kinds of pitches to make it tougher for the batter to hit the ball. Some of these pitches include fastball, curveball, slider, change-up, sinker, splitter, and knuckle-ball.

Catcher

The catcher is considered the unofficial captain of the defense. They sit behind home plate and receive the balls from the pitcher. They also tell the pitchers which pitches to throw and where to throw them.

Additionally, they direct the defense where to stand. To do this, they must carefully study the game and know each hitter on offense who comes to the plate. If the hitter is notorious for pulling the ball, a catcher will call a shift.

First baseman

Perhaps the most important position in the infield, the first baseman is often responsible for recording any out that isn't a pop fly. When a ball is hit to other players in the infield, they will throw the ball to the first baseman. A first baseman must be skilled at catching, as sometimes throws will be off target, so they must scoop them off the ground or try to stretch their body and catch the ball while keeping their foot on the first base bag.

Second baseman

The person playing here positions themselves between first base and second base. They must communicate well with the shortstop and discuss who will cover the bag if the runner from first base steals. They will also often be the in-between player on a throw from the outfield to home plate.

Shortstop

The shortstop stands between second and third base and communicates constantly with the second baseman on who will cover the second base bag on throws. Just like second, they are the in-between on a throw from the outfielder to home plate. A skilled shortstop fields really well and has a strong and accurate arm that can throw the ball across the infield to get a runner out.

Third baseman

This player stands close to the third base bag and must be a good fielder. A skilled third baseman has a strong arm that can throw a runner out at first base. They also must be quick; if there's a bunt down the third base line, the third baseman has to storm in and try to field it and throw the runner out in time.

Outfielder

There are three outfield positions: left field, centerfield, and right field, each guarding that space. The three of them must communicate with each other constantly, particularly on fly balls, so they know who will catch the ball. Failure to do so can cause them to run into each other. Skilled outfielders must be quick so they can track down balls and get to them as fast as possible. Also, they must have a strong arm to try and get the ball into the infield quickly. Sometimes an outfielder will have to throw the ball to home plate to get a runner out.

Designated Hitter (DH)

These are only used in the American League; in most every other league, the pitcher will hit and there is no designated hitter. But a designated hitter plays only offense; they don't go out into the field and play defense. Designated hitters traditionally are good hitters who don't have the quickness and speed to play the field.

Pinch-hitter

Whenever there is a substitution for a hitter, a player comes off the bench to replace them in the lineup. They are called a pinch-hitter. They then go out into the field to replace that player on defense. Similarly, someone who substitutes a runner on-base is a pinch-runner.

Manager

This is the head coach of the team. They are responsible for setting the lineup and the positions in the field. They also take out the pitchers when they feel they are struggling and need a change. The manager must design a philosophy that gives their team the best chance to win a game, and they must also be a good motivator.

3

THE GREATEST OF ALL TIME

The following players were the best at their position. They overcame a great deal of adversity in life to be the best and were all inducted into the Hall of Fame.

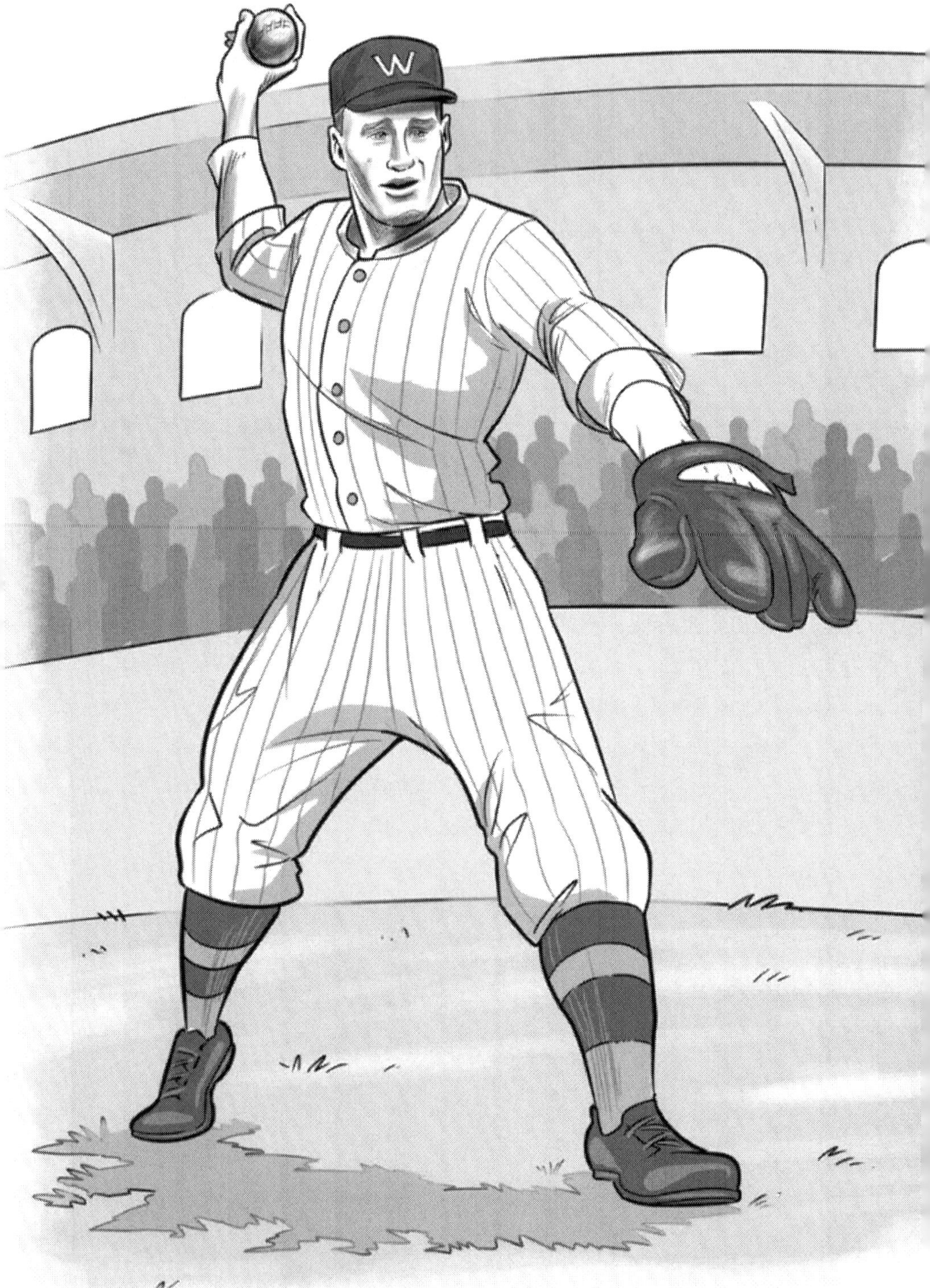
W

PITCHER: WALTER JOHNSON

PITCHER: WALTER JOHNSON

- 110 shutouts (#1 all-time)
- 417 wins (#2 all-time)
- 2.16 ERA
- 3,509 strikeouts (#9 all-time)
- 5,923 innings pitched (#3 all-time)

Biography

Full name: Walter Perry Johnson

Born: Nov. 6, 1887

Nicknames: "The Big Train," "Barney"

Hometown: Humboldt, KS

Uniform Number: N/A

Years Played Professional: 21

Teams Played For: Washington Senators (1907-1927)

Famous quote: "You can't hit what you can't see."

The name Walter Johnson may not be the first name that comes to mind when you think of greatest pitchers, but that's because it's been nearly 100 years since he last stood on the mound. However, there was no pitcher who dominated like "The Big Train."

Inducted into the Hall of Fame in 1936, Johnson holds the all-time record for most 20-win seasons with 10, and they all happened consecutively during the 1910s. He finished his career with 417 wins, more than 3,500 strikeouts, and an amazing 2.17 ERA.

Johnson grew up on a Kansas farm and was the second of six children. Raised in the late 1800s, the country was still trying to recover from The Civil War. The Johnson's grew up poor; Walter had to help out and do all he could on the farm to make sure his family could scratch out a living. He also found time to hunt and fish, the spoils of which they sold to make extra money while his father picked up odd jobs on the side.

The farm life is where many young boys developed a love for baseball. Walter, his siblings, and his friends would find time to play games. Everyone could see how talented Walter was from a young age, especially as his body developed. By the time he was 16, he was already over six feet tall and his body was filling out. When Walter was in his mid-teens, he helped form a sandlot team.

When a horrible drought began to inflict the farm, the Johnson's looked into moving out West where many were finding more opportunities. In 1902, they moved to California, where Walter would play semi-pro baseball, sponsored by his father's employer, an oil company.

As mentioned, Walter was extremely talented as a teenager. Though he played with a bunch of adults, he was the best player on the team. He was mowing down players left and right on the diamond, and word spread to Major League teams about his talent. Johnson believed his talent was fate. "From the first time I held a ball," he said, "it settled in the palm of my right hand as though it belonged there and, when I threw it, ball, hand and wrist, and arm and shoulder and back seemed to all work together."

In 1906, a friend helped Johnson get a job pitching in Southern Idaho for another semi-pro league. He really turned heads his second season, going 14-2 with a 0.55 ERA, striking out 214 batters in 146 innings. Word reached the Washington Senators of this young teenage phenom in Idaho, and they sent scouts out to watch him.

Washington was so impressed with Johnson, they offered him a full contract at just 19 years old. Still a child at heart, Johnson accepted but asked if he could take the train back to California so he could hunt and fish. His family and friends tried to keep him out West and didn't want him to go, but it was an opportunity he couldn't pass up.

It was the best decision he ever made. He went on to pitch 21 years for the Senators, and become arguably the greatest starting pitcher ever. His first season as a 19-year old, he only won five games in 14 games pitched, but impressed teams with a 1.88 ERA.

After that first season, he was incredible. Any ERA under 3 is excellent, and in Johnson's first 13 seasons, he didn't have a single ERA over 3 and only twice had an ERA over 2! His fourth season is when he really began to develop, winning 25 games and producing a 1.36 ERA.

In 1908, with player injuries mounting, Johnson's coach asked him to pitch three games in four days against the Highlanders over Labor Day weekend. Johnson stunned his opponent, giving up just 12 hits in three full games and not giving up a single run! He was the talk of the entire country in just his second season.

He continued to pitch 20-win seasons for the next 10 years, and post ERAs under 2. In 1913, Johnson won 36 games, an all-time record that still stands today for any pitcher after 1908 (before 1908, pitchers had more wins because they started games almost daily). His 36-7 season is considered by many the greatest individual pitching season in the history of Major League Baseball. He led the league with a 1.14 ERA, 29 complete games, and 11 shutouts!

He followed it up the next season with 28 wins and 33 complete games, both leading all of baseball by a mile. Between 1910 and 1916, Johnson's highest ERA was 1.90. He was averaging close to 30 wins per season in that stretch. No pitcher in history has the kinds of numbers he has.

The Senators struggled early on during Johnson's tenure but steadily improved, closing in on the World Series three times but coming up short. Finally, in 1924, the Senators made the championship against the New York Giants. The series went to a decisive seventh game.

With the game tied at 3, Senators manager Bucky Harris turned to Johnson and said, "You're the best we've got, Walter. We've got to win or lose with you." Johnson went in and pitched relief to try and hold the Giants to no runs and hope the offense could produce. It took four innings, but as Johnson shut out the Giants, the Senators finally produced a run in the 12th inning and won the World Series. Johnson had saved the day.

Johnson would pitch 21 years, fading a bit as he approached 40 years old. But he finished 417 wins, the second-most all-time in Major League history. Only Cy Young has more; however, Young played more seasons than Johnson and started nearly 150 more games.

In 1939, Johnson was inducted into the first-ever Major League Baseball Hall of Fame, along with Ty Cobb, Babe Ruth, and Honus Wagner. He would play a role in baseball in different facets for the remainder of his life, including in broadcasting and raising money for charity. During World War II, Johnson and Babe Ruth would help raise money for the war, showing up to different stadiums where Johnson would pitch to Ruth.

Honorable Mention

Cy Young

You've probably heard of the Cy Young Award, which goes to the best pitcher for each league every year. That's because Cy Young was one of the best to ever pitch. He finished his career with 511 wins, an all-time high that will likely never be broken. He also holds the record for most innings pitched (7,356), most career starts (815), and complete games (749). He was inducted into the Hall of Fame along with Johnson.

Mariano Rivera

While Johnson and Young are arguably the greatest starting pitchers ever, there's no doubt that Mariano Rivera was baseball's greatest closer. Rivera ranks No. 1 in Major League history with 652 saves. Only six pitchers in history have even recorded more than 400 saves. Trevor Hoffman is the only pitcher remotely close to Rivera, with 601. Rivera helped the Yankees win five World Series championships, including four in a five-year stretch, and finished with a .891 save percentage. He was inducted into the Hall of Fame in 2019.

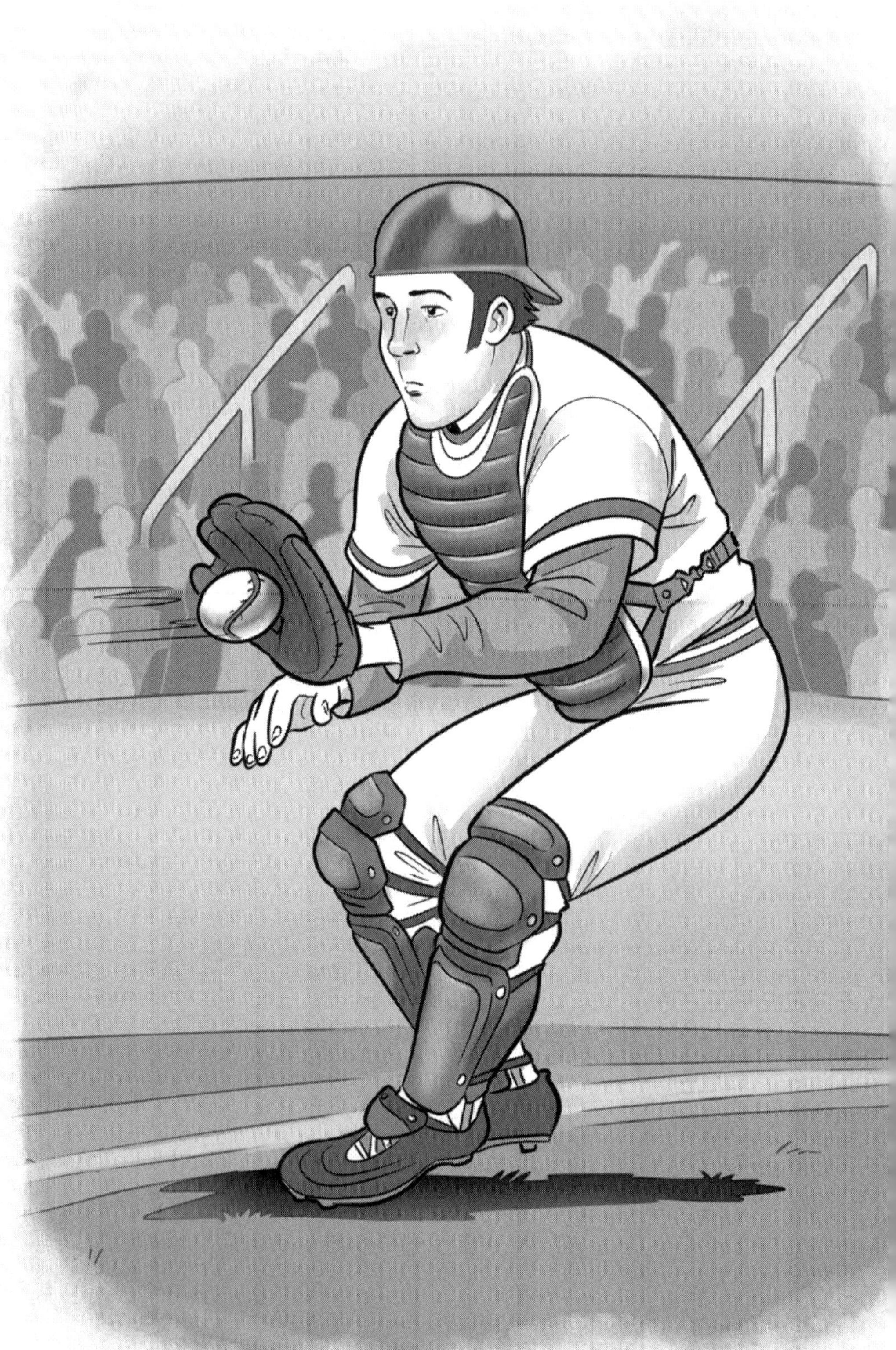

CATCHER: JOHNNY BENCH

- Two-time National League MVP
- 14 All-Star Game appearances
- 1976 World Series MVP
- 389 career home runs (3rd most by any catcher)
- 1968 Rookie of the Year (First catcher to ever win award)
- 10 Gold Glove Awards
- 45 home runs in a single season (#2 all-time for a catcher)

Biography

Full name: Johnny Lee Bench

Born: Dec. 7, 1947

Nicknames: "The Little General"

Hometown: Oklahoma City, OK

Uniform Number: 5

Years Played Professional: 17

Teams Played For: Cincinnati Reds (1967-1983)

Famous quote: "Slumps are like a soft bed; they're easy to get into and hard to get out of."

In the 1970s, the Cincinnati Reds were given the nickname, "The Big Red Machine" for the way they dominated baseball. In fact, they are considered one of the great dynasties of the game. In that decade, they won six division titles, four National League pennants, and two World Series. They had a great supporting cast that included Pete Rose, Joe Morgan, Ken Griffey, Sr., Tony Perez, and Dave Concepcion.

And at the heart of it all was catcher Johnny Bench. There may have been no member of The Big Red Machine who had as much of an influence as Bench did in their winning, and his leadership earned the praise of his teammates.

A catcher traditionally isn't an impact position, especially on offense. They're known more for their defensive skills. A good catcher has a strong arm and can throw runners out at second base who are trying to steal. But Bench was an exception, and he, along with Yogi Berra, who came a little before his time, helped transform the position, becoming true dual-threat powers.

In 17 years with the Reds, Bench was named to an incredible 14 All-Star Games, and he is one of just four catchers in history to win multiple MVP awards. Bench had power, hitting 327 career home runs as a catcher, third all-time. Bench is also third all-time for catchers in RBIs (1,376), ninth for slugging percentage (.476), and fifth for total bases (3,644). Bench is one of 13 catchers in Major League Baseball history with more than 2,000 hits (2,048).

Defensively, Bench was outstanding, and he broke the record for the position at that time by winning 10 consecutive Gold Glove awards. He was known for his strong arm and ability to throw runners out at an alarming rate of 43.4 percent. He was inducted into the Hall of Fame on the first ballot, getting 96 percent of the vote, which at the time was the third-highest ever.

Bench got a lot of his skills from his father, who was a truck driver and semi-professional baseball player. He grew up in the small town of Binger, Oklahoma, just outside of Oklahoma City. Bench grew up delivering newspapers on his bike, playing sandlot pickup games, picking cotton, and spending time with his family, watching and listening to baseball games. He always said you learn just as much from watching the game as you do playing it.

It was his father who coached him and turned him into the superstar he would become. While some kids scoffed at Bench when he said he would become a professional baseball player one day, his father believed in him, and coached him to being the best player in his high school. Bench received scholarships to play not just baseball, but also basketball, in which he was also extremely talented. But when the Cincinnati Reds drafted him in the second round of the 1967 MLB Draft, Bench went all in with the club. He quickly ascended through the Minor Leagues, and within a year had made the Reds Major League club. At just 19 years old, he became the team's starting catcher.

But before becoming a star, Bench's life went through some challenges, two in particular that nearly cost him his life. While riding a bus home with his team from an American Legion baseball game at 15 years old, the bus lost its breaks and spun out of control, skidding off the highway and rolling down the ravine. Bench was rolling on the floor, holding on to his seat for dear life. Two of his teammates died in that crash, but Bench survived, both feet dangling out the window of the bus as he clung to the seat.

Another incident occurred early in his professional year. Already afflicted with a thumb injury that had him sidelined, Bench was driving home and was hit by an intoxicated driver. He was hospitalized but thankfully survived the crash.

Bench made the most out of his second chances at life. His rookie season was the best a catcher had ever had. He hit .275 with 15 home runs and 82 RBIs. He went on to win Rookie of the Year, the first time ever a catcher had won the award.

Bench's best season may have been 1972, when he led baseball in home runs (40) and RBIs (125). He was also a key component in helping the Reds win two World Series titles in the 70s. In the 1976 World Series, Bench hit .533, including two home runs, as the Reds swept the Yankees. He would be named World Series MVP.

Perhaps Bench's career and stardom as a catcher can be best described in a quote by famous Orioles general manager Frank Cashen: "The way I see it, the first thing you want in a catcher is the ability to handle the pitchers. Then you want defensive skill, and, of course, a good arm. Last of all, if he can hit with power, well, then you've got a Johnny Bench."

Honorable Mention

Yogi Berra

Yogi Berra is perhaps known for his infamous quote, "It ain't over 'til it's over." But he was right up there with Bench as one of the greatest catchers to ever play the game. He helped lead the Yankees to 10 World Series championships and played in 75 World Series games, both of which are all-time records. He won three Most Valuable Player awards and ended his career hitting. 285 with 358 home runs and 1,430 RBIs. He later went on to manage both the Yankees and the Mets, leading both teams to World Series appearances. Berra was inducted into the Hall of Fame in 1972.

Ivan Rodriguez

Having spent the prime of his career with the Texas Rangers, Ivan Rodriguez helped shape the present-day catcher. He is the all-time leading hitter for catchers with 2,844 hits. In 1999, Rodriguez won MVP by hitting 35 home runs and posting a .332 batting average. He appeared in 14 All-Star Games and won 13 Gold Glove Awards. He is recognized as one of the most feared catchers for his ability to throw out base stealers, gunning down 661 runners during his career. He was elected into the Hall of Fame on the first ballot in 2017.

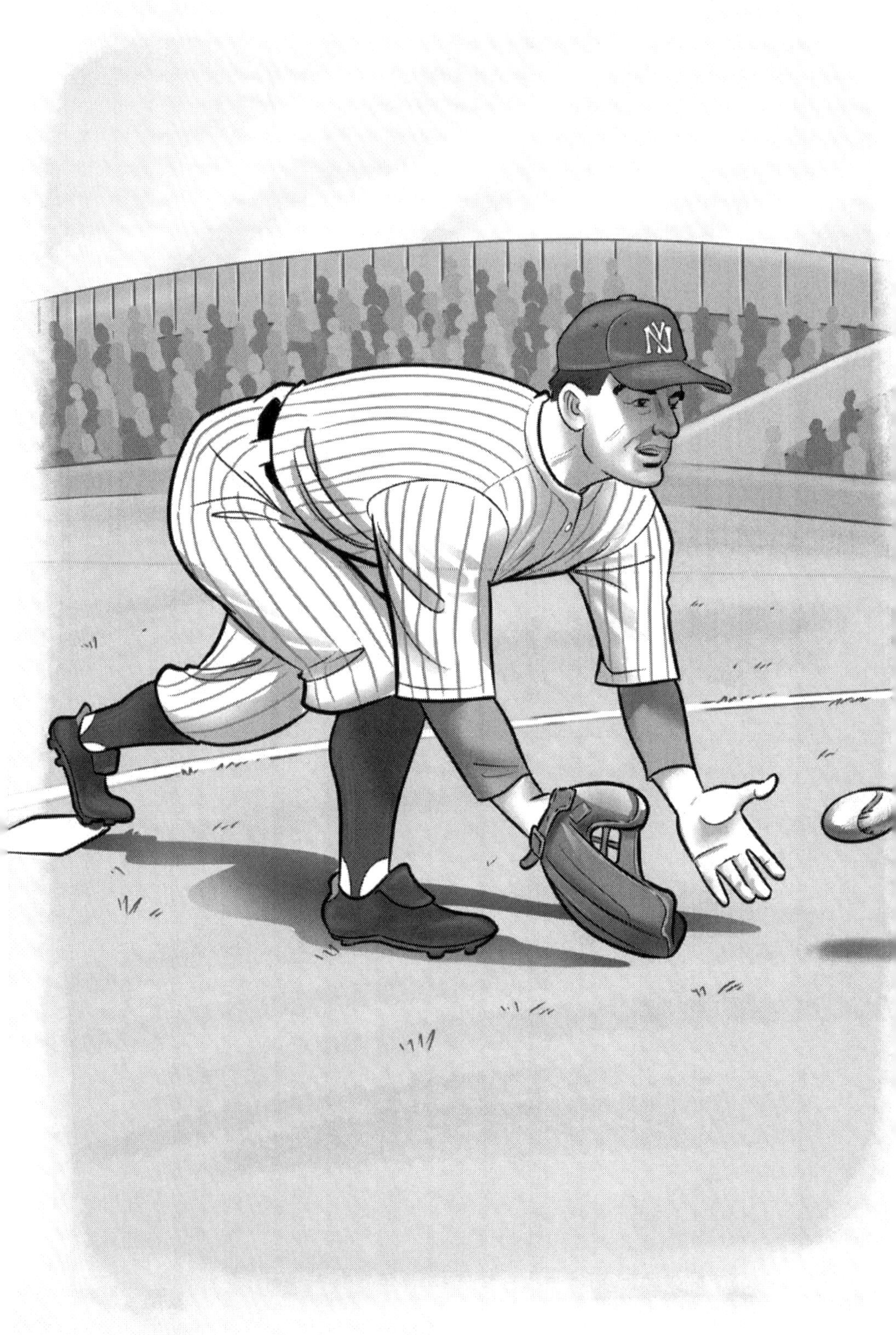

FIRST BASEMAN: LOU GEHRIG

- 1934 Triple Crown winner (Led MLB in average, home runs, and RBIs)
- 493 home runs (#3 all-time for first baseman)
- 184 RBIs in single season (#2 all-time)
- 2,130 consecutive games played (#2 all-time)
- 1 of 15 MLB players to hit four home runs in one game
- 1,995 career RBIs (#2 all-time for RBIs per at-bats)
- 1927 and 1934 American League MVP
- Six World Series rings

Biography

Full name: Henry Louis Gehrig

Born: June 19, 1903

Nicknames: "The Iron Horse"

Hometown: Yorkville, NY

Uniform Number: 4

Years Played Professional: 17

Teams Played For: New York Yankees (1923-1939)

Famous quote: "For the past two weeks, you have been reading about a bad break. Yet today I consider myself the luckiest man alive."

There may be no greater story in baseball than Lou Gehrig's. The man they called "The Iron Horse" is considered today one of the greatest players to ever put on a uniform. Before Cal Ripken came along, Lou Gehrig had what seemed to be an unbreakable record, playing in 2,130 consecutive games. He helped lift the Yankees to an incredible six world championships during his playing career. A two-time MVP winner and seven-time All-Star, Gehrig was not just known as a power hitter, but also a pure hitter, posting .300+ batting averages nearly every season he played. Yet as strong as he was, it was his health that shortened his career and his life.

Lou Gehrig and Babe Ruth were teammates and helped coin the Yankee nickname "The Bronx Bombers" with their incredible home run power during the 1920s and 1930s. Gehrig had five 40+ home run seasons, including two in which he hit 49. In 1931, Gehrig hit an incredible 185 RBIs and followed it up with 46 home runs and 163 runs scored. During his 1934 MVP season, Gehrig led all of baseball with 49 home runs and 166 RBIs. He also finished first with a .363 batting average, achieving something only 14 players in the history of the game have done – The Triple Crown.

Born in New York City in 1903, Gehrig was the son of German immigrants and grew up speaking German. His parents struggled to make a living, doing all they could to earn a penny, and Gehrig helped out, working blue collar jobs on the side. Gehrig was extremely close with his parents, living with them well into his professional baseball career.

Gehrig loved baseball growing up, and was extremely skilled at it. He played at Columbia University and was recruited by the Yankees Minor League team in 1923. He left college early to play in Hartford, Connecticut.

In 1925, Gehrig made his way to New York to play for the Yankees, but was relegated to the bench, where he backed up long-time first baseman Joe Pipp. Gehrig wasn't expected to see much playing time that first season, but Pipp was struggling, and the manager one day gave Gehrig a shot to see what he could do. To say he did well was an understatement – Gehrig didn't see the bench again for 2,130 games.

Gehrig was considered the polar opposite of Babe Ruth. He wasn't boastful and flamboyant, but rather very quiet, stoic, and workmanlike. While Ruth was big and powerful, Gehrig was thin and lanky. The two clashed at times, developing a love-hate relationship that lasted their whole lives. It started in 1927 when Gehrig's popularity in New York began to overtake that of Ruth's.

Ruth was the face of New York; people came to the ballpark to watch him hit home runs for the longest time. But Ruth started to feel a bit forgotten when Lou Gehrig showed up and began hitting home runs at a greater clip than he did in 1927. Gehrig was also leading the league in RBIs and sporting a near .400 average.

Ruth saw this as competition, and the two teammates started trading home runs back and forth, in what became an infamous home run battle. For Ruth, it was a bit of jealousy at first, seeing Gehrig come along and steal the spotlight, but the two would soon bond as they both ascended towards the history books. They pushed each other and achieved great things. Ruth won the home run battle, knocking out a new MLB-record 60 home runs. However, Gehrig took home the American League MVP. In the end, they both won a championship.

The 1927 Yankees went down as one of the greatest teams ever, finishing 110-44-1 and easily winning the World Series. Gehrig finished that year hitting .373 and led the league with 52 doubles and 173 RBIs. Every year after that, the hits kept coming. He sported a .300+ average for 12 consecutive seasons and finished his career with a .340 batting average. He finished his career with 495 home runs, although that number probably would have been much higher if his playing days hadn't been cut short.

Gehrig's 2,130 consecutive games streak ended on May 2, 1939, when he arrived at the ballpark and told his manager he felt ill and couldn't play. Gehrig would miss the next few games, not sure what was wrong with him. When he did return, he wasn't himself, striking out more than usual and making errors. He went to the hospital for a checkup and was diagnosed with Amyotrophic Lateral Sclerosis, better known today as Lou Gehrig's Disease. The disease damages the spinal cord and disrupts brain activity, eventually breaking down the body. Gehrig was dying.

Shortly after the diagnosis, Gehrig had to retire from baseball. The team held a ceremony in his honor in front of 61,000 fans. Everyone knew the pain he was enduring, and how hard it was for him just to stand up. But Gehrig inspired everyone when he told them that despite being given a bad break, "I consider myself the luckiest man on the face of this earth." It was those iconic words that still resonate today as being among the most inspirational ever uttered. Major League Baseball went on to make a special exception and inducted Lou Gehrig immediately into the Hall of Fame, waiving the two-year waiting period after retirement (today it's a five-year waiting period).

After retiring from baseball, Gehrig accepted a position to work with prison inmates in New York, motivating them to see the light during dark days. But just two years into his job, Gehrig's health rapidly deteriorated and he was confined to his home for six months. In June 1941, Gehrig passed away at just 35 years old.

Gehrig was a legend, becoming the first baseball player ever to have his jersey number retired. He was the first athlete to ever be put on the cover of a Wheaties box. He was the first player in the modern-era to hit four home runs in one game, something that not even Babe Ruth could accomplish. He is the only player in history to drive in more than 500 runs in three seasons.

Honorable Mention

Albert Pujols

With 703 home runs, Albert Pujols has more home runs than any other first baseman in history and ranks fourth all-time among all players. Pujols was the 2001 Rookie of the Year and won three National League MVP Awards, including back-to-back honors in 2008 and 2009. While he played with the Angels and Cardinals for pretty much his entire career, his best days came with the Cardinals, including his 700th home run in 2022. Pujols hit 30 or more home runs in each of his first 12 seasons and helped St. Louis to two World Series titles.

Stan Musial

Stan Musial was another St. Louis Cardinals superstar first baseman and outfielder, winning three MVP awards and being voted to 24 All-Star Games. He finished his career with a .331 batting average and 1,951 RBIs. Only Pete Rose, Ty Cobb, and Hank Aaron ended their careers with more hits than Musial (3,630). He helped lead a Cardinals dynasty in the 1940s that won three World Series titles in five years.

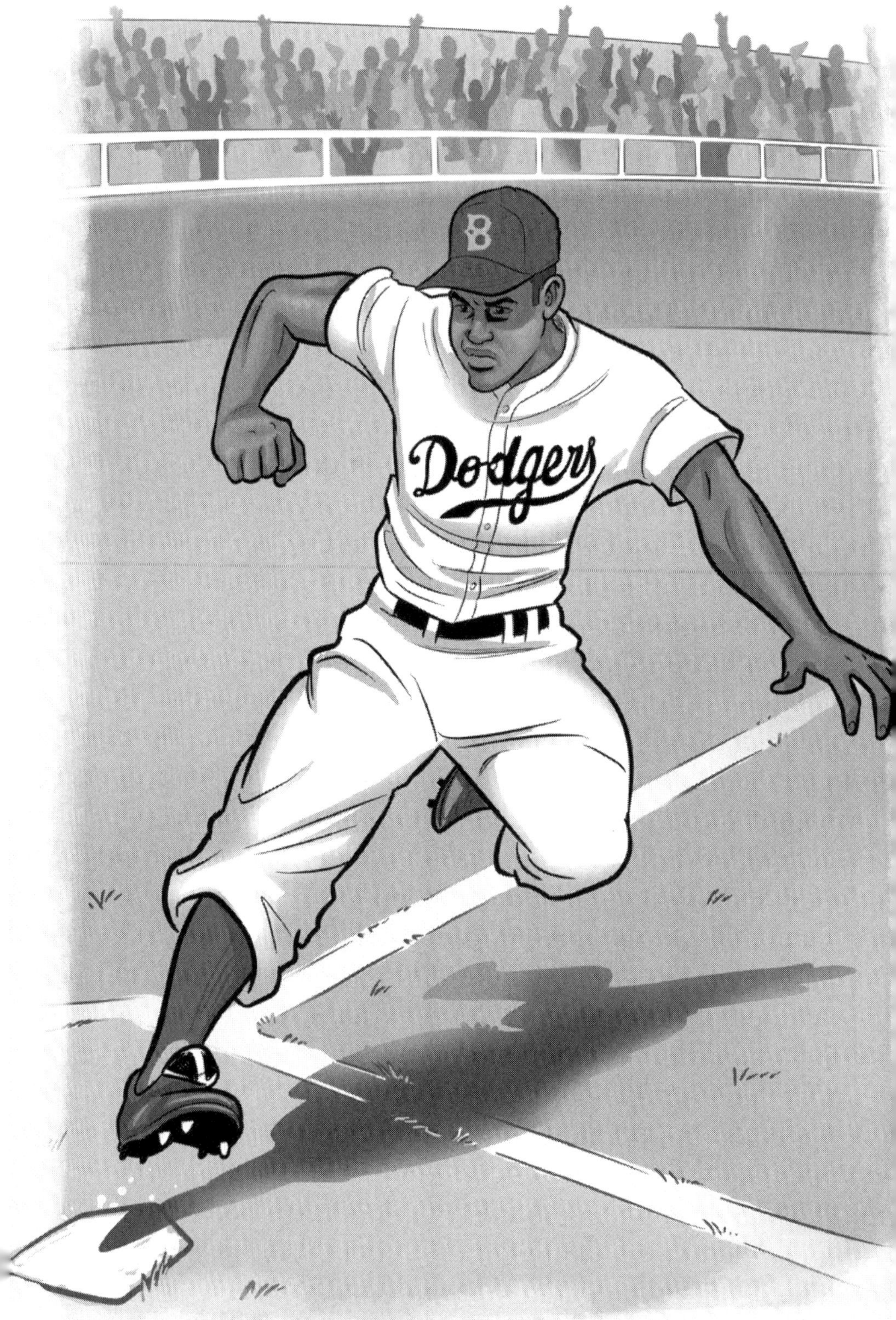
B
Dodgers

SECOND BASEMAN: JACKIE ROBINSON

- 1947 NL Rookie of the Year
- 1949 NL MVP
- First black athlete inducted into Baseball Hall of Fame
- 6 All-Star Game appearances (all consecutive)
- Most double plays for second baseman for four consecutive years (1949-1952)
- Successfully stole home 19 times (#1 all-time)
- Six World Series appearances in 10 seasons played

Biography

Full name: Jack Roosevelt Robinson

Born: January 31, 1919

Nicknames: "Jackie"

Hometown: Cairo, GA

Uniform Number: 42

Years Played Professional: 10

Teams Played For: Brooklyn Dodgers (1947-1956)

Famous quote: "A life is not important except in the impact it has on other lives."

Statistically speaking, was Jackie Robinson the greatest second-baseman to ever play? Maybe, maybe not. Many would say Joe Morgan or Rogers Hornsby were better. However, did anyone have a greater influence on the growth of baseball than Jackie Robinson? No. Did any player face more trials and adversity than Robinson throughout his playing career? No. Is any player looked up to and respected more in the game of baseball today than Robinson? Well, if you want the answer to that, just consider the fact that every year on April 15 (known as Jackie Robinson Day), all Major League Baseball players wear the No. 42 in honor of

Jackie Robinson's debut in Major League Baseball. There is no other athlete in sports that is shown that much respect.

Before Jackie Robinson came along, baseball was strictly a white man's sport. Black players were designated to play in the Negro leagues, which is where Jackie Robinson started out. The game wasn't necessarily segregated, but no owner would take a chance on bringing an African American to play for their team because of how divided the country was and because African Americans were looked down upon. But Robinson dreamed of changing that, as did a particular Dodgers owner. But to do so, Robinson would have to battle through a world of torture.

Born in Georgia, Robinson's family migrated to California when he was young. He was a star athlete, achieving success in football, baseball, basketball, and track. His brother, Mack, was also a great athlete and ran in the 1936 Olympics in Berlin, finishing second to Jesse Owens in the 200 meter dash. Robinson attended UCLA and became the first student athlete to ever letter in four varsity sports. He broke the all-time NCAA broad jump record, 25' 6½".

It appeared as if Robinson was headed towards playing football; he moved to Hawaii to play semi-pro in 1942, but World War II halted his plans. He joined the U.S. Army, serving as second lieutenant during the war. His Army career was cut short, however, when he refused to give up his seat on a segregated bus; he would later receive an honorable discharge, but his fight against injustice was only just beginning.

Robinson turned toward baseball in 1945, playing in the Negro Leagues, where he was one of the premier players. He was noticed by Brooklyn Dodgers owner Branch Rickey, who was blown away by his speed and ability. Rickey, like Robinson, had a dream to change baseball. He took a chance on Robinson, signing him to a Minor League contract with the Montreal Royals. Rickey warned Robinson of the firestorm he was about to enter, but told him not to fight back, no matter how many violent threats, racial slurs, and insults were hurled at him. Sadly, Robinson would face hundreds of such slurs on a daily basis. He would even have to pack up and move several times because of threats to his home or the hotel where he was staying.

Robinson worked his way through the Minor Leagues, leading the International League in hitting and stolen bases. So Rickey made a monumental move, signing Robinson to the Brooklyn Dodgers in 1947. Robinson would become the first African American in the modern era to play Major League Baseball, officially breaking the color barrier.

The move was met with hatred from fans who supported segregation. Even several of Robinson's own teammates disagreed with the move, requesting trades. But manager Leo Durocher stuck up for Robinson, telling the players that he wasn't trading Robinson and didn't want to trade Robinson, and if they didn't want to play with him, to take it up with Mr. Rickey. This scene was played out in the movie "42" about Jackie Robinson, in which Durocher tells his players, "I do not care if the guy is yellow or black, or if he has stripes like a f***in' zebra. I'm the manager of this team, and I say he plays."

Robinson would face unrelenting racial slurs at games, and even was targeted in the head by opposing pitchers. He was issued constant death threats, and he and his wife Rachel were never able to live comfortably. But Robinson, as much as he was boiling inside, stayed calm, cool, and collected, and just played baseball.

Robinson's composure and non-violent actions created sympathy and began to turn the tide of players and fans accepting African Americans into their sport; support grew over time. Teammates rallied around him, and Dodgers fans started cheering him unconditionally at games. One of the turning points came in a game against the Phillies, where manager Ben Chapman constantly hurled insults and threats at Robinson while he was at the plate, repeatedly calling him the "n" word. Robinson never flinched. Chapman's actions would backfire, because Robinson's teammates stuck up for him, and Chapman was asked to pose for a photograph with Robinson as a conciliatory gesture the next time the two teams met.

Another turning point came when future Hall of Famer and teammate Pee Wee Reese became one of Robinson's biggest supporters and helped bring the team together. Reese even put his arm around Robinson at a game in racially-charged Cincinnati. The gesture meant a lot since

Reese was from Cincinnati and many of his family and friends were in attendance. According to Reese, he wanted to show his hometown who he was and what he supported.

It also helped that Robinson was hitting the cover off the baseball. His first season in 1947, Robinson led all of baseball with 29 stolen bases. He hit .297 and drove in 48 RBIs, and at the end of the season, he won Rookie of the Year. Robinson was an integral part in helping the Dodgers win the National League Pennant. And from there, it only got better.

In 1949, Robinson led baseball, hitting .342 and stealing 37 bases. He became the first African American to ever play in an All-Star Game and was voted Most Valuable Player. He went on to make the next six All-Star Games, hitting .300+ in each of those seasons. In 1955, Robinson helped the Brooklyn Dodgers win the World Series.

Robinson began his career at first base but migrated to second base in 1949. He made an immediate impact, leading all of baseball in turned double plays for four straight seasons. Because he didn't start in the Major Leagues until he was 28 years old, Robinson's career was short, but successful and extremely impactful. After he came along, more African Americans joined baseball, including the likes of Satchel Paige, Willie Mays, and Hank Aaron, who were inspired by Robinson. Robinson ended his career with a .311 batting average, a .409 on-base percentage, and 197 stolen bases in eight seasons played. He also stole home plate 19 times.

Jackie Robinson is the personification of courage. He worked with the NAACP to continue African Americans' fight for freedom during the turbulent 1960s, and was awarded the highest civilian honor, the Presidential Medal of Freedom, by President Ronald Reagan in 1984.

Honorable Mention

Rogers Hornsby

Hornsby was without question the most talented all-around second baseman at the plate. He may not have turned double plays or stolen bases like Robinson, but he could hit. His .358 batting average is second all-time only to Ty Cobb. He led the National League in batting seven times and had three seasons where he hit over .400. His .424 batting average in 1924 is the highest batting average in a single season of anyone in the modern era.

Joe Morgan

Like Johnny Bench, Morgan was a member of the "Big Red Machine," helping the Reds to back-to-back championships in 1975 and 1976. Morgan also won the NL MVP during both those seasons and received five Gold Glove awards. Morgan was selected in ten All-Star Games over the course of his career. After his career ended, Morgan went on to become a legendary announcer, becoming the voice of ESPN's Sunday Night Baseball with John Miller for much of the 1990s and 2000s.

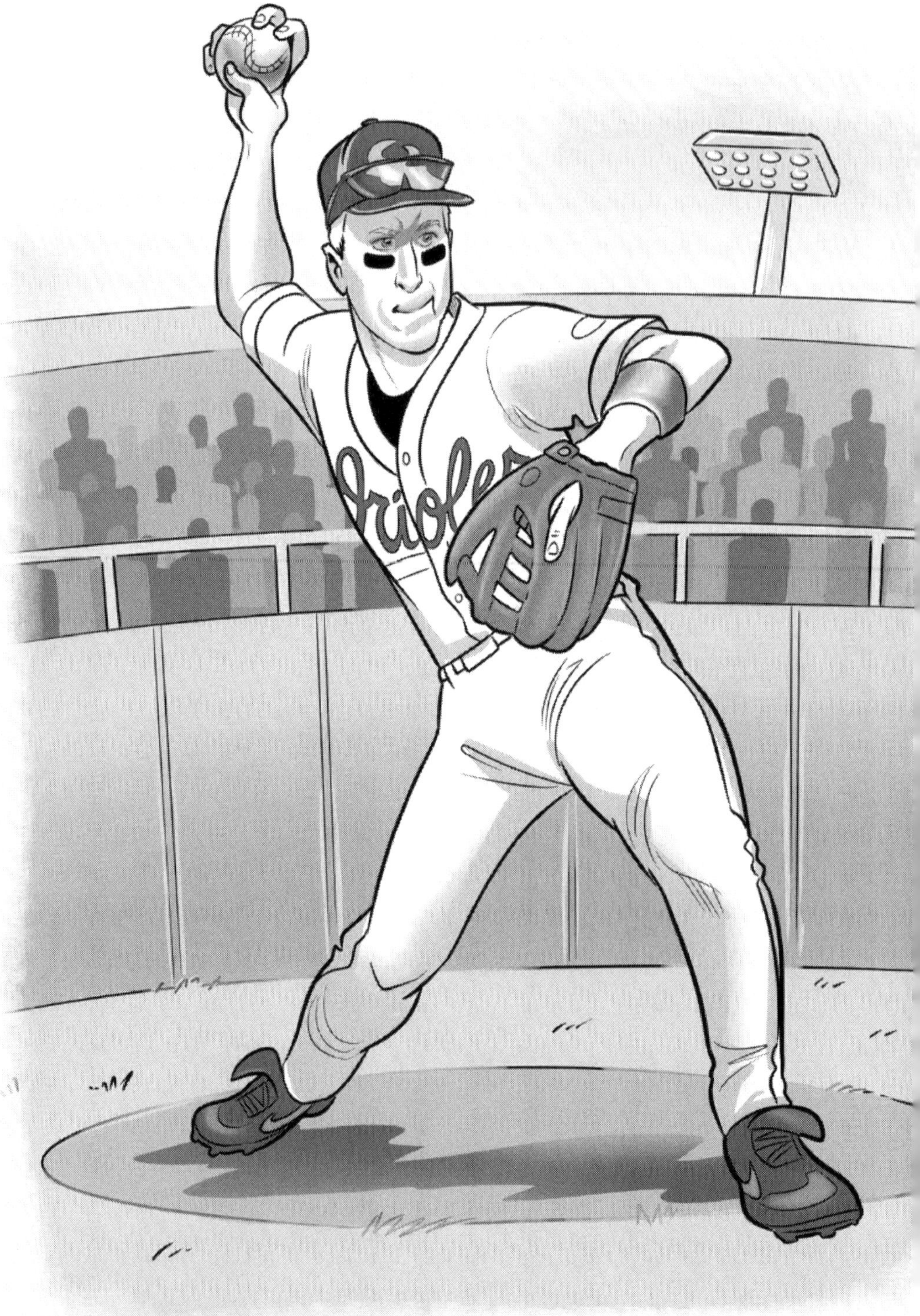

SHORTSTOP: CAL RIPKEN, JR.

- 19-time All-Star
- Two-time AL MVP (1983, 1981)
- 2,632 consecutive games played (#1 all-time)
- Eight Silver Slugger Awards
- 1982 AL Rookie of the Year
- 12 seasons with 20+ home runs

Biography

Full name: Calvin Edwin Ripken, Jr.

Born: Aug. 24, 1960

Nicknames: "The Iron Man"

Hometown: Havre de Grace, MD

Uniform Number: 8

Years Played Professional: 21

Teams Played For: Baltimore Orioles (1981-2001)

Famous quote: "Get in the game. Do the best you can. Try to make a contribution. Learn from today. Apply it to tomorrow."

There are certain records in baseball that are deemed "unbreakable." Joe DiMaggio's 56-game hitting streak has never even been sniffed. Nolan Ryan's seven no-hitters will likely never be touched. Pete Rose's 4,236 hits is likely to stand beyond this century.

But Cal Ripken's 2,632 consecutive games played may be up there above them all.

On September 6, 1995, America was glued to ESPN to see Cal Ripken break Lou Gehrig's historic record for consecutive games played. Not many remember who the Orioles played or who won the game, all they remember was Cal Ripken taking the field for a record 2,131st time and hitting a home run in the process. When he crossed home plate, it was one of the loudest and greatest ovations any player in history has received.

Ripken grew up in a baseball family. His father had played professionally before him for the Baltimore Orioles, but had a short career due to injuries. That didn't stop Cal Ripken, Sr. from managing the Orioles afterwards. But he was also a coach to Cal, Jr. growing up, teaching him how to play the game and become one of the best young baseball players Maryland has ever seen.

Being the son of a Major Leaguer, Ripken, Jr. had a lot of pressure on him as a young man. People expected great things out of him, and his father was especially tough on him, wanting him to follow in his footsteps. There were times when Ripken, Jr. wanted to give the game up because of how hard he was pushed and the fatigue he felt, but he kept pushing forward, and eventually it paid off.

Ripken could have been an All-Star pitcher. In high school, he was one of the best, and pitched his team to the state championship. At 18, he was drafted in the second round by the Baltimore Orioles and worked immediately with their farm team. He was given the choice of becoming a pitcher or shortstop, but years later he told an interviewer that "Pitching was fun, but I wanted to play every day." He quickly ascended to the Major League level, debuting with the Orioles in 1981.

He played third base and shortstop early on but settled at shortstop by 1982. He was tall for his position and could hit, something most shortstops aren't known for. At 6'4", Ripken was one of the tallest shortstops ever.

Ripken was a trend-setter. Before Ripken came along, shortstops were known for their glove, not their bat. He changed that; by the time he retired, the perception of the shortstop had changed. After Ripkin came great hitting shortstops like Barry Larkin, Alex Rodriguez, Derek Jeter, and Jose Altuve.

Ripken quickly elevated the Orioles. He won Rookie of the Year in 1981, and then helped win the Orioles their first World Championship in 1983. Ripken won AL MVP that season, hitting .318 and leading the league in runs, hits, and doubles. He was also selected to his first of 19 straight All-Star Games and won his first of eight Silver Slugger trophies. He started in 17 All-Star Games, an all-time MLB record.

One of Ripken's best seasons came in 1991 when he hit a career-high .323 with 34 home runs. Ripken also won two All-Star Game MVP awards, the most notable in 2001, his final All-Star Game, during which he was honored in front of more than 47,000 fans at Safeco Field. At 40 years old, he had already announced it was his final season, so a brief ceremony was held before the game. He definitely put on a show, hitting a home run to help lift the AL All-Stars to a victory.

Ripken ended his career hitting .276 and 435 home runs. He hit 385 home runs while playing shortstop, the most of any player at his position. He finished his final three years playing third base before retiring as arguably the greatest hitting shortstop ever. Ripken was selected to the Hall of Fame five years later.

Honorable Mention

Derek Jeter

There were many great Yankees that came before Derek Jeter, like Lou Gehrig, Babe Ruth, Joe DiMaggio, and Mickey Mantle. Yet no Yankee had more hits than Jeter (3,465). He was an all-around star, not just because of his .310 career batting average, five Gold Gloves, five Silver Sluggers, and 14 All-Star nominations, but because he was one of the game's greatest leaders. He earned the nickname "The Captain" because of how he helped lead the Yankees to five world championships during his career. His number 2 is retired by the Yankees.

Honus Wagner

Wagner was one of the first great hitters in Major League Baseball. He had 15 straight seasons hitting .300 or better between 1899 and 1913. He led the NL in batting eight times and lifted the Pittsburgh Pirates to the 1909 World Series. He was also known for his speed, stealing home 27 times during his career.

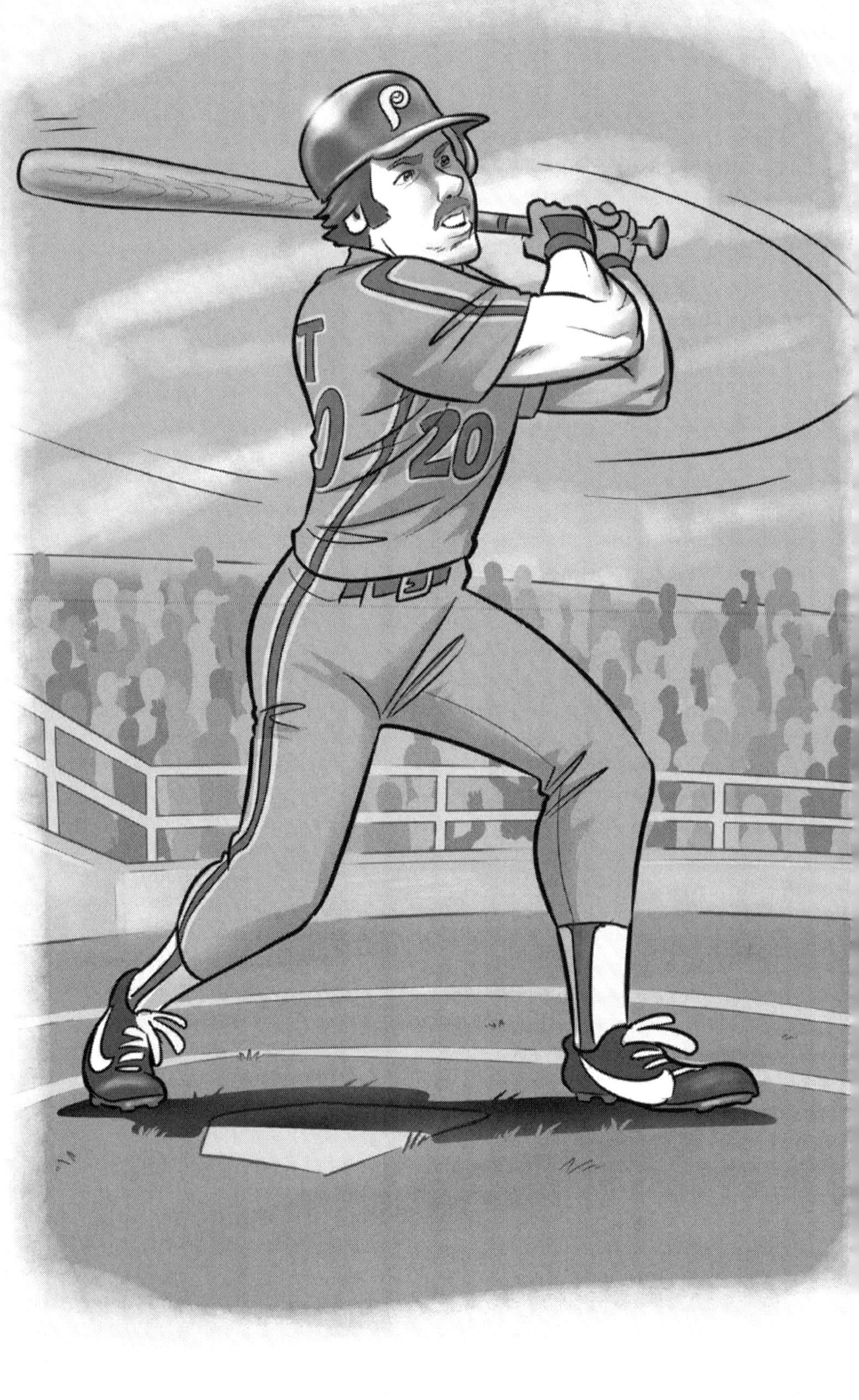
20

THIRD BASEMAN: MIKE SCHMIDT

- Three-time NL MVP (1980, 1981, 1986)
- 10-time Gold Glove winner
- 1980 World Series MVP
- Four-time MLB RBI leader
- 548 career home runs (#16 all-time)

Biography

Full name: Michael Jack Schmidt

Born: Sept. 27, 1949

Nicknames: Schmitty

Hometown: Dayton, OH

Uniform Number: 20

Years Played Professional: 18

Teams Played For: Philadelphia Phillies (1972-1989)

Famous quote: "If you could equate the amount of time and effort put in mentally and physically into succeeding on the baseball field and measure[d] it by the dirt on your uniform, mine would have been black."

Ask any history lover the first name that comes to mind when they think of Philadelphia Phillies baseball, and the name Mike Schmidt will probably be the first thing out of their mouth. He is synonymous with that team, and the city of Brotherly Love certainly fell in love with him.

And why not? Three MVPs. Ten Gold Gloves. 548 home runs. Six post-season appearances. Most importantly, a World Series ring he helped the Phillies win in 1980. He was perhaps the most consistent baseball player in Phillies history.

But Schmidt's full life almost never came to be. When he was a young boy, he fell from a tree and grabbed hold of electrical wires to prevent himself from falling straight down, and perhaps dying. Grabbing the wires did soften the fall, but it also sent 4,000 volts of electricity through him. Fortunately, most of the electricity connected with the ground when he fell. Schmidt would be scarred with multiple burns and bruises as a result, but he lived.

Schmidt took advantage of his second chance at life and turned to sports, playing baseball, football, basketball, and golf. But whether it was fortunate or unfortunate, he damaged his knee in football one year and had to give up both football and basketball, thus leaving his focus on baseball. It was there he found his passion, but his talent was still far off.

Schmidt worked incredibly hard, spending hours with his coaches and his dad in the batting cages. He hit baseball after baseball, trying hard to make himself better. But he struggled to perform consistently in high school, and professional teams, even colleges, turned their backs on him.

Schmidt had to walk on to play baseball at Ohio University, not really recognized for their baseball program. He was almost cut from the team after his first year, hitting just one home run and ending up with a pitiful average. But the team needed bodies, so they kept him.

Schmidt went home and played in a summer league; he practiced day and night, and all of a sudden, something clicked. He found his swing. When he went back to Ohio, he became a hitting machine. He hit a combined 20 home runs in his sophomore and junior year and batted .300. He was named to the All-American team and professional teams started showing interest.

In the 1971 amateur draft, the Philadelphia Phillies selected Schmidt with the 30th overall pick. He began as a shortstop in the Minors but worked his way over to third base. As good as his bat was, he became an even better defensive player, thanks to practice and good coaching.

Schmidt struggled with the Phillies at first, hitting just .200 his first two seasons, but he broke out in a big way in 1974. He slugged 36 home runs, stole 23 bases, won a Gold Glove, and was named to the NL All-

Star Team. He was becoming one of the best all-around players in the game. He would go on to make 12 All-Star teams during his career.

His ability to drive in runs made him reliable. He led the league in home runs eight times and in RBIs four times. The pinnacle of his career came in 1980 when he hit a third baseman record 48 home runs and won the MVP. He helped turn the Phillies luck around; a perennial loser, they began winning games and going to the playoffs in the late 1970s. Then in 1980, with the addition of Schmidt's mentor and childhood hero Pete Rose, the Phillies won the World Series. MVP Schmidt hit .381 in the Series with two home runs.

Schmidt got the Phillies to the World Series a second time in 1983 but came up short to Cal Ripken and the Orioles. Schmidt would retire in 1989 as one of the most decorated Phillies ever. He was inducted into the Hall of Fame in 1995.

Honorable Mention

George Brett

While Mike Schmidt was the NL star and MVP of the 1980 World Series, in the other dugout was Kansas City Royals third baseman George Brett, the AL MVP. Brett would help the Royals win the 1985 World Series and finish his career with a .305 average. Brett ranks 18th all-time with 3,158 hits. He is one of only four players in history to rack up 3,000 hits, 300 home runs, and a career .300 batting average.

Wade Boggs

There was no better hitting third baseman than Wade Boggs. He won eight Silver Slugger awards and was selected to 12 All-Star Games as a member of the Boston Red Sox, New York Yankees, and Tampa Bay Devil Rays. Boggs hit a career .328, the highest-ever for a third baseman. He also finished his career with 3,010 hits and 1,014 RBIs.

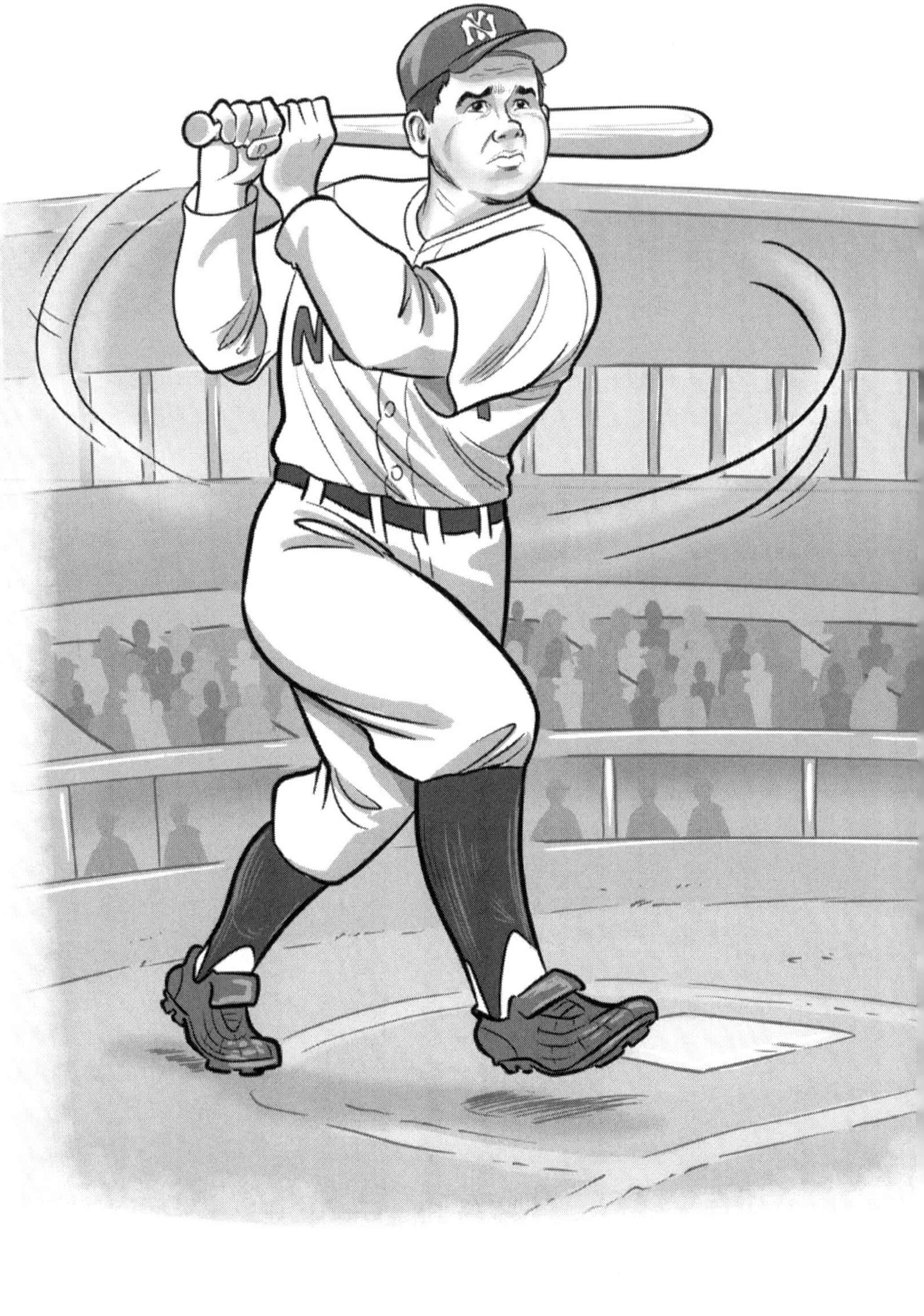

OUTFIELDER: BABE RUTH

- 12-time single-season home run leader
- Seven World Series rings
- 1923 AL MVP
- 714 career home runs (#3 all-time)
- 2,214 RBIs (#3 all-time)
- .690 career slugging percentage (#1 all-time)

Biography

Full name: George Herman Ruth

Born: Feb. 6, 1895

Nicknames: "Babe," "The Sultan of Swat," "The Great Bambino"

Hometown: Pigtown, MD

Uniform Number: 3

Years Played Professional: 22 years

Teams Played For: Boston Red Sox (1914-1919), New York Yankees (1920-1934), Boston Braves (1935)

Famous quote: "Never let the fear of striking out keep you from playing the game."

Picking the best outfielder to ever play baseball is extremely difficult. You're talking about choosing among greats like Ty Cobb, Ted Williams, Hank Aaron, Joe DiMaggio, Mickey Mantle, Willie Mays, and Ken Griffey, Jr.

However, nobody changed baseball the way Babe Ruth did (as explained in the introduction). More than 100 years since his first game, he is still regarded by many as perhaps the greatest and most dominant baseball player to ever take the field.

However, as good as Ruth was, his childhood was difficult. In fact, his parents sent him away because they couldn't handle his aggressive, troublemaking behavior. They sent him to St. Mary's Industrial School in Baltimore, an orphanage for troubled kids who needed behavior reform.

Ruth initially struggled at the school, getting into fights and regularly being disciplined. But then he met Brother Mathias, a monk who changed his life. He taught Ruth how to swing a bat and hit for power, and before long, Ruth was crushing home runs every day during activity time. Brother Mathias and Ruth built a strong bond, and eventually, St. Mary's negotiated Ruth's release to the Baltimore Orioles. He played Minor League Baseball there for six months before being sold to the Boston Red Sox.

Unbeknownst to most, Ruth actually began his career as a pitcher, not a hitter. He was the most dominant thrower in the Major Leagues during his first few seasons. He started 147 games and went 94-46 with a 2.28 ERA. In 1916 and 1917, he won a combined 47 games and posted a league-best 1.88 ERA. His pitching led the Red Sox to three World Series championships in the late 1910s. It wasn't until 1919 when Ruth became a full-time hitter and started playing the outfield.

When management saw how hard and far Ruth could hit the ball and the amount of fans he was drawing into the ballpark, he was put in the lineup more and more often. He lost his desire to pitch and instead wanted to hit. In the words of Ruth, "I liked hitting home runs." His incredible power transformed baseball, and the home run became a new phenomenon that continues to generate excitement today.

But despite how much Boston loved him, owner Harry Frazee and Ruth didn't see eye to eye on his non-baseball life, and in 1920, the New York Yankees paid Frazee $125,000 to acquire Ruth. The Red Sox would forever regret it; Ruth went on to become a legend. The Red Sox wouldn't win a World Series again until 2004, and fans called the drought in between "The Curse of the Bambino."

Ruth's statistics with the Yankees were incredible. He led the Major Leagues in home runs 12 times, including breaking the all-time home run record on three different occasions (twice he broke his own record). In 1927, he and Lou Gehrig competed for the most home runs, with Ruth winning out, hitting 60 that season. Ruth also led baseball in slugging percentage 13 times, RBIs five times, runs eight times, and walks 11 times. He completely dominated baseball.

Ruth finished his career by hitting 714 home runs, an all-time record that stood until Hank Aaron broke it in 1974. His .690 career slugging percentage still stands today as the highest percentage of all-time. His 2,214 career RBIs ranks No. 3, just recently passed by Albert Pujols.

Ruth won seven World Series, four with the Yankees. Perhaps his most famous World Series moment came in 1932 at Wrigley Field against the Cubs. Facing a barrage of boos and fans throwing food at him, Ruth pointed to center field to predict where the next pitch was going. Low and behold, he blasted the next pitch over the centerfield wall, silencing the fans and helping lift the Yankees to the win and the World Series (some question whether he was pointing at the fence or the pitcher, but Gehrig told reporters afterwards that he was indeed pointing at the fence).

Ruth finished his final season in Boston with the Braves and retired in 1935. He was inducted into the Hall of Fame in 1939. He passed away at just 53 years old after contracting cancer.

Honorable Mention

Ty Cobb

There was no better hitter in the game than Ty Cobb. He established 90 records during his playing time, and holds the all-time highest career batting average, .366. Additionally, Cobb ranks No. 2 in career hits (4,1289), No. 2 in career runs (2,245), and No. 3 for single-season batting average (.420). His 4,095 combined runs and RBIs is No. 1 all-time. Cobb helped the Detroit Tigers to three American League pennants, but never won a World Series.

Willie Mays

While Ty Cobb and Babe Ruth were known for their offense, Willie Mays was known for his defense and speed. The Giants superstar won 12 consecutive Gold Gloves, tied with Roberto Clemente for the most by an outfielder. He would have won more if the award was introduced before 1957. But he could also hit; Mays hit 29 or more home runs in 13 straight seasons and won two MVPs. Mays ranks No. 13 on the all-time hit list (3,293), No. 6 all-time for home runs (660), and No. 12 for RBIs (1,909). He finished with a career .557 slugging percentage.

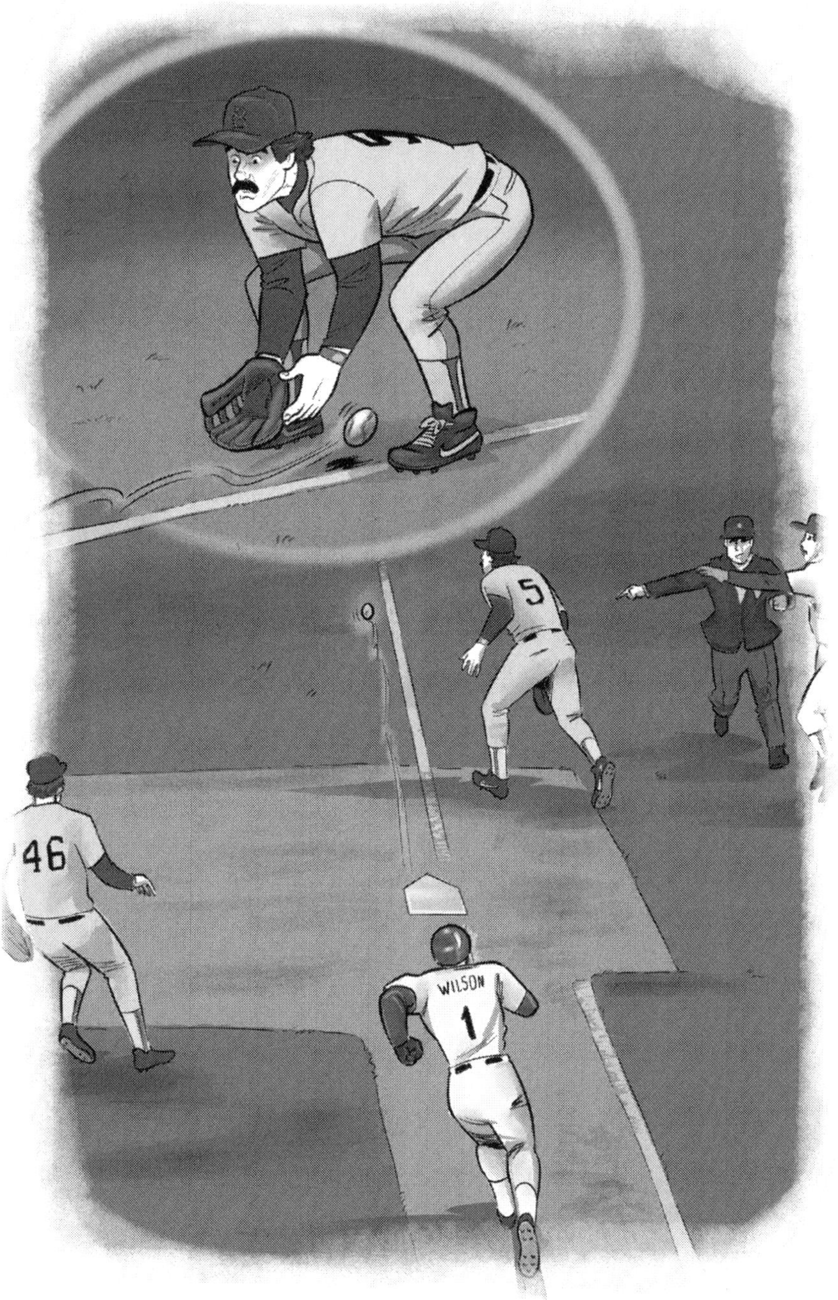
5
46
WILSON
1

4

THE GREATEST GAMES OF ALL-TIME

Baseball has a history of incredible games that left fans on the edge of their seats, particularly in the postseason. The following are some of the most memorable games ever witnessed.

1986 WORLD SERIES: RED SOX AT METS - "THE BUCKNER GAME"

Have you ever heard, "You pulled a Bill Buckner?" Well, if you ever had a ball go between your legs, you may have. The legend that was Bill Buckner was born from this specific game.

It was as classic a World Series as you could ask for. First, it was Boston vs. New York. It may not have been the Yankees, but there was still bad blood between the two cities. You also had two classic rookie pitchers, Roger Clemens against Dwight Gooden. The Mets had their fair share of hot shot players that the media loved to cover, including Lenny Dykstra, Daryl Strawberry, "HoJo" Howard Johnson, Keith Hernandez, Gary Carter, Kevin Mitchell, and Mookie Wilson.

The Mets had home field advantage going into the World Series, but fell behind 3 games to 2 in a best-of-seven series. The Red Sox could win it all in Game 6 at Shea Stadium in New York. If the Mets won, they would force a Game 7.

The Red Sox got out to a 2-0 lead early, and Roger Clemens seemed to be cruising to a championship, but the Mets got the best of him in the bottom of the fifth, tying the game. The Red Sox came back in the seventh to take the lead 3-2, but in the bottom of the eighth against reliever Calvin Schiraldi, the Mets managed to tie the game again at 3, sending Game 6 into extra innings.

Shea Stadium was buzzing, as the crowd rooted the Mets on to force a Game 7. They brought in one of their best pitchers, Rick Aguilera, to try and hold the Red Sox down. But with a man on first, Dave Henderson belted a pitch that quieted the crowd. Home Run! The Red Sox took a 5-3 lead, and it began to look like "The Curse of the Bambino" would be broken.

It looked even more of a sure thing when the Mets' Keith Hernandez flew out to center for the second out in the bottom of the 10th.

Red Sox 5, Mets 3 – Bottom of the 10th. 2 Outs. Nobody on base.

Red Sox fans began to celebrate. The bench players prepared to storm the field. Champagne bottles were actually placed in the Red Sox clubhouse, ready to be opened by the players when they came running in as world champions.

The Mets faces told the story. Fans began to leave. The players backs were against the wall. They were looking for some sort of spark; a miracle, perhaps.

They got a spark when Gary Carter came up and lined a base hit to left field. That at least brought the tying run to the plate. Just two pitches later, Kevin Mitchell lined a hit into center. All of a sudden, the Mets had men on first and second, though still had their backs against the wall.

Ray Knight came up to bat, and quickly got himself into an 0-2 hole. They were now just one strike away from losing. But Schiraldi, trying to jam Knight with an inside pitch, watched as Knight looped a ball over his head and into the outfield for a hit. Carter rounded third and scored, and Mitchell advanced to third. The Mets were now down just 5-4 and had the tying run 90 feet away at third base. Schiraldi, having given up three straight hits, was taken out and replaced by Bob Stanley, who would face Mookie Wilson.

Stanley got the count to 3-2, and tried to put away Wilson, but couldn't. He fouled two pitches off in a row to stay alive. Looking to get Wilson inside, Stanley's pitch was off track and wild, getting away from the catcher and hitting the backstop. Mitchell came sprinting in and scored. The Mets had tied the game. Meanwhile, Knight advanced to second base. All of a sudden, the Red Sox had lost the lead and were on the verge of possibly losing the game. It was slipping away.

The Mets crowd was going crazy. Wilson fouled off another ball, keeping the count at 3-2. But the Mets inning seemed to come to an end when Wilson chopped a slow ground ball to first base for the likely third out. Bill Buckner, known for being one of the best defensive first baseman in the league, crouched down to field the ball, leaving his glove up ever so slightly...

"A little roller up along first," television announcer Vin Scully said after Wilson made contact. "Behind the bag...it gets through Buckner! Here comes Knight, and the Mets win it!"

The ball went right between Bill Buckner's legs. Stunned and in disbelief, the Red Sox watched the Mets celebrate at home plate. The World Series had been right there for the Red Sox. They had it. They could taste the champagne...but it got away from them.

"It was a slow roller with a lot of spin on it," Buckner explained. "I thought I watched it good. I was playing deeper than normally because I didn't want it to get through the infield. If Mookie didn't run so fast, I'd get down on a knee to block it. It bounced and bounced. And then skidded right under my glove. I was waiting for it to bounce. It didn't."

It's a shame for Buckner, given that he was one of the great first baseman in the league. But an injured ankle prevented him from playing at 100 percent and perhaps contributed to the error, although he never admitted that. Many expected manager Bob McNamara to replace Buckner with Dave Stapleton in the 10th inning, a better defensive player, especially after Buckner grimaced in pain after a hit-by-pitch in the top of the inning. Many saw McNamara's decision not to make the substitution as a turning point.

"Bill Buckner has just limped off the field, carrying the weight of the world on his back," Chicago Tribune writer Ray Sons famously wrote after the game. "He can ice those aching ankles all night so he can play in Game 7 of the World Series tonight, but there isn't enough ice to freeze the pain in his heart."

"My legs didn't have any effect," Buckner said after the game. "I felt good out there. It just shows you anything can happen. I feel lousy. Tomorrow, hopefully, will be a different story. We don't have a day or two to forget about it. You can't get down about it."

Many called it "The Miracle of Game 6." Others "The Buckner Blunder." Whatever it was could have been all forgotten if the Red Sox could go out there and win Game 7. For a long time, it looked as if they would. Just like Game 7 in 1975 against the Reds, the Red Sox built a 3-0 lead midway through the game. But the Mets rallied with 3 in the bottom of the sixth, and then Ray Knight hit a clutch home run in the bottom of the seventh to give the Mets the lead. They went on to an 8-5 victory, ensuring "The Curse of the Bambino" remained alive.

2016 WORLD SERIES GAME 7: CUBS AT INDIANS - "BREAKING THE CURSE"

The Curse of the Bambino was bad. The Curse of the Billy Goat was even worse (see Great Facts About Baseball in Chapter 5). The Red Sox ended their 86-year drought by winning a world title in 2004. By 2016, the Cubs had gone 108 years without a world championship.

The 2016 Cubs seemed to have the roster and management to end the streak. The Red Sox general manager from 2004, Theo Epstein, had left Boston to join Chicago. They had successfully pried manager Joe Maddon away from Tampa Bay. They had put together a roster of young superstar talent that included Kris Bryant, Anthony Rizzo, Jason Heyward, and Jake Arrieta. All that stood in their way was the Cleveland Indians.

The Cubs, like the 1986 Mets, had their backs up against the wall. They trailed the World Series 3 games to 1, but strung together two wins in a row to force a winner-take-all Game 7 in Cleveland.

With momentum on their side, they turned a deaf ear to the raucous Cleveland crowd and built a big lead midway through Game 7. After Javier Baez homered to right center and Rizzo singled in a few batters later to drive in Bryant, the Cubs had taken control of the game, leading 5-1.

While the Indians cut it to 5-3, Cubs catcher David Ross came up in the top of the sixth and blasted a home run to center field. It was 6-3 Cubs and they could feel a championship in Chicago, especially when Jon Lester came in relief and shut down the Indians lineup.

By the bottom of the eighth, the Cubs seemingly had control of the game, still leading 6-3 with two outs and just one man on. But Maddon made a questionable decision, pulling Lester for closer Aroldis Chapman, who had just pitched the previous two games. There was concern Chapman had a tired arm. That concern was justified when his usual 100mph fastballs weren't showing up on the radar gun. Brandon Guyer connected with a Chapman fastball and drilled it in the right center gap, scoring Harold Ramirez and cutting the Cubs lead to 6-4. The crowd began to erupt.

Still with two outs, Chapman could get the Cubs out of the inning with little damage. But he just didn't seem to have it, and he left a hanging pitch over the plate to Rajai Davis. Davis connected and blasted a home run that cleared the left field wall. The stadium started rocking.

Cubs 6, Indians 6.

Chapman was able to get the final out, but momentum was all on Cleveland's side, and when the Cubs failed to score in the top of the ninth, their heads were down and the Indians could sense a championship coming, especially when a tired Chapman entered the ninth.

But somehow, Chapman dug deep and found his command, striking out Jason Kipnis and forcing Francisco Lindor and Carlos Santana to pop up, just as the rain in Cleveland started to fall. The game was still tied 6-6, and Game 7 was going into extra innings.

In between innings, a steady rain became an absolute downpour, and umpires had no choice but to temporarily suspend the game. It was a huge advantage for the Cubs, who needed to hit the reset button and regroup. Jason Heyward gave a motivational speech in the locker room to give his team a second life. And when the rain delay ended after 30 minutes, the Cubs came out re-energized, and they showed it with their bats.

With runners on first and second and one out, Chicago's Ben Zobrist drilled a missile to left field, scoring the go-ahead run. Next, catcher Miguel Montero came up and added another single, scoring Rizzo, and the Cubs now led 8-6. Again, Chicago had control of the World Series.

But could they close it out?

Carl Edwards, Jr. came in to relieve Chapman and got the first two outs, putting the Cubs one out from the Series. But after walking Guyer, he had to face the man who had tied the game before, Rajai Davis. Again, Davis came through, this time drilling a base hit to center and scoring Guyer, cutting the Cubs lead to 8-7. The Indians fans were roaring. Could the Cubs get that third out?

Edwards, Jr. was able to get Victor Martinez to hit a ground ball to third. When the ball was successfully thrown to first base before Martinez got there, the umpire called out and the Cubs were world champions for the first time since 1908.

The Curse of the Billy Goat...the Curse of Steve Bartman (see Chapter 5 Baseball Facts) ...whatever you want to call it, had ended, and in dramatic fashion. The Cubs became the sixth team in history to trail 3 games to 1 in the World Series and come back to win it.

1975 WORLD SERIES GAME 6: REDS AT RED SOX "FISK WAVES IT FAIR"

Many call it the greatest game in baseball history. ESPN ranked it as No. 1 on their recent "Greatest Games Ever Played" list. Most people won't remember it since it was nearly 50 years ago, but Game 6 of the Reds vs. Red Sox was as good as it gets.

Seven future Hall of Famers (and Pete Rose) would be on the field between two powerhouses. The Reds, known as "The Big Red Machine" were led by Rose, Joe Morgan, Johnny Bench, and Tony Perez while the Red Sox countered with Carl Ystremski, Carlton Fisk, and Jim Rice. The Reds had won a franchise-high 108 games that season, winning their division by an incredible 20 games. The Red Sox were the underdogs, pulling off the big upset over three-time defending World Series champions Oakland to advance to the World Series. The Red Sox were still looking to shake off "The Curse of the Bambino."

Leading into Game 6, every game of the World Series thus far had been decided by a single run. The Reds had won a critical Game 5 at home, building a 3 games to 2 lead. But to win the world championship, they had to do it in Fenway Park in front of the Boston fans.

But getting to Game 6 wasn't easy. After a designated travel day, the rain in Boston was never-ending; it had already rained out three games before Game 6 was finally able to get underway. That left players, and particularly the pitchers, at the very least, fresh. Red Sox ace Luis Tiant was able to go right back out on the mound after pitching Game 5 and shut down the Reds. Fred Lynn hit an early home run for Boston to give them a 3-0 lead and the crowd at Fenway Park went berzerk.

But after four perfect innings, the Reds bested Tiant in the fifth, and tied the game. Then Ken Griffey, Sr. blasted a double off the Green Monster (the nickname for the field wall) in center to score two runs and give the Reds a 5-3 lead, inching them closer to a world championship. When the Reds' Cesar Geronimo homered in the top of the eighth, the Reds had a 6-3 lead. You could hear a pin drop at Fenway.

The Red Sox clung to hope in the bottom of the eighth when they were able to put men on first and second with two out, and Bernie Carbo stepped up to the plate. He faced a 2-2 pitch. Reds pitcher Rawly Eastwick was looking for a strikeout, but everyone heard the crack of the bat as Carbo connected. The crowd roared as the ball traveled deep to center and over the green wall. Boston went crazy as they tied the game, 6-6.

From there, it was an epic back and forth pitcher's battle that went into extra innings. It looked as if the Reds would break the tie in the top of the 11th when Pete Rose led off with a hit. But when a bunt was laid down to try and advance Rose, catcher Carlton Fisk made a gutsy play and fired to second to get Rose out. The throw made it just in time.

Then with one out and Griffey, Sr. at first, Joe Morgan belted a deep shot to right field that looked destined to go over the wall and give the Reds complete control. Griffey, Sr. broke free and was rounding toward second by the time the ball neared the fence. But Dwight Evans leaped up and made one of the greatest plays in World Series history, saving, at the very least, a run, maybe two. After making the catch, Evans immediately threw to first base, because Griffey was well out in front and was sprinting to get back. The throw reached first base before Griffey could get back–Double Play!

The game remained tied as they went into the top of the 12th. The Reds strung together two hits to put the go-ahead run in scoring position, but pitcher Rick Wise fired a fastball for strike three to retire the Reds and give the Red Sox a chance in the bottom of the 12th.

Up to the plate came catcher Carlton Fisk, who was already 1-for-3 with a run in the game. Pat Darcy, pitching for the Reds, opened the inning with a ball. On the second pitch, Darcy pitched one right down the center at the knees. Fisk smoothly swung and pulled the ball deep down the left field line. There was no question it was going over the fence; the only question was whether it would stay fair.

As the ball traveled for what seemed like an eternity, Fisk was sidestepping down first base, famously waving at the ball to keep it fair. He waved and waved, and the ball passed just inside the foul pole for a home run. The crowd went insane as Fisk rounded the bases. The Red Sox had won 7-6 in 12 innings, tying the World Series 3-3.

The Reds' heads hung low as they walked off the field. They'd lost two World Series in the last four years, and now seemed destined to lose another. They had lost all momentum, and in Game 7, they were down 3-0 early again and the writing seemed to be on the wall. But Tony Perez's home run in the sixth cut the Sox lead to 3-2, and then Pete Rose tied the game in the seventh. With the game still tied 3-3 in the top of the ninth, Morgan came up to bat with two outs and Griffey, Sr. on second. Morgan made contact, and hit a single to the outfield. Griffey, Sr. scored and the Reds took the lead. Then they closed the Sox out in the bottom of the ninth to win the World Series in seven epic games. It's the only seven-game World Series in history where every game was decided by one run.

"After my career was over, I realized what an honor it was to play in Game 6 and in that World Series because everybody remembers it, especially Game 6," said center fielder Fred Lynn. "Everyone remembers it, all baseball fans."

1988 WORLD SERIES GAME 1: ATHLETICS AT DODGERS "I DON'T BELIEVE WHAT I JUST SAW"

The 1988 Oakland Athletics had everything anyone could have wanted in a potential dynasty. They had star pitching, led by Dave Stewart, Rick Honeycutt, and future Hall of Fame reliever Dennis Eckersley. They had "The Bash Brothers," Jose Canseco and Mark McGwire. They had other great hitters like Dave Henderson and Dave Parker. Tony LaRussa was considered one of the best young managers in baseball. They'd won 104 games, dominating the American League, and entered the World Series brimming with confidence.

Then there was the Los Angeles Dodgers, led by manager Tommy Lasorda. They had one ace pitcher, Orel Herscheiser, and a lineup that wasn't nearly as deep and talented as Oakland's. They'd won just 94 games, but after stunning the Mets in Game 7 of the NLCS, a team that had won 100 games and beaten Los Angeles in 10 of 11 games during the regular season, they earned a date with the A's in the 1988 World Series.

To say Game 1 would set the tone for the rest of the World Series was an understatement. Oakland entered as a heavy favorite, and L.A. needed to seize momentum at home. If the Dodgers lost Game 1, most thought the Series would be over quickly. Lasorda put Tim Belcher on the mound to counter Oakland's ace, Stewart, who'd won 21 games in 1988.

While the Dodgers got out to a great start, building a 2-0 lead after the first inning, they immediately ran into trouble in the second inning against Oakland's vaunted lineup. The A's loaded up the bases for slugger Canseco. Belcher, trying to fool Canseco on a curve, left the ball hanging over the plate. Canseco smashed it; the ball sailed deep over the wall for a grand slam and Oakland, as expected, roared out to a 4-2 lead.

From there, pitching and defense dominated, and while the Dodgers were able to scratch out a run to cut Oakland's lead, the A's still led 4-3 through eight innings. Stewart, who'd pitched a stellar game, handed the ball off to closer Eckersley, who many saw as unhittable. Eckersley converted 45 of 47 saves in 1988, striking out 70 over 72 innings and posting a most impressive 2.37 ERA. Any baseball fan would tell you they expected Eckersley to close out Game 1 and give the A's all the momentum going into Game 2.

Eckersley got Mike Scioscia to pop up in the infield for the first out. Next came Jeff Hamilton. Eckersley struck him out. Two outs, nobody on, and fans had pretty much lost all hope. Mike Davis, seemingly their last hope, was able to scratch out a walk to put the tying run on first base.

It was then that Lasorda made a surprising move. Kirk Gibson, 32, had hurt his left hamstring and right knee during the NLCS and was not expected to play much, if at all, in the World Series. He could barely walk and his right knee was horribly swollen. But Lasorda, praying for a miracle, only needed him to swing the bat. If he could get on base, he would put in a pinch runner. Gibson was a talented hitter, batting .290 on the season and slugging 25 homers. But could he hit with two bad legs, and off of Eckersley, a sidearm, low-ball pitcher who rarely gave up a big hit? In fact, NBC flashed a graphic on the screen of how Eckersley had not allowed a home run in two months.

Gibson's entrance onto the field was stunning, for Gibson had just remarked the day before that he was in no condition to play. "I can play with this hamstring, but I can't play with this right knee," Gibson had said. "I couldn't hit today and I couldn't have played today. All I can do is test it out tomorrow."

The crowd went crazy when they saw Gibson limp out to home plate. It was like watching a war hero who had been through battle fight through the pain and stand up to face the music. Gibson took his stance and faced Eckersley.

With the fans going wild, Eckersley delivered his first pitch. Gibson fouled it off, obviously in pain, and hobbled back. He struggled to stand up. He fouled off another. Then on the third swing, Gibson hit it and tried to run. The ball went foul, but watching Gibson was excruciating. He continued to hobble on two bad legs to first, and then back to the plate. Fans tried to cheer him on and encourage him to fight through the pain.

Eckersley tried to get Gibson to lean into a pitch with his bad legs, pitching high and away, but three times, Gibson was patient and didn't swing, and worked the count to 3-2.

With the crowd still going crazy, Eckersley delivered his pitch to home plate, but the ball didn't sink like he wanted but stayed out over the plate. Gibson caught it perfectly, a one-handed swing, and the 70,000-plus crowd at Dodger Stadium erupted as the ball sailed over the right field fence. An absolutely stunning home run that left Tony LaRussa's mouth wide open.

The Dodgers had won!

Perhaps the most iconic memory from that moment came from radio announcer Jack Buck, who delivered one of the most famous calls in baseball history that is still played over and over today.

Buck, in his slow, deep voice, said, "We have a big 3-2 pitch coming here, from Eckersley. Gibson swings. And it's a fly ball to deep right field. This is going to be a home run. Unbelievable! A home run for Gibson. And the Dodgers have won the game, 5 to 4. I don't believe what I just saw! I don't believe what I just saw. Is this really happening?"

Gibson hobbled around the bases. The cameras infamously caught Lasorda running out of the dugout screaming with his arms in the air. Gibson pumped his arm twice as he rounded second base and then needed a push from the third base coach to get him home. The players crowded home plate and the fans screamed at the top of their lungs. The Dodgers incredibly had beaten the A's in Game 1 in the most unlikely of ways, to take a 1-0 Series lead.

On the television broadcast, legendary announcer Vin Scully was silent for a minute after the home run, perhaps in shock, but also to let the audience hear the roars coming from Dodger Stadium. Finally, he broke his silence by saying, "In a year that has been so improbable, the impossible has happened."

It seemed as if the momentum from Game 1 never left them. Oakland struggled to regain their composure after that stunning loss, losing again the next night. The Dodgers then took two out of three in Oakland and shocked the A's to win the World Series in five games.

"First of all, it was like almost some kind of a foolish thing to really go up there and hit just because of the shape I was in," Gibson said as he reflected on the home run. "Just really sitting there in the clubhouse and almost dreaming about doing it, then to go up there and do it, it was like 'Can You Believe It?'

"I remember when I was rounding the bases, my parents went through my mind. Throughout my career, there were a lot of doubters, a lot of people who directed a lot of criticism at me. People would say things to my dad, and initially, early in my career, they had to defend me. I told them, 'You guys don't have to defend me. I'm going to bust it and I'm going to fail sometimes. But we'll have a laugh some day that it will all be worth it.' When I did it, I thought, 'This is the moment.'"

2001 GAME 7 WORLD SERIES: YANKEES AT DIAMONDBACKS "'THE SANDMAN' FAILS"

This wasn't necessarily just a great game; the whole World Series was exceptional. It had everything you could ever want. First, you had the three-time defending champion New York Yankees, winners of the 1996, 1998, 1999, and 2000 World Series. They were the definition of "dynasty," led by greats like Derek Jeter, Paul O'Neill, Bernie Williams, Scott Brosius, Jorge Posada, Roger Clemens, and Mariano Rivera.

The Yankees were a great story in 2001. The September 11, 2001 terrorist attack was still fresh in the minds of the country, and had postponed the season and pushed the playoffs back. Many fans who usually hated the Yankees pulled for them because of the attack and the unity America felt at the time. The Yankees won over the favored A's in the Wild Card, highlighted by Derek Jeter's epic flip to home plate in the decisive game that helped propel them to victory. But then they were heavy underdogs in the ALCS against Seattle, who tied an MLB record with 116 wins. The Yankees beat them easily in five games to advance to the World Series.

""I remember Joe Torre and what he told us," Posada said. "That we weren't only playing for New York. We were playing for everyone in the country."

While the Yankees had all the history, prestige, championships, and attention, the Arizona Diamondbacks were the complete opposite. They didn't have any championships. They were still technically an expansion team, having been established in 1998. They had a lot of star players who had achieved success on other teams, like Randy Johnson, Curt Schilling, and Luis Gonzalez.

But it wasn't necessarily David vs. Goliath because this was a stellar Arizona team, and many saw the Yankees as perhaps past their prime, despite winning three consecutive world titles. Schilling and Johnson had combined for 43 wins alone for Arizona during the regular season. They had outplayed the Yankees for most of the World Series, and won two out of the first three games, outscoring the Yankees 14-3. However, many still thought the Yankees were destined to win, given everything going on in the country, and how they'd miraculously pulled wins out of their hat in Games 4 and 5 to take a 3-2 Series lead. President Bush had even thrown out the historic first pitch at Yankees Stadium.

In those two games at Yankees Stadium, Arizona had led the entire game and just needed to close it out. But in both games, the Yankees hit ninth inning home runs off closer Byung-Hyun Lee, sending the stadium into a frenzy. In Game 4, Tino Martinez tied it with two outs in the bottom of the ninth. Derek Jeter then became "Mr. November," hitting a home run in the 10th inning of Game 4, just after midnight on Nov. 1, officially making it the first ever World Series to seep into the month. The next night, Scott Brosius homered in the ninth inning, again with two outs and off of Lee, tying the game and sending it to extra innings. The Yankees again closed out the D-backs in extra innings.

"The games at Yankees Stadium were amazing," Jeter said. "Probably the loudest I ever heard a crowd."

But Arizona was tough to beat at home, and the last two games were at their home stadium. They cruised to an easy 15-2 Game 6 victory behind ace Randy Johnson. That set up a classic Game 7 pitching matchup: New York's Roger Clemens against Arizona's Curt Schilling.

The two legendary pitchers put on a show. The Yankees offense continued to struggle in Arizona. Schilling shut the Yankees out for the first six innings, and when Danny Bautista doubled to drive in Steve Finley in the bottom of the sixth, Arizona was up 1-0.

But after Jeter scrapped out a hit and advanced to second, Tino Martinez got a clutch two-out hit that scored Jeter and tied the game. Then in the top of the eighth, Alfonso Soriano smoked a home run off Schilling, propelling the Yankees to a 2-1 lead. It appeared as if the

Yankees were about to celebrate their fourth world championship in a row.

But Randy Johnson, who had just thrown 104 pitches the previous night, came in off no rest and incredibly shut down the Yankees continued threat, holding the D-backs deficit to 2-1. The Yankees countered with their best man, Mariano Rivera, known as "The Sandman." Rivera easily disposed of Arizona in the eighth and was just three outs away from a World Series win.

But Rivera had to go through the top of Arizona's lineup in the bottom of the ninth. Unaccustomed to pitching two innings, Rivera was extremely shaky as he began the inning. First, Mark Grace singled to put the lead man on base. Then Damian Miller bunted to try and advance Grace. Instead of going for the safe out at first, Rivera rushed and tried to get Grace at second. It was a mistake; Rivera's throw was off line and ventured into center.

Midre Cummings came in to pinch-run for Miller. Then Jay Bell bunted as well. Rivera again went for the lead man and threw a missile to Brosious at third. This time the Yankees got the out, but now there were runners on first and second with one out.

Tony Womack came up to the plate, and on the fifth pitch, took advantage of a hanger Rivera left over the plate. Womack drilled the ball down the left field line just out of reach for Martinez. Cummings rounded third and scored. Bell advanced to third and Womack took second with a double. The crowd went nuts. It was tied 2-2 and runners were on second and third with only one out. Ninety feet from a World Series title. Rivera, known as the best closer in baseball, was reeling.

It got worse for Rivera. Facing Craig Counsell–who four years earlier had delivered the game-winning hit for the Florida Marlins in Game 7 of the World Series–was plunked (hit) by Rivera, so advanced to first base. This loaded up the bases for Arizona's star hitter, Luis Gonzalez. Still only one out.

Rivera couldn't afford a walk. He had to pitch strikes. The infield was in, ready to throw to home plate on a ground ball. The crowd at this point was as loud as ever, especially when the first pitch missed the strike zone. Rivera tried to jam Gonzalez with an inside strike on the second pitch, but Gonzalez made contact. The ball looped over Rivera's head and just into the lip of the outfield for a hit. Jay Bell, with his arms raised, dashed for home plate. The crowd went bananas when he crossed home, and Arizona had won the World Series with an epic ninth-inning rally.

Nobody could believe what they had just witnessed. The Yankees never blew ninth inning leads, and everyone had been sure that this dynasty would close out the inexperienced Diamondbacks. But it was a lesson to always expect the unexpected. Arizona had won their first, and thus far, their only World Series championship. Johnson and Schilling combined to go 4-0 over 39.1 innings with an incredible 1.40 ERA.

The Yankees held up their heads after the game, particularly Rivera, who went on to finish his career as the greatest closer of all-time. "I think it was the best World Series we ever played in," Rivera said. "Because of the way we had to fight. And just because…of the way we played."

Luis Gonzalez said the win meant everything to him and to Phoenix, but given recent events, they all remembered that there were more important things in the world than baseball. "To be a huge part of Arizona's history, to bring the first world championship here to the state; it's an honor," Gonzalez said.

"I remember as a group we talked about having an opportunity to go out to Ground Zero to pay our respects, to salute all the first responders," he added. "To see the smoke, and all the firefighters, it was crazy. That's when you realize there are a lot more important things in life than just playing the game of baseball."

HONORABLE MENTION

1991 World Series Game 7: Braves at Twins

After moving to Atlanta in 1966, the Braves became perennial losers. They hadn't won a single playoff series, and had only appeared in the postseason twice. So when they made the World Series in 1991, America was behind their Cinderella story as they played the heavily favored Twins, who had won the 1987 World Series. The Braves led the Twins 3 games to 2 and had them on the ropes in Game 6, but in extra innings, Kirby Puckett stepped up to the plate. Jack Buck made another one of his famous calls when he announced, "Into deep left center…and we'll see ya tomorrow night." The home run sent the World Series into a decisive Game 7.

It was a pitcher's duel for the ages. Jack Morris for the Twins against John Smoltz of the Braves. Two future Hall of Famers, and they pitched like it. Neither gave up a single run, and after 9 innings, the game was still 0-0. Rarely does a starter go into the 10th inning, but Morris did, and closed the Braves out to give the Twins a shot in the bottom of the 10th. That's when the Twins bats came to life. They loaded up the bases with one out for Gene Larkin. The Braves brought everyone in, hoping to force a double play. But Larkin hit the ball over everyone's heads and the Metrodome erupted. The winning run trotted home, and the Twins ended the Braves Cinderella story, 1-0, to win the 1991 World Series. The Braves went on to lose the 1992 World Series as well, but finally broke through in 1995.

1956 World Series Game 5: Los Angeles Dodgers at New York Yankees

It was without a doubt the greatest pitching performances in World Series history. Don Larsen faced 27 Dodgers' batters and got all 27 of them out. It was a perfect game, the only perfect game ever recorded in the World Series. The Dodgers' Sal Maglie pitched one of the great games, too, stumping the Yankees dynamic offense for almost the entire nine innings. But Mickey Mantle was able to get one of the Yankees' five hits, a home run in the fourth inning, that put the Yankees ahead.

Leading 2-0 in the top of the ninth, Larsen recorded his seventh strikeout to conclude the greatest pitching performance in championship history.

1960 World Series Game 7: Yankees at Pirates

The Yankees had clearly been the better team throughout the Series, scoring 55 runs while the Pirates only had 17. But the Pirates scratched out 3 wins and forced a Game 7. The deciding game was an offensive classic that went back and forth. First the Pirates darted out to a 4-0 lead, then the Yankees offense showed its firepower and sprang past them with a 7-4 lead in the eighth. But in the bottom of the eighth, Roberto Clemente and Hal Smith both had huge base-clearing hits, netting five runs and putting the Pirates ahead 9-7.

But the Yankees weren't done. They cut it to 9-8, and with two outs and their backs against the wall, Mickey Mantle slammed a hit into the outfield to tie the game, 9-9. In the bottom of the ninth, Pirates second baseman Bill Mazeroski led off. Mazeroski swung at the first pitch he liked and clubbed it over the outfield wall for a home run and the World Series win. The Pirates won 10-9; Mazeroski became the first player ever to win Game 7 with a home run.

1986 NLCS Game 6: Mets at Astros

As we know from above, the Mets won the 1986 World Series, but they had to fight hard to get there. The favored Astros trailed the Mets 3 games to 2 in the NLCS, but had the Mets in the Astrodome and on the brink of defeat. They led 3-0 going into the ninth, and with a win, would be the heavy favorite going into Game 7 with ace Mike Scott pitching. But the Mets rallied, cutting the game to 3-2 in the top of the ninth. Dave Smith, the Astros reliable closer, came in and immediately gave up two walks to load the bases with one out. Ray Knight hit a sacrifice fly that tied the game and sent Game 6 into extra innings.

The game seemed like it would never end. Both offenses failed to produce until the 14th inning, when the Mets scored to put the Astros on the brink of elimination. But with one out and nobody on, Billy Hatcher blasted a home run to tie the game back up and send the

Astrodome into a frenzy. Nobody scored in the 15th and the game went into an incredible 16th inning, where the Mets got a leadoff double from Daryl Strawberry. Knight came up and hit a single to drive in the go-ahead run. The Mets led 5-4. The Astros threatened in the bottom of the 16th but couldn't score, leaving them heartbroken and sending the Mets to the World Series.

1992 NLCS Game 7: Pirates at Braves

After losing the World Series in seven games against the Twins the year before, more people had jumped on the Braves bandwagon in 1992. They got back to the NLCS, but were on the ropes at home against Barry Bonds and the Pittsburgh Pirates. The Braves had made it to the World Series a year earlier by beating the Pirates on the road in Game 7 of the NLCS, and it looked like the favor would be returned (Note: The Pirates had also lost the 1990 NLCS to the Reds).

The Pirates led 2-1 in the bottom of the ninth, but the Braves loaded up the bases with two outs. The Braves fans were all doing the Tomahawk Chop, trying to rally their team. Closer Stan Belinda faced the most unlikely of pinch-hitters, Francisco Cabrera. Unless you were a diehard Braves fan, you'd never heard of the guy. He hadn't played many MLB games. Belinda got behind early on Cabrera, and tried to put a 2-1 fastball past him. Cabrera pulled the pitch and squeezed it between the shortstop and third and into the outfield. One run scored for the tie. Sid Bream rounded third and got the okay to head home and go for the win. Bonds fired the ball from the outfield to the catcher, trying to beat Bream. With the fans going wild, Bream slid to try and avoid the tag. By a split-second, Bream reached out and touched home plate before the glove hit his back. He was safe. Players jumped all over him. The Braves had beaten the Pirates 3-2 in a wild finish to advance to the World Series again, although as we learned earlier, they would ultimately lose it that year.

5

DID YOU KNOW? AMAZING BASEBALL FACTS

Baseball has so many incredible and cool facts that even the greatest historians of the game may not know all of them. Here are ten things about the game's history that may surprise you.

1. **Moon Shot:** Hall of Fame pitcher Gaylord Perry was one of the best to ever throw the ball. But hitting wasn't exactly his thing. In the National League, well, pitchers have to hit. In 1962, manager Alvin Dark joked about his power. "There'll be a man on the moon before he ever hits a home run," players recalled him saying. Well, in 1962, going to the moon was about as likely as someone living on Mars, and Perry lived up to his manager's words by struggling for years at the plate. He went to the plate 546 times and never even came close to the fence. That was until 1969–Gaylor Perry got a hold of one and shocked everyone by hitting a home run…20 minutes after Neil Armstrong stepped foot on the moon! So yes, Alvin Dark's prophecy had technically come true.

2. **Going Out on Top:** Babe Ruth was perhaps the greatest player ever. But like most ballplayers, Father Time got the best of him in the twilight of his career and he struggled mightily at the plate. By 1935, the Boston Braves were the only team who really wanted him, but it was only to fill seats. He was hitting just .170, had a dismal three home runs, his legs

were gone, and he struck out in one-third of his at-bats. But then out of nowhere in Pittsburgh, at one of the hardest ballparks to hit, he blasted not one, not two, but three home runs and stunned fans. He crossed home plate for the final time and told his teammates, "I'm done." Ruth retired from baseball the next day.

3. The Seventh-Inning Stretch: In the seventh inning of every ball game, fans stand up and stretch their legs for the "Seventh-inning stretch." Many times they sing "Take Me Out to the Ball Game," as is customary in Chicago. But how did the seventh-inning stretch get its name? Well, many say it came about in 1910, when President William Taft, a large man, attended a Pirates World Series game and threw out the ceremonial first pitch, the first time a president had ever done that. And in the seventh inning, Taft needed to stand up and stretch his legs and back. Well, when the people saw the President do this, they thought he was going to leave, so out of respect for the office, the entire crowd stood up. Soon after, standing up in the seventh inning became a tradition, and the name "Seventh-Inning Stretch" was born.

4. The Cubs' Curses: We already know what the Curse of the Bambino was about. But the Cubs also had a famous World Series drought that initially became known as "The Billy Goat Curse." It originated when popular Billy Goat Tavern owner Billy Sianis brought his pet goat to Wrigley Field. Sianis was stunned when ushers escorted him and the goat out, citing a policy that animals were not allowed. Sianis was famously quoted saying, "Them Cubs, they ain't gonna win no more." The story grew over time as the Cubs became perennial losers and the media dubbed it "The Billy Goat Curse."

The curse was almost broken in 2003 when the Cubs were on the verge of going to the World Series. They had a 3 games to 2 lead on the Marlins and were up 3-0 in the eighth inning. With runners on first and third and one out, outfielder Moises Alou jumped up to try and catch a foul ball on the edge of the wall for the second out. Unfortunately, a Cubs fan named Steve Bartman reached his hands out over Alou's glove, preventing him from making the catch, infuriating Alou. The Cubs immediately gave up a series of hits following Bartman's interference, went on to lose the game, and then lost Game 7 the next night. Some renamed the curse "The Bartman Curse."

5. Forever the Phillies: We already know the Atlanta Braves are MLB's oldest team. But they've moved around over the years. In 1883, the Philadelphia Quakers were established. Seven years later, they changed their name to the Philadelphia Phillies. Now, 133 years later, they are still the Philadelphia Phillies. That makes them the longest team to retain the same name and stay in the same city in not just baseball, but in any American sport.

6. Facial Hair in Baseball Was Once Frowned Upon: When we watch baseball, or really any sport, we can't help but notice how many players are sporting scruffy faces and beards. But incredibly, from 1914 to 1972, not one MLB player ever had facial hair; there was an unwritten rule against it. But in 1972, the Oakland A's players showed up to spring training with mustaches, mostly as a joke. The A's owner dared his team to keep them, saying he'd pay them $300 each if they kept the 'staches to start the season. When they kept winning, they decided to keep the mustaches much longer because they were too superstitious to shave them off. In fact, they ended up winning 93 games and the World Series!

7. What's in a Nickname?: While nicknames in sports are common, baseball is the king of it. In fact, everyone had one back in the day. Some great nicknames have been born throughout the years. Ozzie Smith was known so much for his defense that he was called "The Wizard." One day Joe Jackson was getting blisters on his feet from his cleats, so he took them off and went out to the field without them. He became forever known as "Shoeless Joe." Reggie Jackson hit 10 home runs and slugged .775 in the October World Series, becoming recognized as "Mr. October." Other popular names include "Catfish" Hunter, "The Crime Dog" Fred McGriff, "The Sandman" Mariano Rivera, and "Say Hey Kid" Willie Mays.

8. The Fast and the Slow: The quickest Major League Baseball game took place on Sept. 28, 1919, when the Giants and the Phillies played a game in 51 minutes! And no, they didn't have a pitch clock. The longest game by innings happened between the Brooklyn Robins and Boston Braves in 1920–a 26-inning marathon that ended in a tie. Time-wise, the longest game was a 1984 contest between the Brewers and White Sox that took 8 hours and 6 minutes. The game went an incredible 25 innings.

9. A Can of Corn: It's a common saying in baseball that to catch an easy fly ball is "catching a can of corn." The term originated in the early 1930s when grocers used to stock cans of corn high on shelves and used a hook to get them down. The hook would knock them off the shelf and the grocer would use their apron to make the easy catch. Announcers Red Barber and Bob Prince were the first to say that outfielders dropped or caught "a can of corn" during a baseball game.

10. Home of the Braves: The Braves started out as the Cincinnati Red Stockings and then relocated to Boston and were renamed the Braves. Besides being baseball's oldest team, they also hold the distinction as the only MLB team to win the World Series in three different cities. They won as the Boston Braves in 1914. They won as the Milwaukee Braves in 1957. Then they won as the Atlanta Braves in 1995 and 2021.

Other Interesting Facts

- Aroldis Chapman holds the record for fastest pitch ever recorded, a 105.1mph fastball on Sept. 24, 2010.
- The Seattle Mariners are the only MLB franchise never to appear in a World Series.
- The New York Yankees hold the record for most championships – 27.
- The 1906 Cubs and 2001 Mariners hold the all-time record for regular season wins, 116. The 1899 Spiders, sadly, hold the record for least amount of wins in a full MLB season, 20.
- Pete Rose holds the record for most games played (3,562) and most hits (4,256). Unfortunately, because he illegally gambled on games, he has been barred from The Hall of Fame.

- Relief pitcher Jack Quinn was the oldest regular player to ever play Major League Baseball at 50 years old. Legendary pitcher Satchel Paige pitched a game in an honorary appearance at 59, but he had officially retired 12 years earlier.
- In 1944, 15-year-old pitcher Joe Nuxhall became the youngest player to ever appear in a Major League game.
- The Dominican Republic is the most represented country outside of the U.S., with 171 active MLB players (as of 2019), which makes up just over 8 percent of the league.
- Ichiro Suzuki broke the all-time single-season hit record in 2004 with 262 hits. He is also the only player to ever have 10 consecutive 200-hit seasons.
- All umpires are required to wear black underwear underneath their black pants, in case their pants rip.
- Fenway Park is the oldest active MLB stadium. They first started playing games there in 1912.
- Major and Minor League teams use wooden bats. However, colleges require players to use metal bats.
- Ed Cicotte became the first pitcher to ever throw a baseball with his knuckles. Thus, in 1908, the "knuckleball" was born.
- Only one team in history has come back from 3 games to 0 to win a playoff series. That was the 2004 Red Sox, who rallied from 3 games down to beat the Yankees. They would then break "The Curse of the Bambino" the following week against the Cardinals in the World Series.
- The New York Yankees were the first team to ever wear a number on their back. They are also the only team in history to not put players' names on the backs of their jerseys.
- Ken Griffey, Sr. and Ken Griffey, Jr. were the first ever father-son duo to play in the MLB at the same time. They also played on the same team (Seattle).
- It's a Major League Baseball requirement that each ball include 108 stitches.
- "A League of Their Own" is the highest-grossing baseball movie of all-time, bringing in a revenue of $107.5 million.

- "Take Me Out to the Ball Game" is baseball's unofficial anthem.
- An average of more than 26 million hot dogs and sausages are eaten during an MLB season, making them the most popular food at baseball games.

CONCLUSION

People have often referred to baseball as "America's pastime" because it gave us something to turn to when times were tough. During the Civil War, soldiers took breaks and put aside their stress and hate to play something they all loved. During the Great Depression, sandlot games were still played in the streets and at local parks, reminding everyone of the good things in life. During the Civil Rights crisis, Americans would find relief from the awful things they saw on television and turned on a baseball game. After 9/11, America tuned in to watch the Yankees and Diamondbacks in the World Series, which helped bring America together.

Other sports have no doubt garnered America's interest in recent years. Still, there's nothing like watching a baseball game to get your mind off the everyday stress that we face. I still love to go home and take my dad to a baseball game because it just seems like all the problems of the world fade away when we're at the game. (In fact, I just got tickets this weekend to a game I'll go to with my dad). Football, hockey, and basketball are great for excitement and an adrenaline-rush. But baseball's perfect for relaxing and smiling. And luckily, excitement usually works its way in as the game goes on.

For kids, baseball is still up there as one of the most popular sports to play. Whether it's t-ball, Little League, or high school, it's become an ideal sport that teaches kids the importance of teamwork, bonding, and development. There's no greater feeling than slugging a hit or maybe even a home run and being welcomed at home plate and celebrating with your teammates. Or watching your mom and dad smile and cheer you on as you walk up to the plate. Or going to a game with your friends and getting an autograph from your hero.

There's just something about it that makes you feel good inside. A feeling that no other sport can give you. It's why it will always be one of my favorite sports to play and to watch in person. Whenever I look for peace of mind, baseball is the perfect antidote.

THE BASKETBALL BOOK FOR BOYS 9-12

THE HISTORY OF THE GAME, BIOGRAPHIES OF THE GREATEST PLAYERS OF ALL TIME, STORIES OF AMAZING GAMES, AND INCREDIBLE FACTS

JIMMY MCCALL

INTRODUCTION

Growing up, my parents always knew where I was. It's not because I told them that I was going to my room, or to the back yard, or down the street. I didn't have to say anything.

They could just hear me playing sports.

Sometimes I'd be tossing a football with friends on the street. We'd lose our minds when someone caught a bomb of a touchdown pass by the stop sign, and did a celebratory dance that made us all crack up.

I would also play baseball in the area, as we tried to direct our scalding line drives away from windows and cars. Instead of using actual baseballs, we'd use tennis balls and aluminum bats to showcase some serious childhood power in the chalk-drawn batter's box.

Basketball also had a special place in my heart during my youth.

When I was in middle school, I remember going to the NBA store and buying a San Antonio Spurs hoop and mini basketball for my bedroom. It was one of those hoops you could attach to the very top of your door. Much to my parents' dismay, the walls were used as backboards for some of the smoothest bank shots and most powerful self-assisted alley-oop dunks in the history of bedroom basketball.

I would later graduate to playing with friends in the neighborhood at the park or in my back yard. While the prospect of grabbing on to the rim after a dunk was out of the question, seeing the basketball go through the hoop while hearing that distinctive "swish" sound made the game even more appealing.

But the truth was, I didn't really need any of these settings to grow my love for the sport. If I wasn't able to get to a hoop, I would get creative. Rolling up socks into a ball, and shooting it into the hamper would've been just as satisfying, especially as a youngster.

There were so many times when an NBA game would be on TV, and I'd look around for any type of clothing (dirty or not) to roll up so I could imitate one of the pros. Don't bother looking for any video footage of this, I promise there wasn't any!

You may be wondering: But wasn't there one moment he can remember that was the true beginning of his love for basketball?

I can't single out one particular magical moment, but maybe that's the point.

Basketball is a sport that highlights the teamwork needed to win a game, and the strategy necessary to come up with a plan to defeat an opponent.

It's a game that tests your physical ability, but also brings out personality traits that you didn't know you had. It teaches lessons of hard work and sacrifice through a sport that you don't need to buy expensive equipment to play.

It's a game that shows you that skill and talent can come from anyone, regardless of what they look like or where they come from.

Basketball is an experience that keeps on giving, and there's nothing in the world I'd trade that for.

1

THE HISTORY OF BASKETBALL

After you've finished your chores and done your homework, tune into an NBA basketball game and take in everything that's going on. When I say *everything*, I mean it.

Focus on the players, the coaches and the referees. Look at the people sitting in courtside seats, at the bench, and the entire arena. Think about how everything has to come together perfectly in order for a two-and-a-half-hour game to take place, to create a product that's beloved by people all over the world.

Check your social media feed during halftime. There's an excellent chance that clips from the game you've been watching are already posted on Instagram or Facebook, and even have hundreds, if not thousands, of comments or likes.

The game has evolved into something that anyone can engage with at home, on the go, or in person at the arena.

But it wasn't always like that.

Celebrities didn't always pay thousands of dollars to feel the breeze of professional players running past them as they sat courtside.

Game officials didn't always have the ability to check instant replay to see if there was a close call.

The games weren't even always broadcast on live TV, which is pretty crazy to think about, right?

Basketball was invented a very long time ago. Over the course of more than a hundred years, the sport has grown into what it is today.

Some of the brightest minds in science are working on ways to allow humans to time travel. But until they figure it out, step into this basketball time machine with me to understand how the sport began, and how it's changed over the years.

HOW IT ALL BEGAN

I don't know where you're reading this book, but there's at least a chance you're in a part of the United States (or the world) that gets mighty chilly when winter arrives. Walking around your neighborhood when the temperature is below freezing and the wind is howling makes it seem like your ears are going to fall off. It's tempting to stay home, curl up in a cozy blanket, and watch TV with your friends and family during these days.

That can be super relaxing, but it can also be boring to do every day until the weather warms up in the spring. Plus, sitting around for several months without exercise isn't good for any kid (or adult, for that matter).

A long time ago, in 1891, a physical education teacher at the International YMCA Training School in Massachusetts, named James Naismith, was given two weeks to come up with a game that would be athletic, not take up too much room, help the track students stay in shape while indoors during the harsh winter months and that was fair for all players.

Naismith asked what materials were available to him, and the janitor brought him two peach baskets. This didn't seem like much help, but it provided the resourceful man some inspiration.

Naismith decided to nail the peach baskets to two balconies on either side of the school's gym. As it turned out, the bottom of the balconies were 10 feet high, which is the same height that regulation basketball hoops are today.

Naismith had no idea what would happen next. Would his rowdy students like the game? Did he have a good enough plan to keep the players safe?

There were only a couple of rules at first, which led the players to engage in all sorts of things that were legal in other sports, but are things we don't recognize in today's basketball games. The students were tackling each other, holding one another, not dribbling and were throwing the ball towards the peach basket rather than shooting it.

It was utter chaos.

Naismith also had to find a way to keep the game moving after someone made a shot. Like any regular basket used for a picnic, these peach baskets had bottoms. As a result, the ball would go into the basket, and just stay there.

To avoid delays, he recruited two men to be stationed on the balconies. They would retrieve the ball from the basket and throw it back down so the game could continue.

This picture isn't exactly the same one we're used to when we think about how basketball is played today. But for something that Naismith came up with so quickly, it was a huge success. His students really enjoyed this new sport, and wanted to keep playing it during the winter of 1891-1892.

But Naismith knew he had to come up with more rules to keep the game from being a free-for-all, and to make sure the players did not get hurt. He introduced the concept of fouls, which would penalize the defense if they committed too many infractions. If the ball went out of bounds, a player could pass the ball back in bounds, but would only have five seconds to do so. That rule is actually still valid today at all levels of basketball!

Of course, it occurred to all the participants that retrieving the ball from the basket was an unnecessary step, so it was later decided that the bottom of the basket would be cut off so a successful shot would go right through the goal.

HOW THE GAME HAS CHANGED

It didn't take very long for word to spread about the sport. In fact, during that same decade, other universities throughout the United States adopted the game. James Naismith himself would go on to work at the University of Kansas, and would serve as the head coach of the Jayhawks, the men's basketball team, from 1898-1906. What's kind of funny is that the Jayhawks lost more games than they won during that timeframe, even though they were coached by the guy who invented the sport!

In the early part of the 1900's, basketball would take off all around the country. The fast-moving nature of the sport, coupled with the idea that specialized gear was not needed to participate, became appealing to the masses. Even though the final score of the games was pretty low, fans enjoyed the continuous action.

During the infancy of the sport, the most popular shot was the two-handed set shot. Players would run around the court looking for open space, and would use two hands to push the ball towards the rim, without jumping off the ground.

In the years that followed, certain players would take it to the next level by shooting towards the hoop with one leg already in the air. We might think of that shot today as a "runner," "floater" or traditional layup. This added to the excitement of the game because players realized they could score without necessarily standing still.

The sport had a solid foundation within the college ranks, but that's where it ended for the time being. After players graduated, there wasn't an obvious next step for them to continue playing professionally. Most players would transition to their adult lives and their regular jobs as firemen, plumbers, doctors, lawyers, and so on.

Even though large arenas like Madison Square Garden in New York would host college games, the sport needed to reach another tier of fame in order to keep growing. An important milestone was when basketball was included as an official sport in the 1936 Olympic Games. The United States would field a team of college players who would play against other young men from Poland, Mexico and Canada. There was only one problem.

The IOC (International Olympic Committee) didn't have a hardwood basketball floor available for games to be played on. It was decided that the competition would take place on a tennis court that was slightly adjusted for basketball. When we say slightly, we mean barely, if at all!

The "court," if you could call it that, was a dirt space with lines to indicate where the court began and ended. Because of the uncertain footing, players were nervous about running too quickly, or dribbling on an area that might be uneven.

The gold medal matchup between the United States and Canada presented one other wrinkle. It rained all day before the game was scheduled to be played, and all throughout the contest as well. The American and Canadian players had to essentially play basketball in the mud, while spectators watched from the stands holding umbrellas. The United States would capture the first basketball gold medal, defeating Canada 19-8 in a very soggy contest. Thankfully, Olympic basketball would never be played outdoors again.

Despite the somewhat questionable presentation of the sport on the world's stage in 1936, basketball was continuing its march into the hearts of American sports fans. Another landmark moment for the game took place in 1927, when a group of traveling showmen named the Harlem Globetrotters played their first game.

Founded by Abe Saperstein, the Globetrotters were created to showcase the fun and exciting side of basketball. The team didn't just want to win; they wanted to put on a show that made fans cheer, laugh and smile. When they first hit the court, they were an actual basketball team, focused on proving that they could beat some of the best collections of talent in the United States.

Thanks to their skills and flair for playing the game with style, the Globetrotters and their classic jingle became popular with fans. They would go on to defeat some future basketball Hall of Famers in the ensuing decades, and basketball Hall of Famers also decided to play with them. The Harlem Globetrotters helped players and fans alike realize what the sport could turn into with their fast break passes, long range shooting and slam dunk plays.

The Globetrotters are still around today, as you may know, and remain committed to making fans happy while running circles around their opponents in what is basically "basketball theater."

With all this positive momentum swirling, there was only one big thing left for the game of basketball to do: Start a successful professional league!

There had been some attempts during this time to play the game at the highest level for money. Regional leagues would pop up in Massachusetts and in cities like Philadelphia and New York, but their interest was limited to people who lived in those areas.

Two leagues were the most successful in the 1940's; the NBL (National Basketball League) and BAA (Basketball Association of America). Both operations had established successful franchises in different parts of the United States and Canada, and in 1949 they decided to join forces to create the league that we know and love today; the NBA!

The NBA would be the go-to destination for big time talent coming out of college in the 1950's and 1960's. Thanks to relocation and business savvy owners, the league would expand to the West Coast and have a following throughout the United States. Things were really taking off, as fans became obsessed with their favorite teams and players.

The league would receive a stiff challenge from 1967-1976 from a new league called the ABA (American Basketball Association). The ABA marketed themselves as a more fun, futuristic league, which could entertain fans better than the NBA could. The ABA had a three-point line, and encouraged high scoring games without too much defense being played.

The ABA was also not afraid to pay their players a lot of money, which attracted some top talent to their league. The NBA was still the most popular league, but the ABA was quickly gaining fans.

As it turned out, the ABA was not able to sustain the business, but they had an important influence on the NBA, and on how basketball would be played moving forward. After the ABA folded, the NBA absorbed four of its teams, and became a more enjoyable sport to watch.

There was another lesson the NBA learned from the ABA. The NBA had some great players, but it didn't always do its best to promote them in the media. Imagine a star player today not being on Twitter or Instagram!

That would all change in the 1980's, as the league welcomed Magic Johnson and Larry Bird. These two players and personalities immediately made the Los Angeles Lakers and Boston Celtics immensely popular, and the league began airing live games at night, when families could watch them together.

Michael Jordan would pick up where Bird and Johnson left off, and NBA commissioner David Stern focused on bringing fans closer to the game in the United States and across the world. In the 1990's, everyone knew how good Jordan was, and how dominant the Chicago Bulls had become.

After Jordan, new stars like Kobe Bryant, LeBron James, Stephen Curry and others continued to bring attention to the game, and international players like Dirk Nowitzki, Tony Parker and Yao Ming helped teams realize that talent could be found anywhere in the world.

THE MODERN ERA

Now that you know how basketball began and evolved over the years, I'll point out some on-court differences from the way the game used to be played compared to how it's played today.

Good Shots

If you asked someone what they thought a "good shot" was in 1981, and someone else what they thought a "good shot" was in 2021, the answer would be completely different.

In 1981, the answer to that question would involve an attempt at the basket that came from eight feet away by one of the team's taller players.

In 2021, the answer to that question would be "the first open shot the team got."

Teams often used to use most of the shot clock in hopes of letting a star player try to put moves on his defender, or pass the ball around. Coaches would become angry when players made an attempt early in their possession, believing that if they were a little more patient, a better shot would come along later.

That thinking isn't as popular anymore, as players and coaches feel like a better shot isn't always guaranteed. It may still be smart to use up most of the time in a late game situation, but for the most part, good shooters have the green light to let it fly when they have room to do so.

Three Point Parades

When the three-point line was introduced to the NBA in 1979, not that many players used it. As mentioned above, people were wired to think that possessions that ended with a shot closer to the basket were most desirable.

But as the years have passed, attitudes towards the three-pointer have changed. In the 1990's, teams used it a little more when they were able to make a few passes that found a player standing wide open behind the arc.

The number of attempts from "downtown" climbed a bit from 2000-2010, but they dramatically shot up starting in 2012-2013. There are a number of reasons for this, but one of the most popular theories is the 'Steph Curr-ification' of basketball.

I may have just made up a word there, but I promise my grammar is pretty good otherwise.

Curry is the greatest shooter in the history of the game by any measure, and has made a habit of swishing three-point shots from extremely far away from the basket. This has led other players to start practicing and attempting these long-range shots, and it's been commonplace ever since.

Players Who Can and Can't Shoot

In previous eras of basketball, there were a lot of professional players who weren't good shooters. Some of those guys still exist today, but that number has decreased significantly.

In the past, players who couldn't shoot well would be valued highly for other skills they brought to the table. Maybe they were great defenders, or unselfish passers who could get their teammates open looks at the basket. Perhaps they were excellent rebounders, and were drawn to missed shots like a magnet.

Today, those skills are still appreciated, but defenses make it hard to keep on the floor players who can't shoot well. Defenses are smarter than ever, and will leave the worst shooting player wide open from the three-point line, while the player "guarding" a below average shooter helps stop another player.

Even though basketball games are supposed to be five on five, sometimes having a player who can't shoot on a team can make it seem like a four on five competition. Back in the day, teams didn't worry about this too much, but they do now.

Post Up Play

As I said earlier, shots closer to the basket used to be viewed as a good thing, while shots taken from far away were thought of as silly.

In order to get closer shots to the basket, teams would pass the ball to a power forward or center who would try to position themselves by the thick rectangle on either side of the paint. This area is generally known as the "low post," which is where big men used to try to back their defender down to get off a close shot.

The entire objective of a possession would be to get the ball to that spot, and everything else that happened would work off the taller player with the ball.

In this day and age, you rarely see these type of post ups anymore. Players are now more spread out from one another, and are usually attempting to dribble past their man rather than back him down.

Double Teams

Because you don't see post up plays anymore, you also don't see defenses trying to double team their opponents as much. A double team is exactly what it sounds like—two defenders try to surround the player with the ball. This is usually done to force the offensive player to panic and make a bad decision, or to simply get the basketball out of their hands and into the hands of what the defense feels is a less talented teammate.

Everyone watching, whether in the arena or on TV, knew where a post up play would take place. The defense could predictably send a double team to that area because they knew what the offense was going to do.

Now, with players so spread out, double teaming is much more difficult. Defenders have to cover a lot more ground on the court after swarming the player with the ball, and offense comes from everywhere on the floor instead of just the post up position.

Coach Interviews During the Game

You may not realize that NBA head coaches weren't always interviewed while the game was going on. This started within the last 10-15 years, when networks wanted to bring fans closer to the game.

Sometimes coaches do reveal their true feelings about how things are going, and other times they offer only one or two-word responses, which can be amusing to fans.

Back in the day, interviewing the coach was never even considered, as fans assumed they were too focused on trying to win and keeping their minds on the game. But this relatively new aspect has been a lot of fun, and it will probably stick around for years to come.

2

HOW THE GAME IS PLAYED

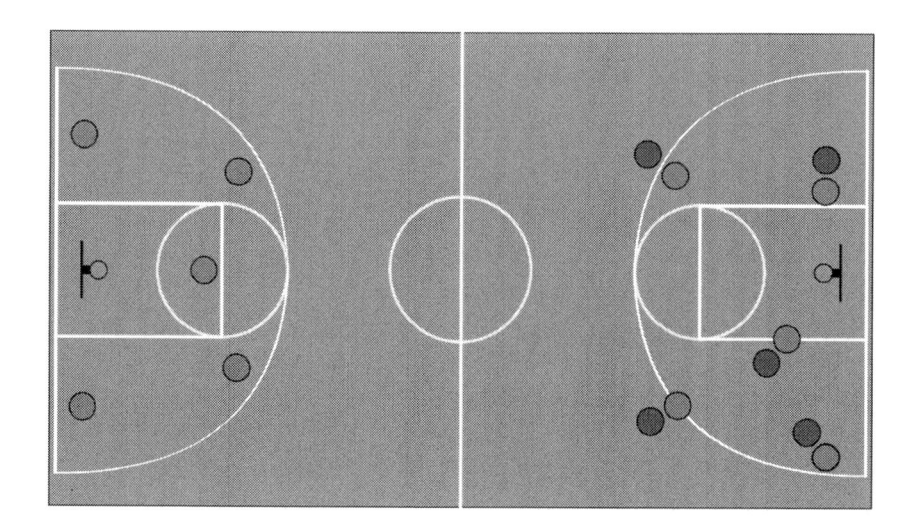

Basketball looks like a ton of fun! Everyone's having a great time running up and down the court, and it's something you'd like to participate in, right?

That's music to my ears. Let's put in our Airpods and jam out to some basketball-related tunes.

While you lace up your sneakers and find your hoops shorts, I've got to fill you in on a few things. The sport is fantastic, but just as with anything else, there are things you can and can't do.

Read up on the regulations below, so you can step on to the court with a clear idea of how to play.

BASIC RULES

Ball handlers

Basketball is a pretty easy game to understand. The objective is to put the ball in the basket, but there are a few things to keep in mind to make sure you aren't called for a violation.

Dribbling, or bouncing the ball, is required if you have possession of the ball and are moving around the court. Once you receive the basketball, you can start dribbling at any time and move as you please around the court. But once you stop dribbling, you have to stop moving, and can take no more than two steps towards the basket after your last bounce.

If you stop dribbling and you're not intending to shoot, you must pass the ball to a teammate. The dribbling rules described above begin again for that teammate. If the ball is passed back to you, you can dribble and move with the ball again.

There's a phrase in basketball that's called "keeping your dribble alive." Of course, it's not like watering your plant or feeding your pet. Keeping your dribble alive means continuing to bounce the ball until you decide what you want to do next (pass or shoot).

When you jump with the basketball (ideally to shoot, but sometimes to pass), you cannot land with the ball still in your possession. While you're in mid-air, the ball needs to leave your hands.

Offensive Players Without the Ball

If your team is on offense, but you don't have the ball, you can pretty much run around wherever you want on the court.

There's one thing to be aware of, though. There's a rectangle in front of the basket that is commonly referred to as "the paint." You get three guesses as to why that is, but you'll probably only need one.

It's usually full of color, painted with a color that matches the home team's uniform. As an offensive player, you can only stand in that area for three seconds at a time. You are welcome to visit the paint for three seconds, leave for one second, and come back in for another three, but each trip can't be more than three seconds.

If you're caught violating this rule, you can be whistled for "three in the key," and the ball goes to the other team.

Scoring

Putting the ball in the basket is the name of the game, but how much is each shot worth?

Three points—If your feet are behind the curved arc behind the paint and the free throw line when you take a shot, you'll be awarded three points if you make it. Because these attempts are taken the furthest from the basket, you get the most points per shot for making them. The reward is greater, but so is the difficulty.

It's important to note that if any part of your foot (yes, even that tiny pinkie toe) is on the three-point line when you shoot, the basket will count as only two points.

Two points—If you make a shot anywhere on the court inside of the three-point line during regular game play, the basket will be worth two points. These shots tend to make up the majority of points scored by a team, even though three pointers have become much more popular in recent history.

One point

If you're fouled when you have the ball on offense (more on this below), you may have the chance to take shots at the free throw line with no one guarding you. The free throw line is located at the top of the colored rectangle described earlier.

Each basket made from this area for a free throw attempt is worth one point.

Timing

An NBA game lasts for 48 minutes, and is played with four 12-minute quarters. College basketball games last 40 minutes, and are usually played with two 20-minute halves.

Games at lower levels of basketball are shorter, with high school games usually lasting 32 minutes over four 8-minute quarters. In middle school and elementary school, quarters will usually run for five or six minutes.

In college basketball and professional basketball, a shot clock is used. It's another timer that ensures an offensive team takes at least one shot within a certain period of time. The NBA has a 24-second shot clock, and college basketball has a 30-second shot clock. The clock resets if the ball hits the rim on a shot attempt or if possession changes.

Coaches also can take timeouts throughout the course of a game to speak to their team about strategy, or stop a run of points from an opposing team. The number of timeouts available to coaches varies at each level.

Fouls

We've spent a lot of time talking about offense and how it works, but there's another important element to the game. A common phrase in basketball is that "defense wins championships," and stopping the opponent is arguably just as important as putting the ball in the basket.

A good way to describe a basketball guarding position is to picture someone who doesn't want to be caught sticking their hand in the cookie jar. If your mom or dad finds you in the kitchen and asks why there are crumbs on the countertop, you'll stand straight up with both hands in the air proclaiming, "I didn't do it!"

(Be careful, they might catch you next time!)

In any event, standing with your chest pointed straight ahead and your hands above your head will keep you away from unnecessary fouls in basketball. It's when you start to reach towards the offensive player, perhaps even leaning on them or striking a part of their body with your hands or arms, that fouls are called.

In college basketball or lower levels of the game, each player is allowed to commit up to five fouls. In the NBA, each player is allowed six fouls. At any level, if a player reaches the maximum number, they are considered to be "fouled out," and cannot return to the game.

Fouls can result in the offensive player being allowed to take one, two or three free throws, which again are worth one point each.

Important Terms to Know

Assist: A pass made by a player that directly leads to a basket by one of his teammates. For example, your friend passes you the ball, and you catch it and immediately score. You get the points, and your friend gets the assist.

Other terms for assist: dime, helper

Rebound: Catching the ball after a missed shot attempt. A rebound most commonly takes place when a ball bounces off the rim, but it could happen when the basketball hits the backboard, or misses the rim entirely.

Other terms for rebounding: cleaning the glass, hitting the boards, 'bounding.

Steal: Taking the ball away from an offensive player without committing a foul.

Other terms for steal: picking a pocket, swipe.

Block: When a defensive player slaps/knocks the ball away from an offensive player while they are about to release a shot, or have already released the shot.

Other terms for block: rejection, stuffed, protecting the rim.

Goaltending: When a player tries to block a shot that an offensive player already released, but the shot is moving in a downward direction towards the basket.

Charge: An offensive player cannot run full speed into a defensive player. This will always result in a foul called against the offensive player. Also, if the defensive player is positioned with their hands up in front of an offensive player, and they are crashed into, a foul will be called on the offensive player.

This is one of the hardest calls for a referee to make, because they have to judge whether a defensive player was able to fully establish a stance in front of the oncoming offensive player. Even though it can be difficult to determine, it is a rule, and is called a charge.

Double Dribble: Remember when I said you can't dribble again once you stop? If you try to dribble again after stopping, you will be called for a double dribble and the ball will go to the other team.

Traveling: Similarly, if you've stopped dribbling, and you try to continue taking steps, you'll hear a whistle. This is called traveling, and the ball will go to the other team.

I also want to review the responsibilities each player has on the floor. You know that basketball continues to evolve and grow with each passing year, so some of this information is based on what players at certain positions have historically done. As you watch games moving forward, you will realize that the responsibilities can be shared amongst several players.

Point Guard

Making short jokes might seem pretty funny to you, but it wouldn't be wise to tease your point guard about their height. They're usually the shortest players on a basketball team, but a point guard has a lot of responsibility! For starters, they're the ones who dribble the ball up the floor the most consistently, so most offensive possessions will start with the ball in their hands.

Because of this, it's important for point guards to be smart and observant when it comes to making decisions that will affect their entire team. They have the freedom to keep the ball if they believe that they will be able to get a good shot at the basket, but shooting every time is usually not wise.

The point guard is supposed to get their teammates involved, and make sure the ball is going to the player who has the best chance to score.

On defense, they will also be tasked with trying to make life difficult for the opposing point guard, who will also be trying to smoothly start his team's offensive possession.

Shooting Guard

This might sound like the most fun position to play on a basketball team. Shooting guard—that means you get to shoot all you want, right? Bombs away!

Yes and no. It's true that a shooting guard is generally expected to be the most skilled player on the team at scoring points, and it's essential for them to be able to consistently make jump shots. It's also helpful if a shooting guard has solid dribbling ability. They may not be as good as a point guard at handling the ball, but they should be good enough to take the ball to the basket around a defender.

Sounds like a pretty sweet deal, right? It is, but there are other things this player has to do as well.

Shooting guards often have to run around the court more than the other players, and are often the main target of an opposing defense. This makes sense, because if a team knows that a shooting guard is the best scorer, they will try to stop them from making easy baskets. As a result, a shooting guard needs to be in excellent physical shape, as they cannot afford to get tired when a shot has to be made.

While a shooting guard generally has the green light to take shots, it's important that they don't take bad shots. For example, if a shooting guard is leaning away from the basket, with two players guarding him, shooting may not be the best idea. Another player on the court might be more open than the shooting guard in that situation, so they should pass the ball if there's time to do so.

Small Forward

Have you ever heard the term "Jack of All Trades"? You might think this refers to a boy named Jack, who was skilled at trading bad sweets for the good stuff at lunch in the cafeteria.

But the term actually refers to someone who is good or talented at many things. The player who comes closest to being a "Jack of All Trades" on the basketball court is the small forward.

A small forward's height is usually the median (pay attention in math class!) of his teammates. Because they're not the smallest but also not the tallest player, they have the ability to contribute in many different ways.

For example, if the point guard wants a break from dribbling the ball up the floor, a skilled small forward might be able to cover for them once in a while. They can also help out by scoring themselves, or by rebounding the ball.

Perhaps a small forward's biggest impact comes on defense, though. They should be able to guard the opposing small forward, but are also not in a bad spot if they need to switch to defending a shorter or taller player. This can be extremely valuable during the course of a game.

Even if a small forward isn't the best player on the court at any one skill, they should be able to respectably fill in where needed when called upon.

Power Forward

As we continue our trek through a basketball lineup in size order, our next stop brings us to the power forward. The name of this position might be a little confusing, since basketball doesn't seem like a game where power would be needed. If it was, we would need to buy a helmet and shoulder pads, right?

But strength and toughness is important in basketball, especially as you get closer to the basket. That's where you'll find taller players like the power forward, who are actively using their lower bodies to try and move opponents out of position on defense.

Power forwards are also expected to be a force in the rebounding department, and to prevent opposing teams from having multiple chances to score a basket. That's where a little bit of grit and determination comes in handy. There are a bunch of hands, arms and bodies swarming to the basketball after a missed shot, and a power forward is tasked with overcoming all of them to come down with the ball.

Offensively, power forwards traditionally have been the least skilled players on the floor, although that has changed in recent basketball history. Back in the day, it would be surprising for a power forward to take and make a shot from more than 15 feet away, since their job was to stay close to the basket. In this day and age, however, power forwards have extended their range considerably, and can make three-point shots just like smaller players.

Center

Hopefully you're in a comfortable spot while reading this book, but we may have to adjust our necks a little bit as we look up at the player in the center position. They're usually the tallest on the court, and have been known to duck under the top of door frames so they don't hit their heads. There's a hilarious scene in *Space Jam* where former NBA center Shawn Bradley smacks his head on the ceiling—check it out!

Our vertically gifted friends can affect a game in multiple ways. They are usually pretty adept at scoring close to the basket, and can attempt different types of shots without the fear of being blocked. Because they usually shoot close to the basket, the percentage of shots they make is usually greater than players at other positions.

They're also used as "screeners" or are asked to "set the pick" in a pick and roll situation. This is a basketball play where a teammate runs to a spot and stands still, keeping his arms within the frame of his body. The ball handler will "use the pick," which will slow his defender down as the defensive player either runs into or around the screener. Centers are usually the biggest players, which is why it makes sense for them to be screeners.

On defense, a center has one of the most important jobs in the game. They are assigned to the other center, and will need to make sure that they don't get chances to score easy shots. Centers are also responsible for helping their teammates by challenging opposing teams' shots at the basket. Even if a center cannot block a shot, getting in front of a player and putting their arms up can make a shot at the basket much more difficult.

Just like with power forwards, the expectations and skill levels for centers have changed and evolved over the years. Centers' defensive responsibilities have not changed that much, but their offensive jump shooting range has, as well as their ability to dribble the basketball.

3

THE GREATEST OF ALL TIME

We've reached that point in the book where it's time to talk about GOATS. Wait, what? *What do farm animals have to do with basketball?* you might be asking yourself.

The answer is nothing. While you might come across a goat during a school field trip to the zoo, I'm talking about a completely different kind of GOAT. These are the human kind, and don't make noise when they want to be fed (in most cases).

In the last few years, GOAT has come to stand for "Greatest of All Time," and is commonly used in sports to give the very best players their proper respect.

The GOATs made their mark in the game of basketball by winning championships, scoring a lot of points, making their teammates better, and playing great defense. They're extremely famous NBA players whose talent and skill rose above most of their peers. They also loved the game more than anything else, and worked extremely hard to continue getting better and better.

But there's another thing that all of these players have in common. Any guesses?

They were once all children with dreams about what they wanted to be when they grew up. The path to greatness wasn't always easy, but they continued to believe in themselves every step of the way.

Let's learn a little bit more about the 10 players who rank as the greatest of all time.

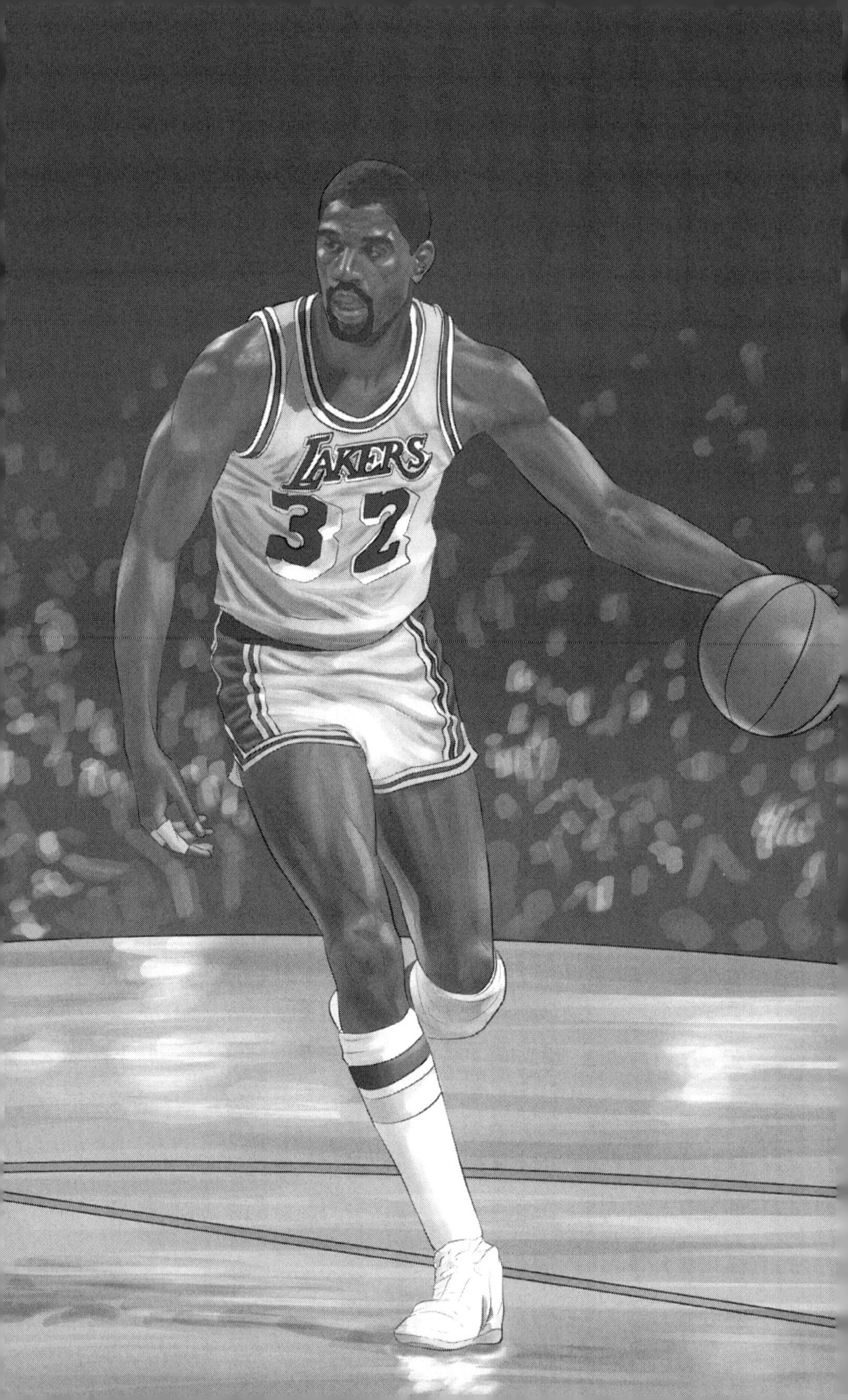
LAKERS
32

MAGIC JOHNSON

Full Name: Earvin Johnson Jr.

Nickname: Magic

Born: August 14, 1959

Hometown: Lansing, Michigan

College: Michigan State

Year Turned Pro: 1979

Total NBA Seasons: 13

Height: 6'9"

Position: Point Guard

NBA Team: Los Angeles Lakers #32

Notable Quote: *"Ask not what your teammates can do for you. Ask what you can do for your teammates."*

There may not be a happier player in NBA history than Magic Johnson. If your parents let you watch YouTube or social media and you can pull up old video of Magic, you'll see that he was always smiling!

But life wasn't always full of sunshine and roses for the man everyone called Magic. He had nine brothers and sisters, and his parents worked really hard to make sure they had food on the table every night. Young Earvin didn't have TikTok to showcase his vocal skills, but he would pass the time singing in the neighborhood with his friends.

When he wasn't busting out a tune, Magic would obsess over the game of basketball, even when he couldn't get to a hoop. On his way to the convenience store on cold Michigan days, he would dribble his ball with his right and left hand. While most kids sleep next to stuffed animals or action figures, Magic would snuggle up to his basketball when he went to bed each night, like it was a teddy bear.

His love for the sport would continue as he attended Everett High School, and later, Michigan State University. Magic had a wonderful college career, which ended with him leading the Michigan State Spartans to a national championship in 1979.

Because of his accomplishments in college, he was already a popular player before he entered the NBA. The Lakers were lucky enough to have the first pick in the NBA Draft in 1979, and Magic's exciting brand of basketball seemed like a perfect fit for them.

There was one major question though. The Lakers' best player when Johnson arrived was Kareem Abdul-Jabbar, a center who played close to the basket. Johnson loved to push the ball up and down the court on the fast break. Would the two stars get along and play well together?

The answer would come in the Lakers' very first game. Abdul-Jabbar would make a shot at the buzzer to defeat the San Diego Clippers, and Magic jumped into his arms in celebration, as if he was his best friend. It was clear from that moment forward that both players were willing to work together to win championships.

One of Magic's most special moments came in the 1980 NBA Finals, in his first year as a player. Abdul-Jabbar was forced to miss the game in which Los Angeles had a chance to clinch the championship, and the Lakers had to decide who to replace him with at the center position. The head coach decided that Johnson, their 6'9" point guard, would be the best choice.

It turned out to be the right move. Magic had one of the best games of his career, totaling 42 points, 15 rebounds and seven assists. Because of him, the Lakers would go on to win the title!

It was this type of unselfishness that made Magic one of the greatest players in NBA history, and so successful over the course of his career. He would grab a rebound, push the ball up the floor and willingly pass it to the teammate who had the best opportunity to score. Knowing this would motivate his teammates to sprint down the court next to him.

Magic would lead the Lakers to four more NBA championships in the 1980's, making the Los Angeles Lakers a dynasty. One of his other iconic moments came in the 1987 Finals against the Boston Celtics. With only seven seconds left in the game, Johnson hit a running hook shot that gave Los Angeles a victory that would help them win the title a few days later.

Magic Johnson's basketball career in the NBA ended a little early because of an illness, but despite the setback, he would still be a part of two unique basketball experiences that are part of his legacy.

Despite not playing in an NBA game during the 1991-92 regular season, Johnson was voted into the 1992 NBA All Star Game by the fans. He would put on a show with a memorable performance, as he led the Western Conference to a victory and became the All Star Game MVP.

Magic was also invited to be on what many fans consider to be the greatest basketball team ever put together. As part of the 1992 Dream Team, Magic Johnson's talents were on full display for basketball fans all over the world, as the United States team brought home the gold medal in the Olympics.

Even after his basketball career ended, Johnson remained famous and heavily involved with the Lakers. He has served as their coach and president of basketball operations at different stages of his life. He has also been a sports commentator on TV, sharing his thoughts and viewpoints on current players and teams.

As if Magic was not already cemented as a Los Angeles legend, he was also part of a group that purchased the Los Angeles Dodgers, the city's baseball team!

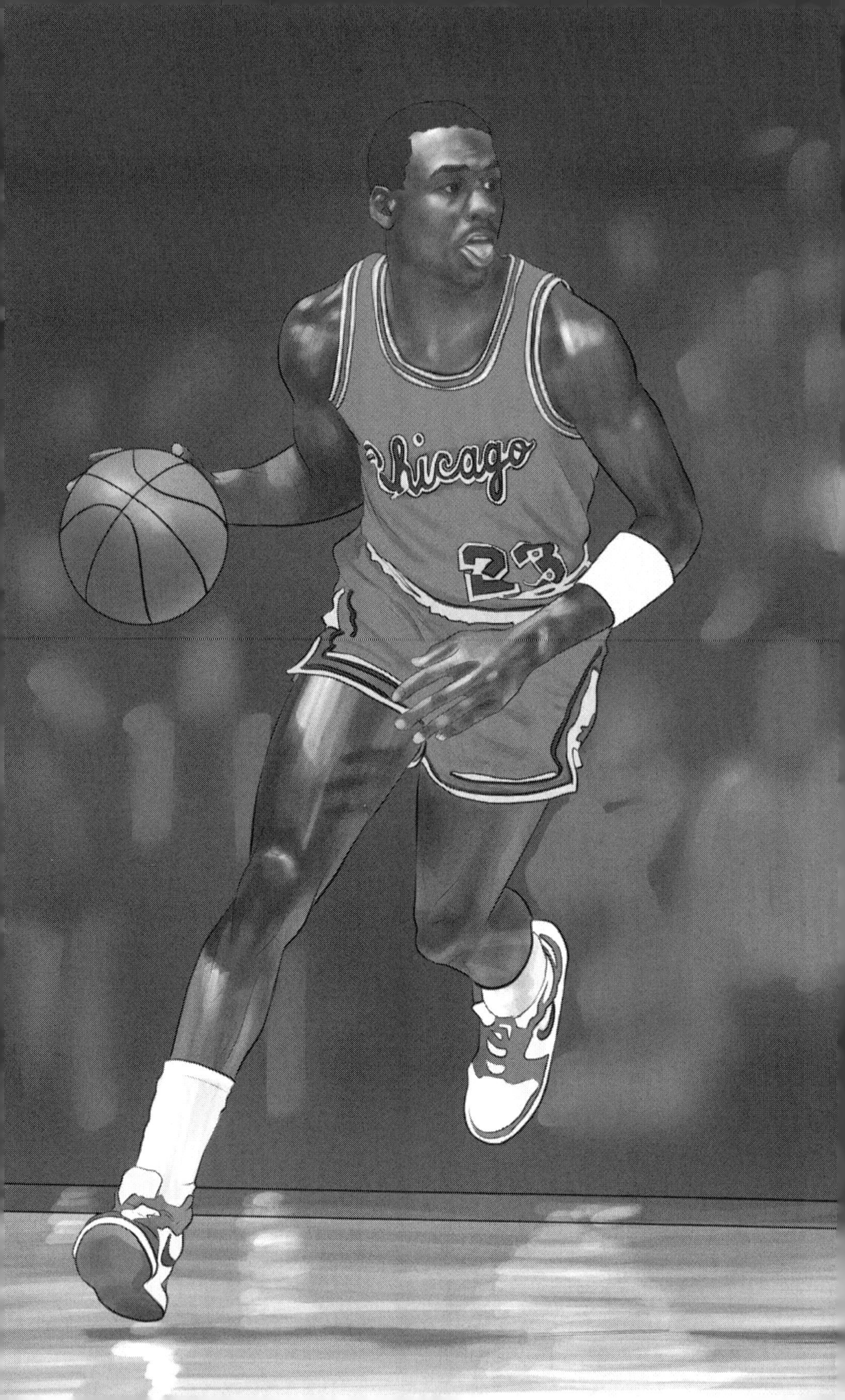
Chicago
23

MICHAEL JORDAN

Full Name: Michael Jeffrey Jordan

Nickname: His Airness

Born: February 17, 1963

Hometown: Brooklyn, New York

College: North Carolina

Year Turned Pro: 1984

Total NBA Seasons: 15

Height: 6'6"

Position: Shooting Guard

NBA Teams: Chicago Bulls #23, Washington Wizards #45

Notable Quote: *"I can accept failure, everyone fails at something. But I can't accept not trying."*

"Like Mike… if I could be like Mike!" Those were some of the catchy lyrics to the theme song, "Be Like Mike" in a Gatorade commercial featuring Michael Jordan, and a bunch of kids who wanted to be like the Chicago Bulls star.

Before he had such a large fanbase amongst young people, Jordan was just a kid himself growing up in New York and later North Carolina. He was a normal boy who loved to play sports, but also didn't like to study that much. When he started high school, he became more focused on his classes, while also dedicating time to the game he loved so much.

While he was a sophomore at Laney High School, Jordan would be told that he wasn't good enough at basketball. Yes, you read that right. One of the greatest players in basketball history, and in sports, did not make the cut for his high school varsity team.

A lot of teenagers would have stopped playing the game if that had happened to them. They might go home and feel sad, or blame the coach for not realizing how good they were. But Michael Jordan decided to continue to work on his game so he could be ready to try out again as a junior.

He would make the team the following year, and average 25 points per game in his two years on the varsity squad.

His excellent play in his final years of high school attracted the attention of the University of North Carolina coaching staff, who were excited to keep Jordan close to where he grew up. As a member of the Tar Heels basketball program, Jordan would display great athleticism against other college players. Most people know Jordan from his incredible play in the NBA, but he also made one of the biggest shots in NCAA basketball history.

In the 1982 championship game against Georgetown, Jordan would receive the ball in the corner, and nail a game winning jump shot to clinch the title for North Carolina.

Number 23 would enter the NBA in 1984, immediately showing otherworldly talent as a Chicago Bull. While Jordan quickly became one of the best players in the league, his team struggled to win in the playoffs.

He would still have the chance to wow fans all over the United States and around the world with his physical abilities. Jordan would dazzle basketball die-hards in a few Slam Dunk Contests, which showcased the best athletes in the league. In 1987, he took off from the free throw line and jammed it home, which is one of the farthest leaps any player has ever taken in dunk contest history.

As the 1980's came to a close, there was only one thing missing on Jordan's elite resume; an NBA title. He would end up achieving that dream for the first time in 1991, as he led the Bulls to a championship over Magic Johnson's Lakers. Jordan would end up playing in five more NBA Finals, winning every time. His performances would deny titles to other great players like Clyde Drexler, Charles Barkley, Gary Payton, Karl Malone and John Stockton.

The six-time champion would bring the popularity of the NBA to new heights in the 1990's, which helped the league become more famous in different parts of the world. Many of the international stars we watch in today's NBA started playing basketball because they'd watched Jordan as children.

He also became more popular with children after the 1996 film he starred in called *Space Jam*. Playing on a team with Bugs Bunny, Daffy Duck, Yosemite Sam and many other Looney Tunes, Jordan encouraged and trained the cartoon characters to beat the evil squad known as the Monstars, who stole the talent of NBA players.

What makes Jordan's accomplishments even more impressive is that he left the NBA for nearly two years when he was at the peak of his abilities in order to play professional baseball for the Birmingham Barons. Of course, he eventually returned to the Bulls to win more rings.

The star shooting guard would retire from the game in 1998… but it would not be for good. In fact, Jordan ended up working in the front office for the Washington Wizards, which meant he was able to pick who would play on the team, and in 2001, Jordan joined the Wizards on the court!

Even though he was pushing 40, Jordan showed he could still play with the young guys. He made two more All-Star teams while he played for Washington.

After his time in Washington, Jordan bought the Charlotte Bobcats (now the Charlotte Hornets) in 2010. He is often seen sitting courtside at their games. Naturally, the players always want to play their best in front of the basketball legend!

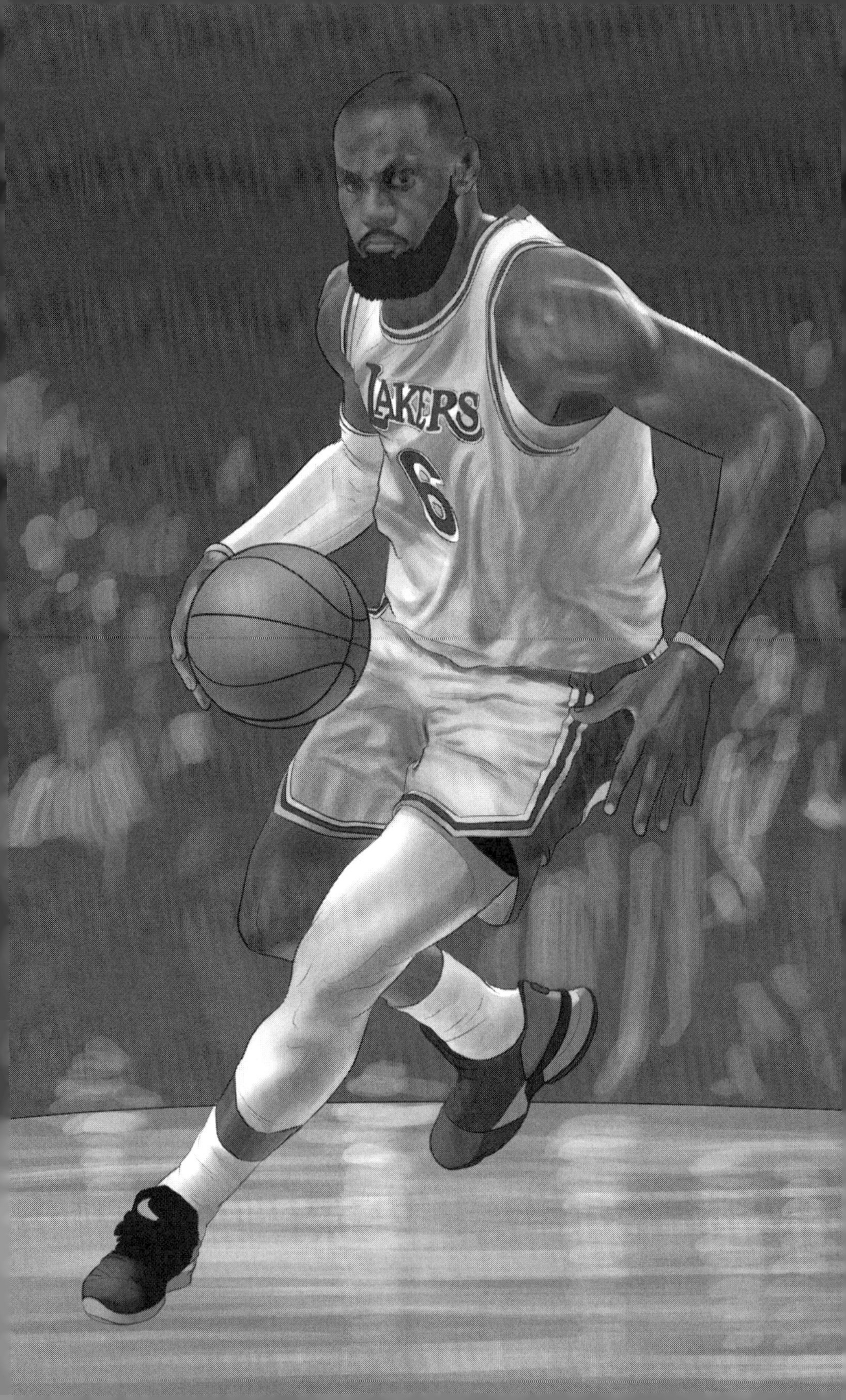
LAKERS
6

LEBRON JAMES

Full Name: LeBron Raymone James

Nickname: King James

Born: December 30, 1984

Hometown: Akron, Ohio

College: Entered NBA Straight from High School

Year Turned Pro: 2003

Total NBA Seasons: 20 (and counting!)

Height: 6'9"

Position: Small Forward

NBA Teams: Cleveland Cavaliers #6, Miami Heat, Los Angeles Lakers #23

Notable Quote: *"Basketball is my passion, I love it. But my family and friends mean everything to me. That's what's important. I need my phone so I can keep in contact with them at all times."*

Most of the GOAT's that you'll read about in this book were identified at a young age for their special basketball talent. However, only a couple of them grew up in the era of smart phones and social media, which means that fans across the country and the globe could take video of their every move.

LeBron James has had the spotlight on him ever since he was a teenager. He made the cover of *Sports Illustrated* magazine as a 17-year-old, with the title "The Chosen One" on the side of his picture. There are so many times in sports that teenagers are expected to become legends before they've ever played a professional game. In the case of James, however, those expectations were realized.

Before he became the best player in the NBA, LeBron and his mother Gloria had to deal with some challenges. When young LeBron was just five years old, he and his mom had to move five times in one year. Imagine packing up your Xbox, favorite jerseys, iPad, posters and everything else you own five times in a single year. It would be really hard!

James was determined to overcome those hardships and ultimately became one of the best basketball prospects in decades. His games at St. Vincent-St. Mary's High School were on ESPN for everyone to watch, and it seemed like destiny that he would be the next great NBA star.

It is quite rare for players to become great close to where they grew up, but James would start his NBA career with the Cleveland Cavaliers, not far from his hometown of Akron, Ohio. It was easy for his friends and family to watch him play, which made the jump from high school to the pros a little bit easier for him. He was also already used to playing games on TV, so he didn't feel too much added pressure when he joined the NBA.

Within a couple of years, the Cavaliers became one of the main attractions in the NBA, thanks to James. In 2007, when fans were not yet expecting Cleveland to contend, 22-year-old James led the team all the way to the NBA Finals. The team was swept by the San Antonio Spurs and fellow GOAT Tim Duncan, but the future for James and his teammates was extremely bright.

The Cavaliers would get very close to making the NBA Finals again during the next couple of seasons, but would fall short. In 2010, James' contract with the team was over, and he could choose to play for whatever team he wanted. Most of the teams in the league tried to persuade him to sign with them, but in the end, he chose to play for the Miami Heat. This allowed him to play with his friends Dwyane Wade and Chris Bosh.

The Heat would end up winning two championships while Lebron was on the team. He learned from Wade and Miami Heat president Pat Riley what it took to win a title. James would realize how to take over games when his team needed him to, while also deferring to his teammates when they were playing well. These were lessons that would serve him well for the rest of his career.

When James left Cleveland to play for Miami, his hometown was disappointed and saddened by the local Ohio kid's decision to leave. It did not seem like they would forgive him. But LeBron, after accomplishing his ultimate goal with the Heat, was looking for his next challenge, and in 2014 he returned to the Cavaliers, who now had some new young talented players on the roster, like Kyrie Irving and Tristan Thompson.

The Cavaliers were one of the few teams in the NBA that had never won a championship, but James put his heart and soul into changing that fact. In the 2016 NBA Finals, Cleveland was down three games to one to the Golden State Warriors, and it seemed like they were going to lose again. The Cavaliers never gave up, though, and forced a Game 7. In Game 7, James would block Warriors forward Andre Iguodala's shot from behind, and this single move completely changed the momentum of the game. Kyrie Irving would make a three pointer after that to give the Cavaliers the win, and their first NBA championship!

LeBron would ultimately make yet another move—this time, out west. He signed with the Los Angeles Lakers in hopes of continuing his quest to win more championships. The Lakers would send a lot of their good young players and draft picks to the New Orleans Pelicans to receive Anthony Davis, who was one of the best big men in the NBA. Together, Davis and James were magnificent during a playoff run in 2020, which led to the Lakers winning the NBA title. This ring would be James' fourth.

King James is still with the Lakers, and is hoping to achieve more team and individual success. The small forward is looking to break the all-time scoring record held by Kareem Abdul-Jabbar.

James is also enjoying being a father, and watching his sons, Bronny and Bryce, chart their own basketball journey in Southern California.

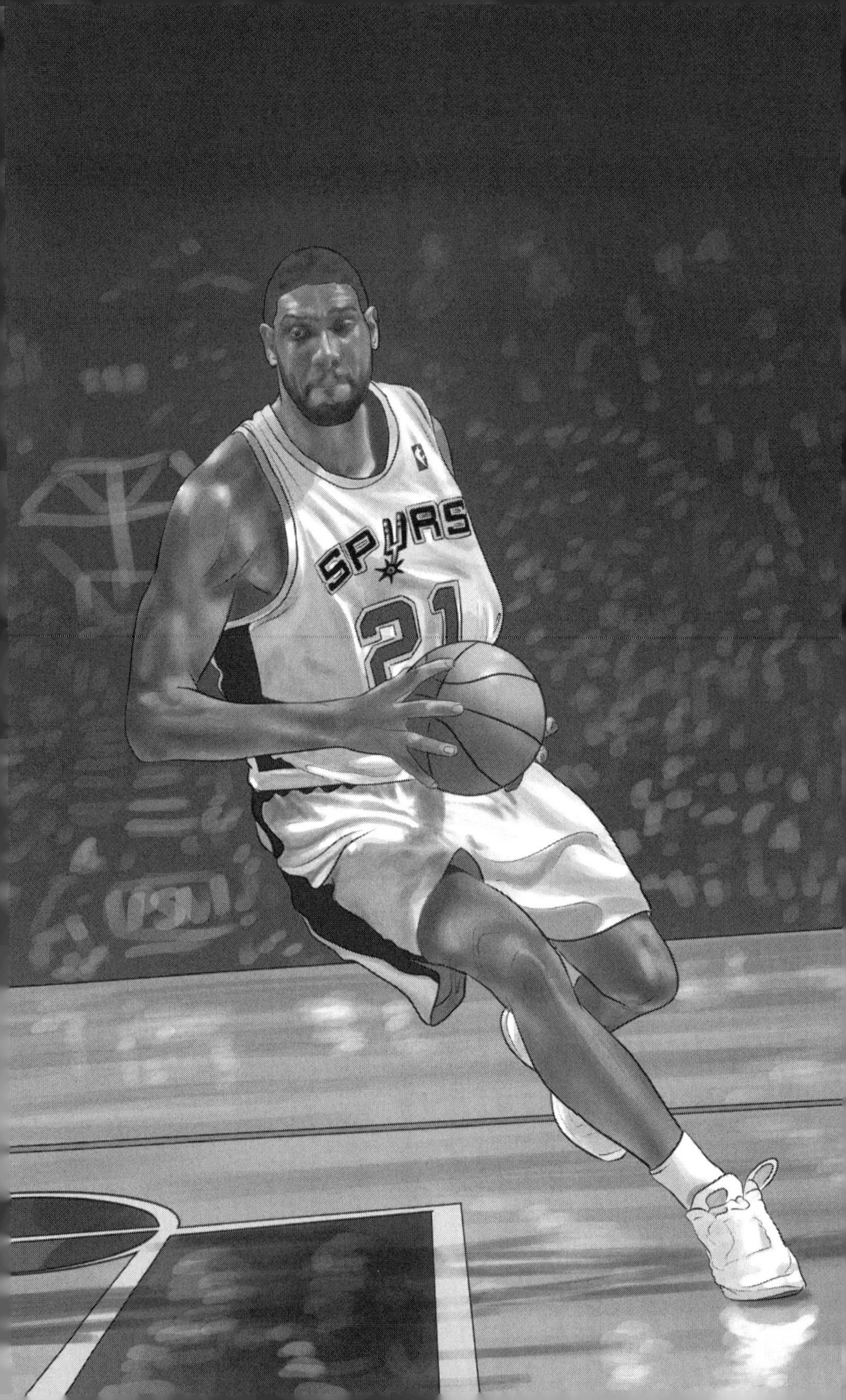
SPURS
21

TIM DUNCAN

Full Name: Timothy Theodore Duncan

Nickname: The Big Fundamental

Born: April 25, 1976

Hometown: St. Croix, U.S. Virgin Islands

College: Wake Forest

Year Turned Pro: 1997

Total NBA Seasons: 19

Height: 6'11"

Position: Power Forward

NBA Team: San Antonio Spurs #21

Notable Quote: *"I enjoy jokes, smiling, and making people smile. I may be a little different, but that's OK, who wants to be normal anyway?"*

It may seem hard to believe, but Tim Duncan became one of the greatest basketball players of all time by accident. Most of his childhood was not spent dreaming about the sport, or how he would go on to have one of the most decorated NBA careers in history. That's because Duncan spent the majority of his early years in a pool.

That's right! Instead of lacing up basketball sneakers and putting on basketball shorts, Duncan was walking around the Virgin Islands in his flip flips and swim trunks. There were days he would swim close to five miles. Enter that distance into your computer or smartphone, and you will quickly realize that it's a very long way to swim!

Unfortunately for Duncan, his childhood dreams of excelling in water sports were dashed by Hurricane Hugo, which destroyed the main pool where he trained. He was already a natural athlete in fantastic shape, so he had to find another sport to focus on. When he was 14 years old, he began to play basketball.

This was going to be an interesting experiment, to say the least. Duncan was obviously tall, but he had very little prior experience to fall back on. He did not have a youth coach or mentor who taught him drills when he was in elementary or middle school. Duncan would have to catch up quickly, but he was extremely intelligent and observant.

In an unlikely turn of events, the boy from St. Croix would turn himself into a legitimate player, one that noted college basketball programs in the continental United States were interested in. Wake Forest University in North Carolina did a lot of homework on the evolving post player, and were amazed by what he could do, considering he had only been playing the sport for a couple of years.

The Demon Deacons coaching staff wasted little time getting Duncan into their lineup. He started 32 games as a freshman, and averaged 10 points and 10 rebounds. What was even scarier for opponents was that he averaged nearly four blocks per game in his first college season, which made it very hard to score on Wake Forest.

As his college career progressed, Duncan's ability to score improved, as he would make baskets on the box next to the painted area, and make bank shots that hit the backboard before going through the hoop.

His offensive ability and his defensive prowess made him an attractive player to the NBA. The San Antonio Spurs already had an All-Star big man in David Robinson, and usually NBA teams like to add players in areas where their current players are not that good. However, the Spurs realized how special Duncan was, and believed that he and Robinson would find a way to play well together.

San Antonio was absolutely right. When Duncan first joined the team, and it was clear that he could play well with Robinson, the two players were nicknamed "The Twin Towers." Scoring at the rim was very difficult for teams with the 6'11" Duncan and the 7'1" Robinson ready to jump.

After finishing with one of the NBA's worst records in the season before they added Duncan, the Spurs transformed into one of the league's best squads. During the 1998-1999 season, San Antonio made somewhat of a surprising run to the NBA Finals, where they squared off against the New York Knicks. The Spurs had a lot of experienced players on that team, but relied on their young star to deliver during the biggest games of the season. Duncan did just that, and his play led the team to the title, and earned him the NBA Finals MVP award.

It would have been easy for Duncan to think more about himself and seek out even more attention as one of the best NBA players at such a young age. Instead, the quiet superstar remained humble, and always spoke about the team first, and what they could do better. When San Antonio brought international stars Manu Ginobili and Tony Parker onto the team, Duncan was delighted to help them improve so the team could get back to winning more championships.

With a potent big three, the Spurs would again win titles in 2003, 2005 and 2007. Even though they were dominant, they didn't receive a lot of press from the media… but that's precisely how Duncan liked it.

After their 2007 title, it did not appear that the Spurs would make another run at the championship. Duncan was getting older, and there were many other talented teams in their conference.

Then in 2013, San Antonio made it back to the Finals, and were within seconds of winning a title against the Miami Heat. However, a miraculous shot by Heat guard Ray Allen forced a Game 7, and Miami managed to secure the trophy that year.

The following season, San Antonio was determined to win the title, thinking that they'd let a golden opportunity slip away the year before. They won 62 regular season games, and earned a rematch with the Heat in the 2014 Finals. This time, the Spurs completely blitzed Miami, and won the title, the fifth of Duncan's illustrious career.

Duncan would retire in 2016, and not surprisingly, he would stay out of the spotlight. He did briefly become an assistant coach for the Spurs, because of his strong relationship with head coach Gregg Popovich, but soon returned to private life away from the bright lights.

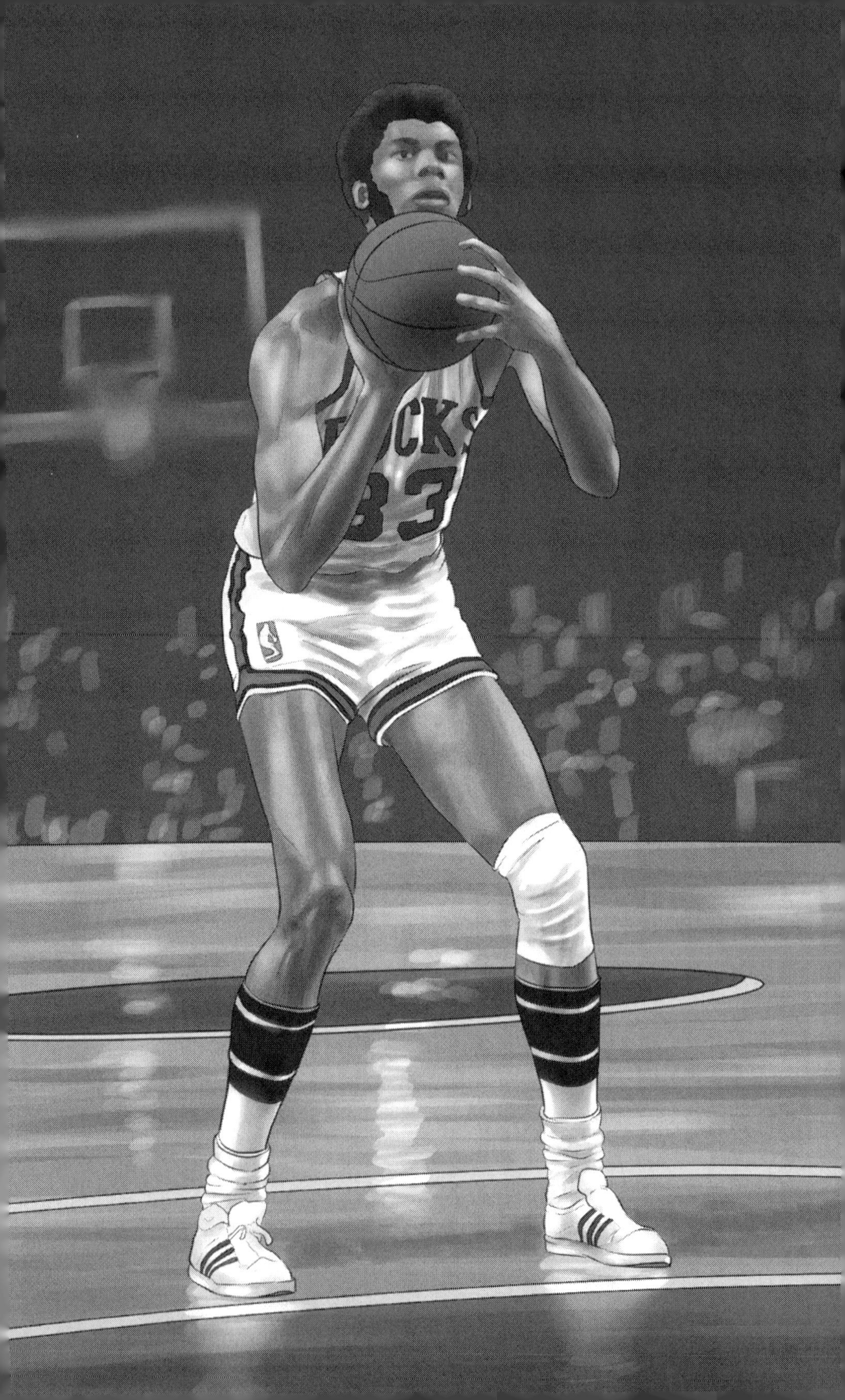

KAREEM ABDUL-JABBAR

Full Name: Kareem Abdul-Jabbar (born Ferdinand Lewis Alcindor Jr.)

Nickname: Big Fella

Born: April 16, 1947

Hometown: New York, New York

College: UCLA

Year Turned Pro: 1969

Total NBA Seasons: 20

Height: 7'2"

Position: Center

NBA Teams: Milwaukee Bucks #33, Los Angeles Lakers #3

Notable Quote: *"One man can be a crucial ingredient to a team, but one man cannot make a team."*

When you look at the record book of achievements in NBA history, one of the most impressive numbers you'll ever see is 38,387. What does that number signify, you ask? That is the number of total points Kareem Abdul-Jabbar scored in his NBA career. It's the most points any player has ever scored in league history.

Think about that for a second. How many shots do you take when you play basketball at the park or your local gym? On a good day, you're probably playing with your buddies for a few hours, and do a lot of shooting during that time. But can you ever imagine making 15,837 two-point shots? How about 6,712 free throws?

That's how many shots it took Abdul-Jabbar to score all of his points (except for three), and it took him a long time to get to that number. He played in the NBA for 20 years, which is probably around twice the amount of time you've been alive!

A lot happened in Abdul-Jabbar's life before he became the NBA's career leader in scoring. He was born with a different name, Lew Alcindor, in New York City. He was a tall boy who was determined to learn from wise older people and follow his love of basketball. This helped divert his attention from the troubles his family experienced. For example, sometimes his mom couldn't afford to buy everything she needed for her family. Because of such financial difficulties, life was often sad for her and her young son Lew.

During high school, Lew became one of the most dominant players in the entire country. Everyone wanted to know where he would play basketball when he graduated. It was important to him to find a college program that would help him improve on the court, but would also teach him important life lessons and challenge his brain.

Many people thought he would end up playing college basketball in New York, but Alcindor ended up choosing a school far away, in Los Angeles, California. UCLA had a strong program, and Lew really felt a connection with head coach John Wooden. Wooden would teach Alcindor skills on the court, but wanted to pass on other knowledge as well that would help him for the rest of his life.

It turned out to be a great decision. The UCLA Bruins only lost two games during the three years the young center was with the team, and they won the college championship every single season. For his college career, Alcindor averaged over 26 points and 15 rebounds per game.

He had one of the best college careers of all time, and every NBA team would've loved to have him when he left school, but it was the Milwaukee Bucks that ended up drafting him in 1969. They were really lucky, because they could pair him with Oscar Robertson, who was also one of the best players in NBA history.

Shortly after joining the NBA, Alcindor would officially change his name to Kareem Abdul-Jabbar. It did not matter what his name was, or what people thought of him, as Abdul-Jabbar proved right away that he was going to go down in history as a special player. In just his second year as a professional, Abdul-Jabbar and Robertson led the Bucks to an

NBA championship. It's not easy for a young player to be one of the best, but Abdul-Jabbar clearly was!

Abdul-Jabbar would end up playing six seasons for Milwaukee, and then spent the final 14 years of his NBA career with the Los Angeles Lakers. When Magic Johnson joined the team in 1979, the two would form one of the greatest duos in NBA history. Abdul-Jabbar would win five more championships in Los Angeles.

Now that you know more about Abdul-Jabbar's background, let's return to all those points he scored. How was he able to accomplish that? After all, he only made one three-pointer in 20 NBA seasons, so he was only adding to his total one or two points at a time.

The answer is that he had a secret weapon… a shot that no one before Abdul-Jabbar or anyone who played after him has ever mastered. It was called the sky hook.

Already tall, standing 7'2", Abdul-Jabbar's sky hook shot made him pretty much unstoppable. After a few dribbles, he would take the ball in one of his large hands, and then spin the ball towards the basketball with his super long fingers. The ball would go high in the air towards the sky, and gently fall into the hoop.

It was a beautiful shot, and it helped Abdul-Jabbar remain a threat to opposing teams even as he was in his final NBA seasons.

Now go ahead and count to 38,387… after you finish reading the book, of course.

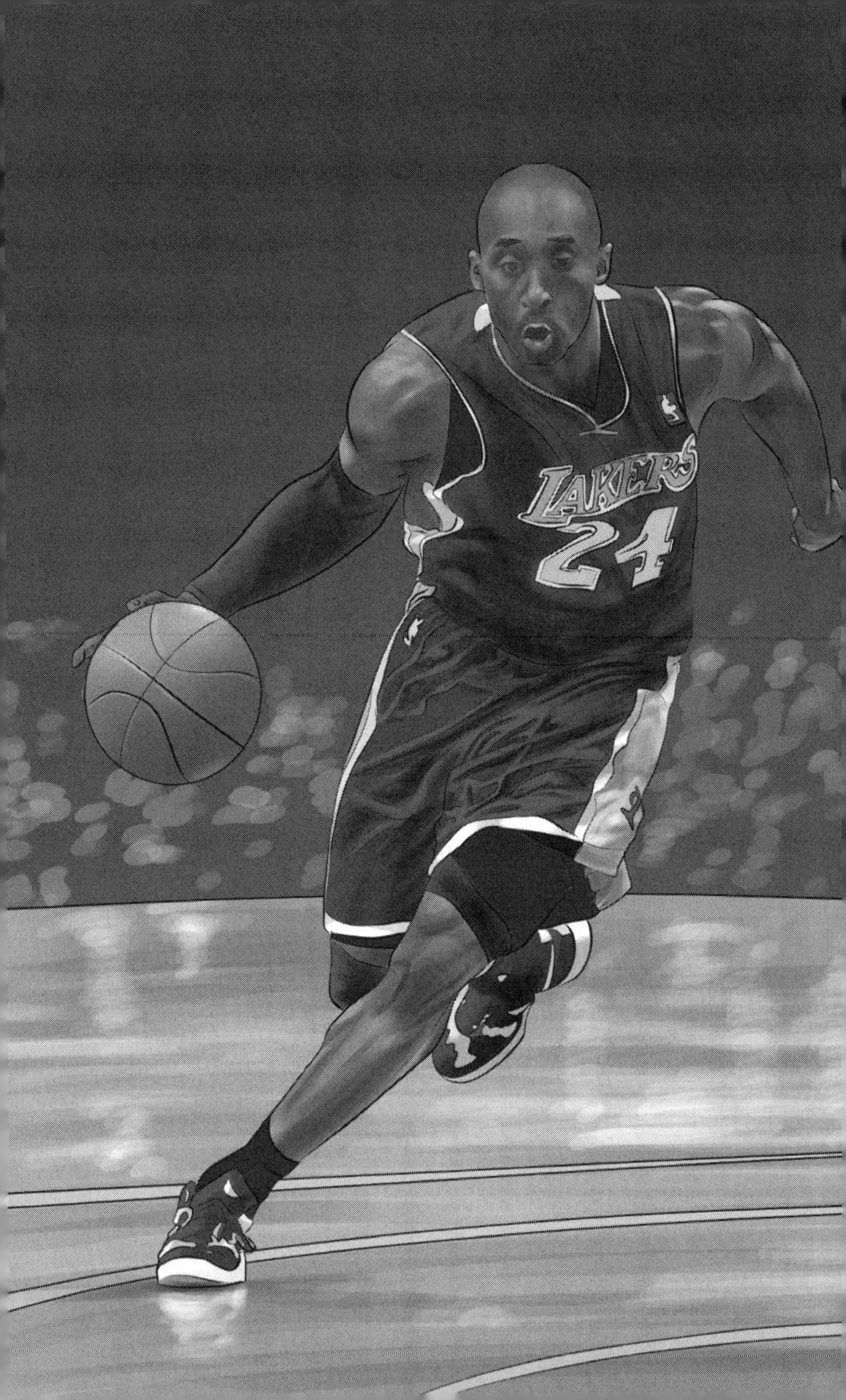
LAKERS
24

KOBE BRYANT

Full Name: Kobe Bean Bryant

Nickname: Black Mamba

Born: August 23, 1978

Hometown: Philadelphia, Pennsylvania

College: Entered NBA Straight from High School

Year Turned Pro: 1996

Total NBA Seasons: 20

Height: 6'6"

Position: Shooting Guard

NBA Team: Los Angeles Lakers #8 & #24

Notable Quote: *"Sports are such a great teacher. I think of everything they've taught me: camaraderie, humility, how to resolve differences."*

When you go by only one name, you know you've accomplished something great. Add Kobe to that list. Kobe Bryant was one of the best shooting guards in NBA history. He had a desire to be the best, and was willing to put in a lot of work to accomplish his dreams. When other people were sleeping, eating or goofing off, Kobe was in the gym exercising or practicing basketball.

There was no guarantee that Kobe Bryant would ever become one of the greatest basketball players of all time. As a boy, change was one of the only constants in his life. What if you had to go to a new school without much warning, and make new friends without saying goodbye to your old ones?

That was Kobe's life for much of his childhood, as his family moved to follow his father's professional basketball career. There was even a short time when young Kobe lived in Italy. Not only did he have to make new friends; he had to learn a new language just to be able to speak with other kids.

Moving so often was not easy, but it taught Kobe to be flexible, and to learn how to succeed in different types of situations. He and his family would eventually make their way back to the United States, and Kobe would be a popular high school player at Lower Merion High School near Philadelphia. The NBA was interested in him during high school, and how good he could be even without playing college basketball.

It is not always smart to skip college, but Bryant did that, and it worked out for him. He was acquired by the Los Angeles Lakers in the 1996 NBA Draft, which is where he would spend his entire career.

You might know that Kobe won five championships in his career with the Lakers, or that he was one of the greatest players to have on your team when the game was close and you needed a basket. But you might not know that performing in the clutch didn't always work out for him.

Before Los Angeles became one of the best teams in NBA history from 2000-2003, Bryant had to go through some growing pains. The Lakers would lose in the playoffs, and Bryant badly airballed a shot against the Utah Jazz one year, which left people wondering if he would ever become a great player.

There were no more doubts about that after the 2000 NBA Finals, as Kobe put on a show in one of the most important games of the series. Fellow superstar Shaquille O'Neal fouled out of Game 4, and someone else needed to step up to carry the team to victory. Enter the 21-year-old Bryant, who was not afraid of the moment. He was spectacular in the final moments of the game, and the Lakers would go on to win the title thanks to his efforts.

The reason the Lakers were so amazing during that time was because Bryant's skills improved, but also because he learned how to be a better teammate. At first, it wasn't always easy for him to play with O'Neal, who preferred to play the game a little more slowly than Bryant. However, through communication and a shared goal of winning, the two greats were able to come to an understanding, and the results spoke for themselves.

During the course of his career, Bryant proved that he would do whatever it took to help his team win. He is known for his exceptional scoring, but was also named as one of the top defenders in the NBA in 12 different seasons! He had a great ability to move his feet, and keep the offensive player he was guarding in front of him. Bryant would give maximum effort jumping to try and make the offensive player's attempt to score more difficult.

Remember I mentioned that Kobe had to learn Italian back when he was kid? He also learned Spanish as an adult, so he could communicate with teammates and opponents. This came in handy when speaking to one of his favorite teammates later in his career, Pau Gasol.

The Lakers were not the best team in the last couple years of Bryant's career, but he finished his legendary stint in the NBA with one final game that everyone remembers. Against the Utah Jazz, the same team against which he'd shot the airballs early in his career, Bryant finished with 60 points in the last game he would ever play in the NBA. All of his friends, family and former teammates were at the game to cheer him on, and pay their respects to one of the best players to ever play the game.

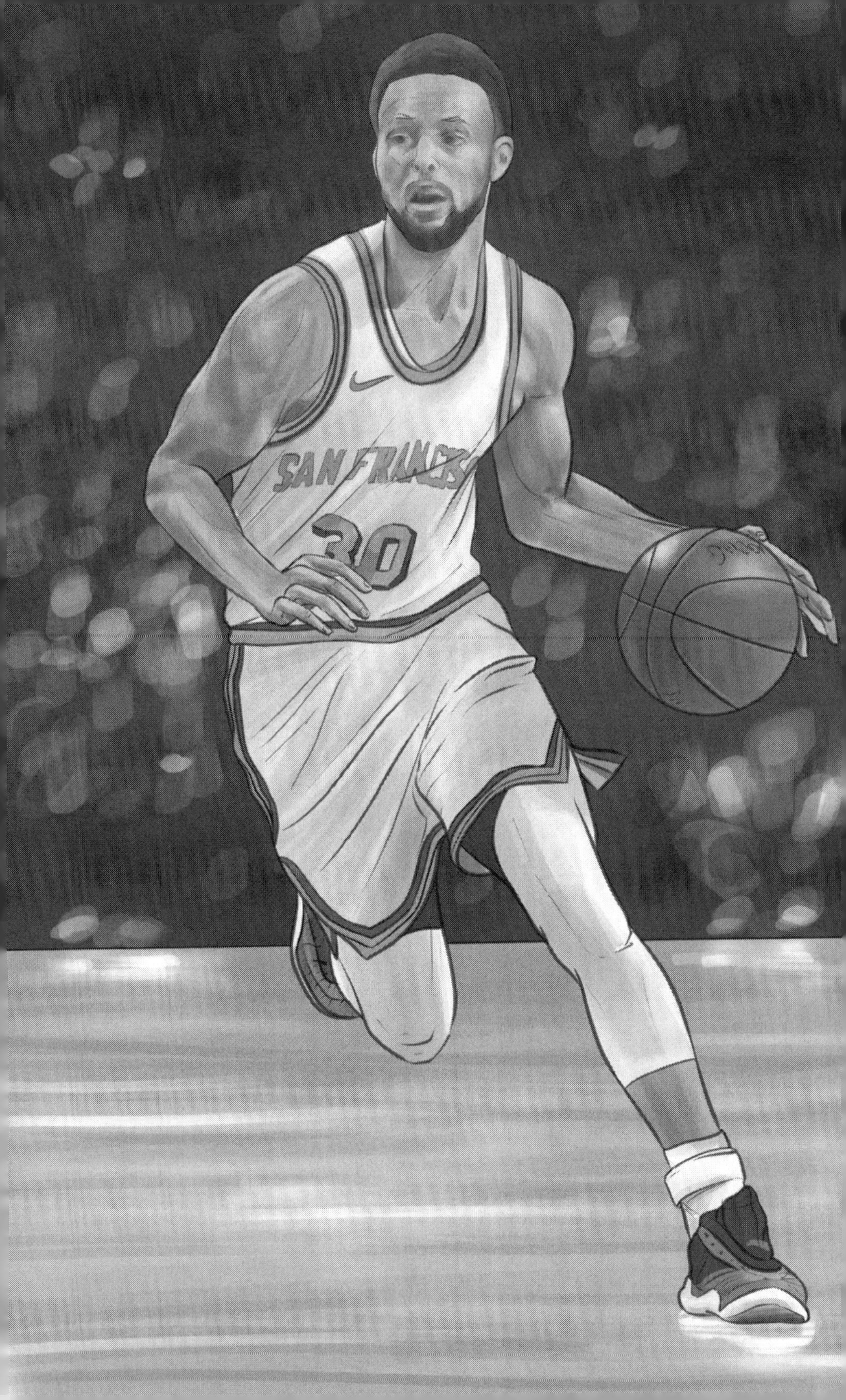
30

STEPHEN CURRY

Full Name: Wardell Stephen Curry II

Nicknames: Steph, Chef Curry

Born: March 14, 1988

Hometown: Akron, Ohio

College: Davidson

Year Turned Pro: 2009

Total NBA Seasons: 13 (and counting!)

Height: 6'2"

Position: Point Guard

NBA Team: Golden State Warriors #30

Notable Quote: *"I try to make it look easy, but the behind-the-scenes stuff is the challenge."*

Let's pick up Stephen Curry's story right from his own words in the above notable quote. To say he makes playing the game of basketball look easy might be the understatement of the century.

You don't even need to watch him play in a game to understand just how "Stephortless" the sport is for him. Pay attention to the type of shots he takes in warmups and pregame. There has arguably been no player who fans have wanted to show up early to watch *practice* more than Curry.

He routinely connects on shots from half-court that are extremely challenging for other professionals. On certain layups, Curry tosses the ball very high in the air, almost like he's just playing around... only for it to come straight down into the hoop. He'll also make long distance shots while sitting on the bench, or while standing in the tunnel entrance players walk through to get to the court.

It truly is remarkable, as his game feels like an actual performance, and his stage is the basketball court and everything around it.

It's fair to say that Curry feels at home on an NBA court because he's spent so much time on it, both as a child and as an adult. He is the son of Dell Curry, who played 16 years in the league, and would let his sons shoot with professionals when they were young boys. There are a lot of really cool pictures of Steph as a kid sitting next to NBA stars of the 1990's and 2000's.

Stephen Curry would have a lot of fun playing basketball as a child, but was also smart enough to speak with his dad and his teammates about the best way to succeed in the sport. This was a unique thing, as Curry was trying to learn by watching the game just as much as he was improving with a basketball in his hands.

It was pretty clear that Curry was always going to be able to shoot the ball, but there was concern that his body was not strong enough to compete against other players. Even though his frame was slender, Curry was still able to put up points at every level he played at. When he was 12 years old, he used a move that his coach wanted to teach adults. This level of skill and prowess with the basketball allowed him to overcome his skinny build.

Even though he had an amazing high school career in the Charlotte area, a lot of the powerhouse basketball college programs did not want to take a chance on the small-ish guard. But one university welcomed him with open arms, and Curry proved to the world that he was one of the best players in the country.

While attending Davidson College in North Carolina, the future NBA star consistently drained three-pointers from distances most players would not even consider attempting. It didn't really matter that he didn't look as sturdy as other players—as long as he had a little bit of space to shoot, there was an excellent chance he would score.

During the 2008 March Madness college basketball tournament, Curry made a dazzling display of shots that put him on the map. Because of his stellar play, Davidson was beating some of the best teams in the nation, which many college basketball fans were very surprised about.

When he announced he was leaving Davidson to enter the NBA Draft, there were still questions even then about how he would hold up playing against grown men. But the Golden State Warriors saw enough from the Davidson guard to choose him in the 2009 NBA Draft, and the rest is history.

There were a couple of years early in his career where Curry battled ankle injuries, but he would overcome them to show that his skill set is amongst the most potent in league history.

There are two things that most people will remember about Curry even after he retires from the NBA. There is no doubt that he is the greatest shooter of all time, as he drains long distance shots both off the dribble and standing still. There hasn't been anyone who has even come close to Curry in terms of the amount of three-pointers he's made in his career. Curry set the all-time record for three-pointers in 2021 against the New York Knicks. Ray Allen had the record before Curry, and was there to congratulate him and give him a hug.

The second accomplishment of Curry's career that will never be forgotten are the four championships he has won (so far). Before the Warriors started their dynasty in the middle of the 2010's, there were very few teams that had ever won a title by primarily shooting a bunch of jump shots. Golden State was so good at doing that, though, that it didn't matter that they weren't always close to the basket when they tried to score.

There have been and will continue to be great players who play at the NBA level, but arguably no one player has changed the sport more than Curry. Other players and children now have the confidence to shoot from great distances because Curry does, which has made the three-point shot more of a factor than it ever was before.

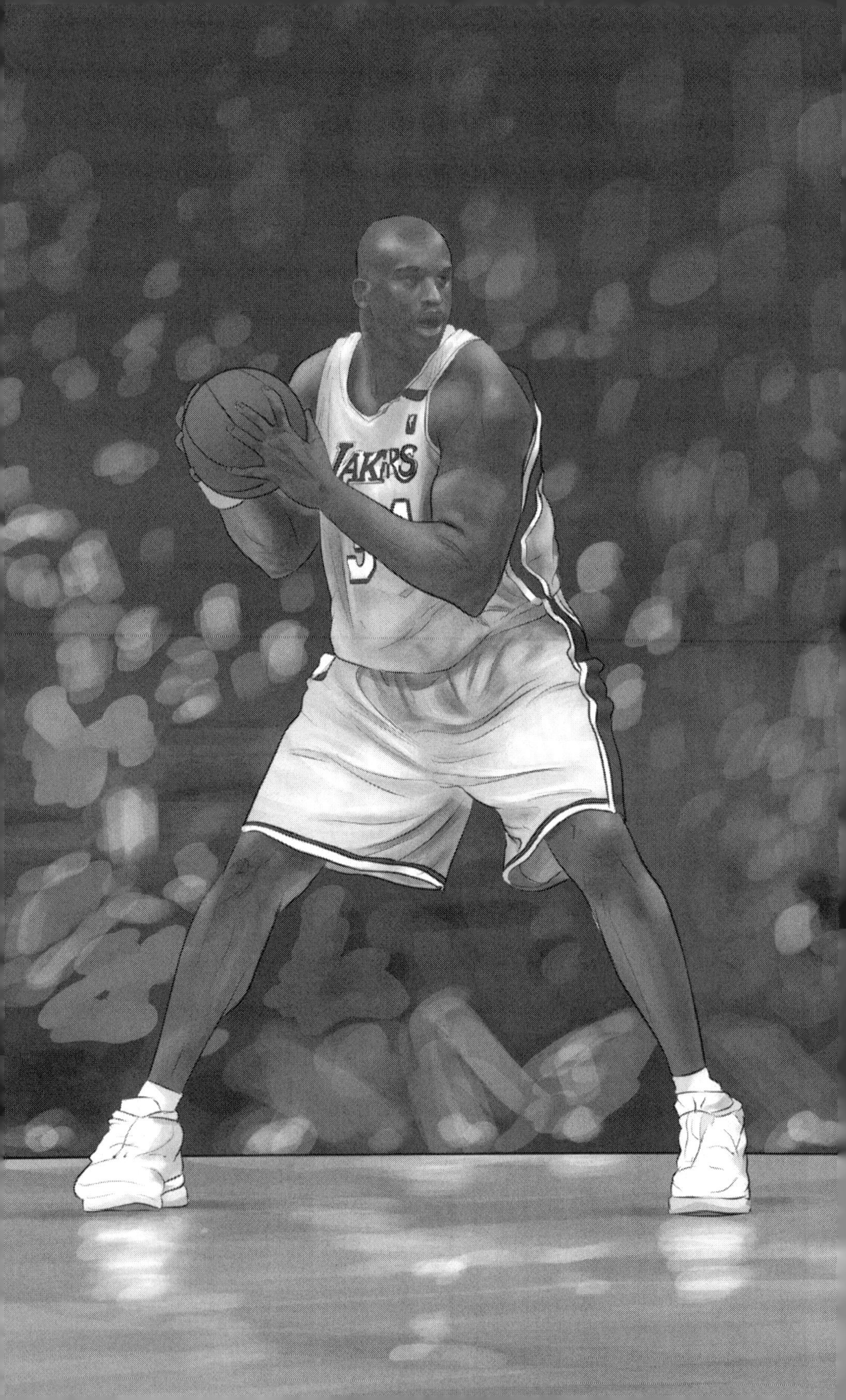

SHAQUILLE O'NEAL

Full Name: Shaquille Rashaun O'Neal

Nickname: Diesel

Born: March 6, 1972

Hometown: Newark, New Jersey

College: LSU

Year Turned Pro: 1992

Total NBA Seasons: 19

Height: 7'1"

Position: Center

NBA Teams: Orlando Magic #32, Los Angeles Lakers #34, Miami Heat #32, Phoenix Suns #2, Cleveland Cavaliers #33, Boston Celtics #36

Notable Quote: *"I never worry about the problem. I worry about the solution."*

Shaquille O'Neal deserves to make this respected list of GOATs because of his stellar NBA career, but he also has one of the most entertaining personalities of any athlete. When the game was on the line and plays had to be made, O'Neal was always locked in on what needed to be done. But before the game started, and even after it was over, his trademark grin and never-ending jokes entertained everyone and ensured people thought well of him.

Today, O'Neal is known for the commercials he does, and for his contributions to TNT's pre-game, halftime and postgame coverage of NBA games. He and Charles Barkley always seem to make each other laugh, or throw playful jabs at one another. And even though he is best known for his accolades in the world of basketball, he also has many fans outside of the sports world as well.

For as goofy a guy as he can appear to be sometimes, Shaq grew up with a lot of rules and discipline that helped him become one of the most dominant basketball players ever. He credits his stepfather for keeping him on track and showing him how to build good habits and stay away from things that can prevent kids from achieving their dreams.

There were times when Shaq did not like the amount of structure placed on him, and was not happy with his stepfather. It didn't seem fair that other kids had more freedom than he did. But as an adult, Shaq was extremely thankful for the blueprint of how to become a successful person, and admitted he probably wouldn't have achieved his goal of being a basketball player if it hadn't been for those rules.

Shaquille O'Neal is a large man, so it makes sense that he was a sizeable boy as well. He would play to his strength, literally, by using his backside to back down smaller players until he was at the rim. Even though he was taller and stronger than many of his opponents as a child, O'Neal was also very athletic. When he kept in peak shape, O'Neal was able to beat his opponents down the court and finish with rim-rattling dunks.

He would go on to play college basketball at Louisiana State University, where he put up some mind-boggling statistics. He averaged over 24 points, five blocks and 14 rebounds per game when he was a sophomore and junior at LSU. Talk about getting the job done on both ends of the floor!

It wasn't all that difficult for NBA teams to envision what Shaquille O'Neal would look like on an NBA court, because he was already a full-grown man in college. The NBA centers who played the game at the time were much more methodical and plodding, whereas O'Neal liked to run and jump as if he was a small forward.

The Orlando Magic selected O'Neal with the very first pick of the 1992 NBA Draft, meaning they felt he was the best player available that year. He came in right away and proved he belonged, and was named the NBA Rookie of The Year in the 1992-1993 season.

During that year, he also did something that would be watched over and over again for many years. He dunked the ball ferociously in a game against the New Jersey Nets, and the entire backboard was brought to the ground! While this ended up stopping the game for several minutes, it was a sign of O'Neal's unbelievable strength.

After a few magnificent years with the Magic, O'Neal joined the Los Angeles Lakers, where he would have the best seasons of his NBA career. He learned many lessons during his time in Orlando, and that experience helped him become a champion in Los Angeles.

He made the NBA Finals in 1995 with Orlando, but the team was swept against a much more prepared Houston Rockets squad. O'Neal would not let that happen to him again, and was laser-focused when the Lakers made it to the Finals in 2000, 2001 and 2002. Led by the big fella, the Lakers would win the title each of those years, staking their claim as one of the best basketball teams in NBA history. O'Neal and Kobe Bryant would also form one of the best tandems the game has ever seen.

Los Angeles made it to the NBA Finals again in 2004, but lost to the Detroit Pistons. After that, the Lakers decided to build the team around Kobe, and Shaq was traded to the Miami Heat. Many wondered whether O'Neal's best days were behind him, or if he could help transform the Heat into a legitimate title contender.

It turned out that O'Neal (nicknamed The Diesel) had a lot of gas left in the tank. In his second season in Miami, he provided the physicality in the painted area of the court that the team needed, while still being able to pour in points at the rim. He also offered leadership to a team that had been entrusted to the young Dwyane Wade. The blend of teamwork, youth and experience was a wonderful combination, and allowed Miami to win the championship in 2006.

To round out his storied career, O'Neal would play with the Phoenix Suns, Cleveland Cavaliers and Boston Celtics. His numbers and contributions would decline in his final years, but everyone involved with those three teams loved having such a fun person on the team.

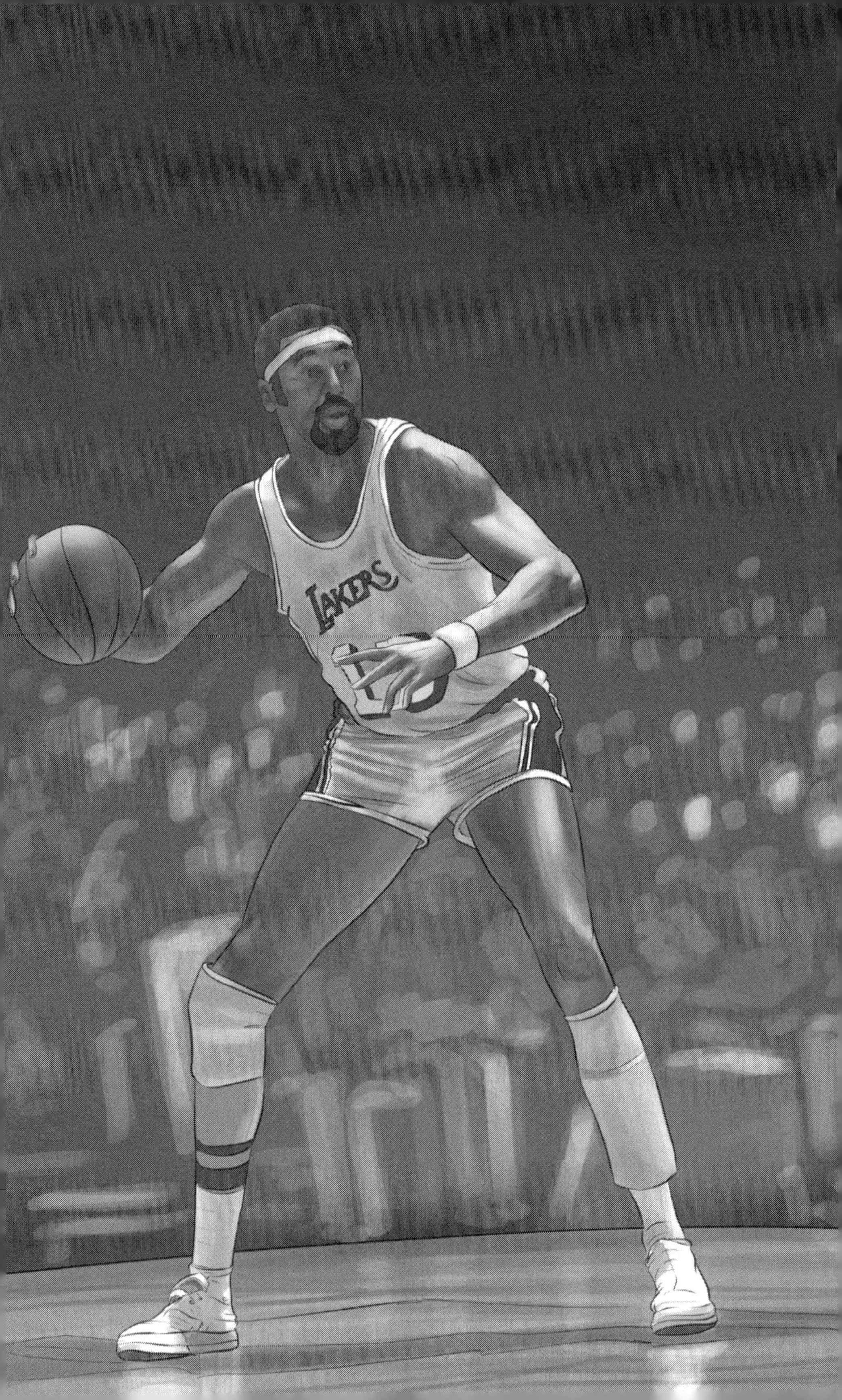
LAKERS

WILT CHAMBERLAIN

Full Name: Wilton Norman Chamberlain

Nickname: The Big Dipper

Born: August 21, 1936

Hometown: Philadelphia, Pennsylvania

College: Kansas

Year Turned Pro: 1959

Total NBA Seasons: 14

Height: 7'1"

Position: Center

NBA Teams: Philadelphia/San Francisco Warriors #13, Philadelphia 76ers #13, Los Angeles Lakers #13

Notable Quote: *"I couldn't have come close without my teammates' help because the Knicks didn't want me to make 100."*

When you play a sports video game, you're usually allowed to increase or decrease the skills of players you create. For example, maybe in a basketball video game, the default shooting, passing, dribbling and jumping ability is 75. If you're having a little fun, you could toggle those numbers up to 95, to create a player who is essentially unstoppable. Feel free to thank me later for that idea!

The closest thing in real life we have ever seen to a video game-like character and player was Wilt Chamberlain. Some of the things he achieved on a basketball court feel like they are made up. Like the fact that he scored 100 points in a single game. Or that he averaged over 50 points a game for an entire season. Or that we actually don't really know how great he truly was, because the NBA did not keep track of blocks when Chamberlain played from 1959-1973.

That's the kind of legacy Chamberlain had in those days, and even after he retired. He was a larger-than-life figure who could do things that most other people couldn't.

Chamberlain loved to participate in track and field as a kid, running faster than the competition. However, he grew very tall very quickly! He was 6'11" in high school, which is pretty remarkable. Let's just say he didn't have to jump to reach the top of his door frames at home.

As you might imagine, there wasn't much other high school kids could do to stop Chamberlain on the basketball floor. He scored more than 2,200 points in three seasons as a high school basketball player, which is hard to believe. Rumor also has it that his teammates would miss shots on purpose, so that their towering center could take the ball and put it into the basket without much resistance.

This was also when Chamberlain earned himself a few different nicknames. It's important not to call people by names that make them feel bad, but Wilt enjoyed being called the Big Dipper. The name was in reference to a constellation of stars in the sky, but it also came about because the extremely tall student often had to dip his head to avoid hitting the ceiling.

The frenzy of attention around Chamberlain as he dominated the high school game was remarkable. Everyone across the country wondered where the teenager would decide to attend college. Since he was from Philadelphia, locals were hoping to continue to watch the massive player break all kinds of records in eastern Pennsylvania. Chamberlain would have a big decision to make, as he was recruited by over 200 universities across the United States.

But there was one college that seemed to want him the most. The University of Kansas would send prominent alumni to visit Chamberlain and talk with him about their experiences at the school. Head coach Phog Allen wanted the prospect to feel comfortable on campus, since he would be moving far away from where he'd grown up.

Chamberlain did end up becoming a Kansas Jayhawk, and is arguably the greatest player to ever play for the program. The competition was no match for the 7'1", 275-pound behemoth. In two phenomenal college seasons, Chamberlain would average nearly 30 points per game, and over 18 rebounds as well. He won the Most Outstanding Player award in 1957 for his efforts.

Before he joined the NBA, Chamberlain spent a year on the Harlem Globetrotters. They were (and still are) a team of players focused on making sure fans have fun at their games. The team does many fancy tricks with the basketball, and makes shots from great distances. Chamberlain's physical feats were a perfect match for the traveling roadshow.

There wasn't much doubt where Chamberlain would begin his NBA career. Back in those days, the league had something called a territorial draft, where teams could take players who grew up in their geographical area. The NBA did this so that hometown players could drive interest from fans who may have remembered them playing before they became professionals. This meant Chamberlain got to return home, because the Philadelphia Warriors selected him with the first pick.

Even though Chamberlain would go on to accomplish many things with the Warriors/76ers, as well as with the Los Angeles Lakers later in his career, he will always be remembered for what he did on March 2, 1962 in Hershey, Pennsylvania. The hoops legend would score a single-game record 100 points against the New York Knicks that night!

The gargantuan player would make 36 baskets for the game during the regular course of play, and he would make 28 free throws as well. Chamberlain was not known as a prolific free throw shooter, so the fact that he made 28 out of 32 attempts at the line was pretty remarkable.

One of the most iconic photos in basketball history was taken after that game, and it shows Wilt holding up a piece of paper with the number 100 written on it.

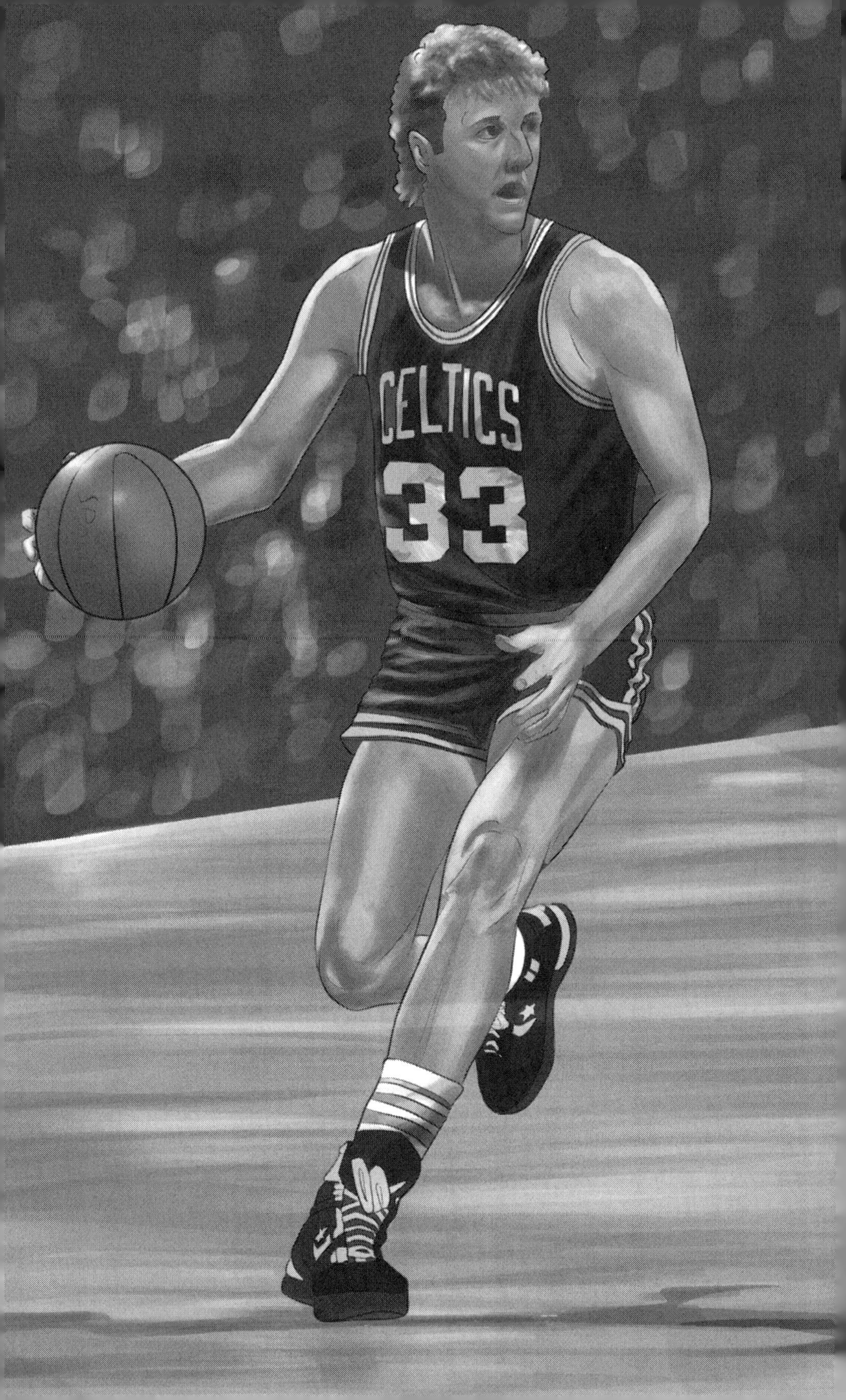
CELTICS
33

LARRY BIRD

Full Name: Larry Joe Bird

Nickname: Larry Legend

Born: December 7, 1956

Hometown: West Baden, Indiana

College: Indiana State

Year Turned Pro: 1979

Total NBA Seasons: 13

Height: 6'9"

Position: Small Forward

NBA Team: Boston Celtics #33

Notable Quote: *"I have a theory that if you give 100% all of the time, somehow things will work out in the end."*

You may not realize it now, but you have many traits that you inherited from your parents. These can be anything from a physical feature, like when people tell you your eyes look like your mom's, to a personality quirk, like if you tell funny jokes just like your dad. It might even be something you don't want to admit to your friends in elementary or middle school because it's not cool to be like your parents... but one day that will probably change.

For NBA great Larry Bird, he and his mother might as well have been two peas in a pod. He watched her work very hard to earn just enough money to put food on the table for her six children. She was not easily rattled, and did not give up when things did not go her way. Larry himself would be known as someone who gave every bit of effort he could in life.

The two would end up needing to stick together, since his parents divorced when he was in high school and his father died when he was 18.

Through all of the trials and tests Bird faced as a boy, he was able to get away from it all doing one thing he loved more than anything: playing basketball. A hoop was hung on the back of a barn near where he grew up, and Bird would spend countless hours outside shooting there. It wasn't what someone in this day and age would call a proper court, but for Bird, it was a sanctuary where he could try everything that came into his mind.

The ability to feel comfortable taking any type of shot was something that Bird worked tirelessly to achieve. He would practice with both hands, and was sure to get a good amount of arc on his shots, to give the ball a chance to bounce in if his attempt wasn't perfect.

Even though he spent a lot of solo time improving his shot, Bird had a natural feel for how the game should be played. He was talented enough to take and make most shots, but understood the importance of getting his teammates involved. If the other players on the court had confidence and played well, that would only help give Bird better opportunities at a shot.

This unselfishness and team-oriented attitude was on full display during Bird's college career at nearby Indiana State. While averaging over 30 points per game, the savvy forward was still able to put up over four assists and more than two steals per contest. The numbers and the highlights showed that Bird would do anything it took for his team to win the game.

During the 1978-1979 college basketball season, the Indiana State Sycamores did a lot of winning. In fact, they won every single game leading up to the national championship. The Sycamores would play the Michigan State Spartans, led by Magic Johnson, in the title game. While Indiana State fell short of finishing off a perfect campaign, a historic basketball rivalry would start that night between Bird and Magic Johnson.

The Boston Celtics had their eyes on Bird for a couple of years, as they hoped to rebuild their roster with a young player that could take the NBA by storm. He would do just that from day one, as Bird won the league's Rookie of the Year award, and also helped Boston increase their win total immensely.

It would be the beginning of a great run for the Celtics, who would go on to win three NBA championships in the 1980's thanks to Bird's masterful play. In an era that featured many other future Hall of Famers, Bird stood out as one of the very best, capturing three Most Valuable Player awards in the decade as well.

The 6'9" forward could do anything the team asked of him. Bird could match up with other forwards on the perimeter defensively, while also crashing the glass and serving as a de facto point guard. He was fearless, and loved a challenge. One of the best examples of this was his duel with Dominique Wilkins of the Atlanta Hawks in the 1988 playoffs. Wilkins poured in 47 points in a win or go home Game 7, but Bird scored 20 points in the fourth quarter to secure the victory.

Bird also has one of the coolest distinctions in league history. The NBA introduced a three-point shooting competition as part of their All-Star weekend festivities in 1985, and the Celtics' sharpshooter won the event in each of its first three years. It helped kick off what would eventually become a three-point revolution in the game, so it's only fitting that one of the best marksmen in history started it off on a good note.

In the last couple years of his career, Bird struggled to remain healthy, but would finish his playing days strong. He was named to the 1992 United States Olympic basketball 'Dream Team,' where he would play with two other GOATs, Michael Jordan and Magic Johnson. The last game Bird ever played was the gold medal matchup with Croatia, which added another accomplishment to the Indiana native's resume.

BABY GOATS

There are some who might think that other names should have cracked my GOAT top 10 rankings. While I feel pretty good about my list, here are five other players who deserve to be mentioned, and who fell just short of the top 10.

Bill Russell

Put simply, Bill Russell is the NBA's ultimate winner. There is a great picture of the former Celtics legend holding all 11 of his championship rings, with a wide smile plastered across his face. No player in the history of the sport can claim that many titles.

Even though Russell could score, he made his greatest impact on the defensive end of the floor. As his notable quote suggests, he wanted offensive players to feel like they were going to get their shot blocked any time he was in the area. Jumping in the air with his hands held high on every possession is how he made his presence felt.

Hakeem Olajuwon

Even though he was seven feet tall, you would have a difficult time finding anyone who was more coordinated than Hakeem Olajuwon. His athleticism allowed him to move around slower centers, and he could trick other players with a bunch of fakes that left him with open shots.

Olajuwon was a master at using his feet in order to make the defensive player uncomfortable, to get himself into a position to lay the ball into the basket. He was the main reason the Rockets won two consecutive championships in 1994 and 1995, but Olajuwon always shared credit with his teammates.

Oscar Robertson

In basketball statistics, one of the most impressive accomplishments is a triple double. While it's a funny name, it's pretty easy to understand. A triple double is when a player gets 10 or more of something in three different basketball categories. For example, if someone scores 15 points, makes 13 assists, and grabs 10 rebounds, they've accomplished a triple double.

For many decades, there was no player who was more associated with a triple double than Oscar Robertson. In order to do that once, let alone 181 times, which Robertson did, you have to be a player who is good at multiple things on the basketball court. Robertson certainly was, and his numbers proved it.

Kevin Durant

At every level of basketball, there are certain players who just seem to be able to score points easier than others. Whether it's a fellow youth player with a smooth jump shot, or an adult who makes athletic layups at the basket, some players just get buckets no matter what!

Kevin Durant absolutely falls into that group. There isn't a lot a defender can do to stop him, so the best they can hope is that he will take a difficult shot. Durant is so skilled that he can make those tough attempts even far away from the basket, and it feels like he has a move for every type of game situation.

Jerry West

Take a good look at the NBA logo. It seems like the player is about to drive the ball to the basket with his left hand, ready to go up for a shot or maybe set up a teammate for an easy shot. It's one of the perfect images to associate with the game of basketball.

But that silhouette wasn't just randomly picked. It was actually modeled after a real picture of Jerry West. He was one of the sport's greatest players in its early years, and was known for making baskets at the end of games.

One of the most famous shots he ever made came in the 1970 NBA Finals, when he made a basket from beyond halfcourt to send the game into overtime!

4

AMAZING GAMES

As I'm sure you already know, basketball can be so much fun! There are many different ways players can contribute to a game, and the excitement of getting together to play is truly special.

Whether you've played in hundreds of games, or only a few so far, I have no doubt that there are certain games that stick out in your mind more than others, for different reasons. Maybe you were playing at the hoop in your schoolyard during lunchtime and someone made a game-winning basket just as the period was about to end. Perhaps your buddy made a crazy reverse layup that surprised everyone on the floor. Maybe it's a defensive performance that is memorable, where you helped slow down a really talented player.

Even at the highest level of the sport, there are a handful of special games that come to mind faster than the rest. I've compiled a list of some of the most amazing games in NBA history, which unfolded with about as much drama as some of the best books you've read in school.

I'll explain who the main players were, and why the game was so important in NBA history. Get ready to feel like you were a part of the action as we go through some outstanding performances and endings.

I encourage you to use your imagination to picture how the games played out as I describe them, and then go ahead and pull up highlights of these games later. You won't be disappointed.

2002 WESTERN CONFERENCE FINALS (WCF) GAME 4: SACRAMENTO KINGS AT LOS ANGELES LAKERS

In the early 2000's, the Los Angeles Lakers were an unstoppable freight train that no one could seem to stop. They had won back-to-back NBA championships in the 2000 and 2001 seasons, and there didn't seem to be any strong challengers who could knock them off the throne.

Enter the 2002 Sacramento Kings, who did not quite have the star power of the Lakers, but played team basketball. Each player happily passed the ball to their teammates, and willingly moved without the ball to find open shots. Their unselfishness made them very difficult to guard, and they had a fantastic regular season that year.

Led by Kobe Bryant and Shaquille O'Neal, however, Los Angeles just seemed to be too powerful for Sacramento to beat. The two teams would face one another in the 2002 Western Conference Finals, and the winner would go to the NBA Finals that year. Whichever team won four games first out of a possible seven would win the series.

It became pretty clear early on in the Western Conference Finals that the Kings were going to give the Lakers a lot of trouble. Their style was unique, and Los Angeles had not really faced a team like them, whose ball movement was so sharp.

The Kings would win two out of the first three games, setting up a massively important Game 4 in Los Angeles. If Sacramento won, there would be a very good chance that the Lakers dynasty would be over. If Los Angeles was victorious, they would reclaim momentum on their way to a third straight title.

The game started brilliantly for Sacramento, and disastrously for Los Angeles. In the first half, it felt like the Kings made every open jump shot, while the Lakers struggled to get their offense going. Things appeared to come easily for Sacramento, while every attempt to score for Los Angeles seemed hard.

Now, even though it didn't seem too important at the time, Lakers forward Samaki Walker made a shot from halfcourt at the buzzer at the end of the first half. Los Angeles was still losing, but this raised the spirits of the players and their fans. Fans watching on TV noticed that Walker actually did not release the ball before the buzzer sounded... so the points shouldn't have counted, but back then, referees could not check the replay, so the three crucial points remained on the board.

(Today, of course, referees can double check to see if a shot was released before the clock ran out.)

When the players returned to the court for the second half, the score got extremely close. The Lakers' defense tightened up, and they were able to find a rhythm on offense. The game would come down to the last few seconds of the fourth quarter.

With under 10 seconds to go in the game, Sacramento had a 99-97 lead. Los Angeles had the ball, looking to extend the game into overtime, or even win it. Bryant drove to the basket, and flipped up a shot that went off the rim. O'Neal caught the rebound, but his shot was short and came off the rim hard.

At that precise moment, it seemed like the Lakers dynasty might be over. Sacramento would take a 3-1 lead in the series, and a new team would represent the Western Conference in the NBA Finals.

Except... something crazy happened.

Kings center Vlade Divac tipped the ball back towards the three-point line after O'Neal missed the putback shot. He did this trying to waste time and keep the ball away from the Lakers' stars.

There was only one problem - the ball bounced right to Los Angeles forward Robert Horry, who was standing behind the three-point line. With supreme confidence, Horry took the shot, and the ball went in at the buzzer. The Lakers won!

The crowd went absolutely bonkers, and the series was even at two games apiece. Los Angeles would go on to win the series, and then the championship. But they wouldn't have gotten there if not for the amazing shot by Horry.

2007 EASTERN CONFERENCE FINALS GAME 5: CLEVELAND CAVALIERS AT DETROIT PISTONS

For several years, the story surrounding Cleveland Cavaliers star LeBron James was that he was different. He was the most special prospect to come into the league in a long time, and greatness was expected from him from the first day he played in the NBA.

James displayed his remarkable talent literally from his first game, and was showing that he could affect a game in many different ways. His tremendous athleticism allowed him to finish plays with thunderous dunks that revved up the crowd. James was also an incredible passer, finding his teammates cutting to the basket or spotting up for open three-point shots.

Of course, he was also able to put the ball in the basket himself, averaging 20 points as a rookie and then 27 as a second-year player.

His sensational talent did help the Cavaliers win more games each year, but it wasn't translating into enough victories to be serious playoff contenders.

However, that would all change in the 2007 season, as James and the Cavaliers would make a surprising run to the Eastern Conference Finals against the Detroit Pistons. Detroit would be a really tough opponent for Cleveland, because of Detroit's historic ability to play excellent defense and stop teams from scoring.

Detroit clamped down on the Cavaliers in the first two games of the series, beating Cleveland in both matchups while limiting them to just 76 points in each game. But Cleveland was able to make some changes that helped them score more points in Games 3 and 4, and they were able to beat Detroit in those games, which surprised many.

With the series tied at two games each, the winner of the crucial Game 5 would have an excellent chance to advance. The fifth game was in Detroit, so Pistons fans would be thunderously loud and try to distract the Cavaliers.

The game was close throughout, and was tied at 70 when it entered the fourth quarter. It seemed like Detroit's tough starting five would wear down Cleveland, but James put his team on his back.

Game 5 would remain tied after the fourth quarter, and after the first overtime as well! It went into a second overtime, and the Cavaliers eventually won when James scored a layup with 0.2 seconds remaining.

That's how it ended, but you may be wondering how the Cavs got there. During the final period and overtime, James was spectacular. He made difficult jump shots, determined drives to the basket, and threw down some ferocious dunks. The funny thing was, the Pistons knew exactly who the ball would go to on every possession, but they couldn't stop him.

At one point in the fourth quarter and then during the two overtimes, James scored 25 straight points for the Cavaliers, without anyone else on his team scoring during that stretch. It's safe to say that this game proved that the emerging superstar would be as great a player as everyone expected him to be.

The Cavaliers would win that series, making the NBA Finals, but lost the championship to the San Antonio Spurs.

1995 NBA FINALS GAME 1: HOUSTON ROCKETS AT ORLANDO MAGIC

Michael Jordan missed the entire 1994 NBA season and most of the 1995 season when he decided to take a break from basketball to play professional baseball. The rest of the league's eyes lit up during this time.

Other teams would now have a chance to win a title!

The Houston Rockets took full advantage of His Airness' absence in 1994, putting together a strong team that defeated the New York Knicks in the NBA Finals that year. The roster was built around superstar center Hakeem Olajuwon, who was one of the most skilled players in the league at that time.

In 1995, the Rockets had an uneven performance during the regular season, and it didn't seem like they were a strong bet to defend the title. But they squeaked into the Western Conference playoffs that year.

Meanwhile, the young, hungry, athletic Orlando Magic team dominated its way through the Eastern Conference. Led by youthful stars Shaquille O'Neal and Penny Hardaway, the Magic cast a spell on the rest of the league.

While the veteran Rockets were able to use their intelligence and experience to return to the Finals in 1995, the Magic used the enthusiasm of their fresh-faced stars to get to the title series.

It was such an interesting matchup, because O'Neal and Olajuwon would go head-to-head, but they had different styles. Game 1 would set the tone.

Orlando came out on fire, outscoring Houston 30-19 in the first quarter. It seemed like the Rockets' veterans were a step slow early on.

But sure enough, the defending champs would bounce back. They took over the game in the third quarter, scoring 37 points to Orlando's 19 in that period. This meant Game 1 would come down to the fourth quarter.

With a few seconds remaining, the Magic were clinging for dear life to a three-point lead. The Rockets had to foul Orlando in order to extend the game, so they fouled Magic forward Nick Anderson.

At that point, Anderson had scored 22 points, and was playing very well. If he could make some free throws, the chances that the Rockets could come back would significantly decrease.

Anderson stepped to the line and missed his first attempt. It wasn't a big deal. If he made the second shot, Orlando would have a four-point lead.

But he missed the second shot too! There was a scramble for the rebound, and the ball ended up back in Anderson's hands, who was fouled once more. Second chances don't always present themselves during games, but Anderson had a chance to make up for his earlier misses.

Unbelievably, Anderson missed two more free throws, and the Rockets came down with the next possession and made a game-tying three-pointer to send the game to overtime!

In the extra period, Houston's experience proved to be the difference, and they won Game 1. They would also be victorious in Games 2, 3, and 4, so were on their way to a second consecutive title.

The Rockets' determination cannot be ignored, but it is also important to point out how the Magic responded to Anderson's missed free throws in the first game. They did not blame their loss on their teammate, or make him feel worse when he was already upset.

Orlando players said that if they had made a couple more plays earlier in Game 1, it would not have come down to those free throws at the end. That is an example of a team sticking together no matter what happens.

1997 NBA FINALS GAME 5: CHICAGO BULLS AT UTAH JAZZ

The combined scores of the first four games of the 1997 NBA Finals were separated by a total of two points. Not surprisingly, the Chicago Bulls and Utah Jazz each won two games, and the winner of the championship would need to take two out of the next three games to bring home the trophy.

The math was simple enough, but there was only one problem for the Bulls. Michael Jordan was sick heading into Game 5.

There have been a lot of different stories about this illness over the years. One version involves Jordan getting hungry late in the evening the night before Game 5. There weren't any restaurants open when the Bulls star wanted a bite to eat, so his options were limited. Someone located a pizza place in Utah that was still open and would deliver a pie to Jordan's hotel.

The pizza showed up at Jordan's door, and he devoured it. Now he could go to bed feeling full and wake up fresh and ready to go the next morning. Except that didn't happen. Jordan's stomach went topsy turvy in the middle of the night, and he couldn't get to sleep. He was also weak.

And that's the legendary pizza-gate tale!

Another version of the story involves Jordan having the flu. You know those days when you have a headache, fever and your nose is stuffed up? Maybe your parents keep you home from school and make you stay in bed, bringing you soup and ginger ale.

Jordan could have stayed in bed and missed Game 5, but he was determined to play. But he did not look like himself, and was already very sweaty at the beginning of the game. He did not run up and down the court with the same energy he usually had.

One thing he did on the bench during that game, which so many of us do when we are sick, was drink a lot of fluids. This helps an illness pass through your body more quickly, which is what Jordan hoped would help him feel better.

Despite everything that was tried to make him feel better, it was still a struggle. Jordan was even seen leaning on Scottie Pippen's shoulder, as Scottie tried to help him through the game. Shockingly, number 23 somehow played 44 out of a possible 48 minutes in the game.

The amazing thing about the "Flu Game" was that Jordan played better than most players who were healthy! He scored a game high 38 points, and the Bulls needed every single one. Chicago ended up winning the game by a final score of 90-88.

It was one of the most inspirational performances in NBA history, as perhaps the greatest player of all-time continued to display greatness when he should have been sick in bed.

Chicago would go on to win Game 6 as well, and capture their fifth championship of that decade.

2016 NBA FINALS GAME 7: CLEVELAND CAVALIERS AT GOLDEN STATE WARRIORS

The weight of a tortured basketball fanbase versus the prospect of being crowned as the greatest team of all time. Sounds like a big-time showdown, doesn't it?

That's precisely what was at stake during the 2016 NBA Finals, which featured the Cleveland Cavaliers taking on the Golden State Warriors.

The Cavaliers were a franchise that had approached the mountaintop on several occasions throughout their history, but could never quite get over the top. Though there were some solid Cleveland teams led by head coach Mike Fratello in the 1980's and 1990's, and one that made a surprise run to the NBA Finals in 2007 but lost, things never broke right for the Cavs when it mattered most.

Adding insult to injury was the departure of favored Ohio son LeBron James during the summer of 2010. In a highly public free agent courting, James was wooed by other teams to sign a contract to leave Cleveland, and he ended up going to the Miami Heat. The Cavaliers' chances to contend for a title walked right out the door with James.

But after his four seasons with the Heat, James decided to return to his first NBA home. In 2015, he led the Cavaliers back to the NBA Finals, though they lost in six games to the Warriors.

Now let's flip our attention for a moment over to Golden State's story. Their 2015-2016 regular season was incredible. It started off with one of the longest winning streaks in NBA history. The Warriors won their first 24 games to start off the campaign. They continued to breeze through their schedule, dropping only four games before the All-Star break in the middle of the year.

It was clear early on that they were going to clinch homecourt advantage throughout the playoffs, so they had to decide whether they wanted to set the regular season wins record, or rest their players ahead of a long playoff run. Golden State decided to try to set the mark, and maintained their wonderful winning ways. The Warriors won their 73rd game, the final game of the regular season, which was the most wins in any single season in league history.

The anticipation, buildup and excitement of this matchup culminated in a historic Game 7 of the NBA Finals. A lot was at stake, and you could feel the intensity through your TV screen.

As things grew tense, shots were missed, and the two teams combined for the lowest point total in Game 7 than in any other game of the series. Both teams upped the pressure defensively, as the Cavaliers' taller players tried to keep Warriors guard Steph Curry covered in pick and roll situations.

For four straight minutes near the end of the fourth quarter, neither team could make a hoop! Someone was going to have to do something extraordinary to secure the championship for their team.

Then, with less than two minutes left, it seemed like the Warriors were going to score easily on a fast break layup by Andre Iguodala. As Iguodala was going up to score, James sprinted back on defense and swooped in for a legendary chase down block, which denied Golden State the easy basket. It was an enormous play that swung the momentum back in Cleveland's direction.

On the other end, the Cavaliers had a chance to take the lead for good. What type of play would they run for such an important possession? Somewhat surprisingly, the ball was given to Kyrie Irving, who would try to get a good shot up over Curry. After a few dribbles, Irving pulled up for three, and nailed the basket!

Golden State was not able to answer, and the Cavaliers were NBA champions for the first time in their history!

1970 NBA FINALS GAME 7: LOS ANGELES LAKERS AT NEW YORK KNICKS

In the early days of the NBA, there were a few franchises that were the gold standard of the league. For the first two or three decades, many of the original teams in the biggest cities had the most attention paid to them.

When the Los Angeles Lakers and New York Knicks met in the 1970 NBA Finals, fans on both coasts were pumped. You had the concrete jungle that is New York City, compared with the glitz and glamour of Los Angeles. It was like a script for an edge-of-your-seat action movie!

Of course, a film is only as good as the actors involved in the production, and this one had some pretty big stars. You had Wilt Chamberlain playing center for Los Angeles, who was still putting up astronomical statistics. Jerry West was a humble star, but he was one of the NBA's best clutch players at that time.

New York had a sensational backcourt, led by Walt "Clyde" Frazier and Earl "The Pearl" Monroe. The Knicks also had a great center in Willis Reed, who would need to do battle with Chamberlain if they had any hope of winning the title.

While there were several amazing games to choose from in this series, including nailbiters in Games 2 and 3, we're going to lock in on a Game 7 that would decide whether the championship was headed to the East Coast or the West Coast.

Through the first four games, Reed had more than stood up to the task of performing against Chamberlain. He played exceptionally, including a 38-point, 17-rebound masterpiece in a Game 3 victory.

It seemed like the two big men would duke it out for the remainder of the series, but the plot changed dramatically in Game 5. Reed would tear a muscle in his thigh (yikes!) during that contest, and was only able to play eight minutes. While the Knicks were able to hold on to win that game, they lost to the Lakers in Game 6.

New York's spirits were a little down heading into Game 7, because it looked like they weren't going to be at full strength for the ultimate game. Reed was injured, and it didn't seem like the Knicks would have enough to fend off the mighty Lakers.

Remember how we set this up as a movie? What does any good flick have?

A shocking ending!

During pregame warmups, Reed hobbled on to the court to shoot around with his teammates. But no one ever thought he would be able to suit up. Reed later said that this was going to be his best chance to win a title, and he did not want to look back and regret not trying to play.

Somehow, some way, Reed was able to play 27 minutes in Game 7. He made two iconic baskets to begin the game. Although he would not score again, those shots gave the Knicks a huge emotional lift at the most pivotal point of their season. It was a gutty effort that would be remembered throughout NBA history.

Add to that the fact that Clyde Frazier had arguably the best game of his career that night, recording 36 points, 19 assists and seven rebounds. The Knicks would go on to win the NBA title, their first in franchise history.

1965 EASTERN CONFERENCE FINALS GAME 7: PHILADELPHIA 76ERS AT BOSTON CELTICS

There are very few teams in sports history who are identified by their team name and a decade. The 1920's New York Yankees. The 1980's Edmonton Oilers. The 1970's Pittsburgh Steelers. Fans just know the type of excellence demonstrated by these franchises over that memorable period of time.

Right at the top of the list are the 1960's Boston Celtics, who were a juggernaut during that decade. They won a remarkable 11 titles in a 13-year stretch from 1957 through 1969. Legendary head coach Red Auerbach was known for celebrating on the bench when it was clear that Boston would take home the victory. The Celtics were truly the first NBA dynasty.

While their roster was stacked with future basketball Hall of Famers, their approach to each game involved doing whatever it took to win. It didn't matter who scored the most points, who made the game-winning shot, or who got the most attention. If the team brought home the championship, everyone would be able to bask in the glory of being the best.

When you've finished your homework and completed your chores, take a look at some of the scoring averages for Boston's players during that time. You may notice that a lot of their opponents have one or two players getting most of the baskets, but with the Celtics, it's pretty evenly distributed across multiple players.

For example, in the 1964-1965 season, six players averaged 10 or more points per game. This means that players bought into the idea of passing the ball to the player with the open shot on most possessions.

During that season, Boston was looking to win its seventh straight championship, but as you might imagine, other teams in the league were getting a little tired of the Celtics' dominance. One of those teams was the Philadelphia 76ers, who had fallen to Boston in the playoffs for several years prior.

Wilt Chamberlain was on the roster at the time, and was casually averaging 30 points and 22 rebounds per game—no big deal. The 76ers were centered (pun intended) around their center, and everyone else kind of fit in around him.

As it turned out, the 76ers and Celtics would cross paths again in the 1965 playoffs, and their Eastern Conference Finals playoff series would be one for the ages. Each team alternated wins for the first six games of the series, setting the stage for a monumental Game 7. Boston's dynastic run was in serious jeopardy, and it would take a strong effort to keep the streak alive.

The game was close throughout, as the stars came to play in this critical matchup. Chamberlain played incredibly, while Bill Russell and Sam Jones also laid down remarkable performances. The right to represent the Eastern Conference in the NBA Finals came down to the final seconds.

It seemed like Boston had things wrapped up. They were up by one point, and had the ball. One of the Celtics players was likely to be fouled, and to put the game away with two free throws (there was no three-point shot at this time). All they had to do was inbound the ball.

That proved to be a challenge. Russell tried to pass to a teammate, but the basketball struck a wire that was linked near the backboard. The ball fell back out of bounds, and Philadelphia found themselves with one opportunity to win the game.

All they had to do was inbound the ball...

Philadelphia's Hal Greer tried to pass it to a teammate, but Celtics forward John Havlicek stole the ball, in one of the most iconic plays in NBA playoff history.

The play is made even more electric by the call of Celtics radio play by play announcer Johnny Most, who loses his mind when it happens. "Havlicek stole the ball!" has actually been its own exhibit at the Basketball Hall of Fame in Massachusetts.

Boston's streak of excellence would continue thanks to Havlicek's cat-like quickness as the most important point of the season.

2013 NBA FINALS GAME 6: SAN ANTONIO SPURS AT MIAMI HEAT

Do you know what a heat index is? Usually, it has to do with the weather in the summertime, and is a number used to explain how hot it actually feels outside.

Basketball fans think of the Heat Index (yes, in capital letters) as something else. It was created to watch every move of what many call the first super team in NBA history. In the summer of 2010, star free agents Chris Bosh and LeBron James would join Dwyane Wade on the Miami Heat. Everyone was extremely curious to find out how successful a franchise with that much talent was going to do. Would they all be willing to sacrifice for the greater good of the team?

When the Heat introduced Wade, James and Bosh together for the first time, they openly wondered how many championships they would win.

Before the 2012-2013 season, the answer to that question was one. Miami had fallen in the NBA Finals in 2011 to the veteran-laden Dallas Mavericks. But in 2012, the Heat would prevail over the talented but youthful Oklahoma City Thunder.

The Heat would continue to march through the competition during the regular season and postseason, qualifying for a third straight NBA Finals in 2013, this time against the San Antonio Spurs. This would be a much tougher test than the previous two title series, since the Spurs had athleticism, experience and chemistry from many years of playing together.

San Antonio's Tim Duncan, Manu Ginobili and Tony Parker had won three titles together, and were searching for their first championship since 2007. Forward Kawhi Leonard was an emerging star, thanks to his relentless toughness and the physical defensive pressure he could put on the opposing team's best players.

This blueprint created a lot of trouble for Miami, who found themselves down three games to two heading into a must-win situation in Game 6.

San Antonio had been through high profile close-out games before, and would not make mistakes that would give Miami easy opportunities. The Spurs had a 10-point lead in the fourth quarter, and were positioned to finish off their opponent.

The Heat were down three points with 20 seconds left in the fourth quarter. They could decide to go for a quick two points, and then foul the Spurs to extend the game, or they could go for a three-pointer to try and tie things up.

Miami would choose the second option, and ran a play to get James a wide open look at a three pointer. The ball bounced off the rim, and it seemed like the Heat were going to lose in devastating fashion.

But that's not what happened. Bosh jumped high for the rebound, and secured the ball. There was now less than 10 seconds left in the fourth quarter, and he had to think fast. So did every one of his teammates, including Ray Allen.

By that point, Allen was nearing the end of his amazing NBA career, and was on the Heat in order to space the floor with his pinpoint shooting ability. In his younger days, he'd been a star, and plays would be designed to get him chances to score. With Miami, Allen's role was to roam around the perimeter and knock down open shots to keep defenses honest.

Allen had taken thousands of three-point shots in his life, and knew he had to act quickly while Bosh gathered himself. He back-peddled to a spot behind the three-point line in the corner of the court. Bosh looked up and passed him the ball.

With Parker closing in on him quickly, Allen rose up and drilled a three pointer to tie the game!

It would eventually go into overtime, and Miami was able to hold on to force a Game 7.

Game 7 was a defensive struggle, but the Heat would prevail over the Spurs and win their second title in three years. None of it would've been possible had it not been for Allen's heroics.

2006 REGULAR SEASON: TORONTO RAPTORS AT LOS ANGELES LAKERS

I hope you've learned many cool facts in this book that you can share with your friends and family. One of those little nuggets was that the record for most points scored in a single game by a player is held by Wilt Chamberlain, who scored 100 points against the New York Knicks in 1962.

Here's one of the most fun debates to have about basketball. Do you think it's possible for anyone to ever break that record? It would take someone getting video-game level hot with their shooting, and it might also involve teammates consistently passing a player the ball to help him get the record.

Needless to say, a lot of things would have to go right for anyone to even come close to challenging Chamberlain's mark.

But on one Sunday night, while many NBA fans were already tucked into their beds, a player actually did come close to that seemingly unreachable number.

Los Angeles Lakers legend Kobe Bryant would have a banner night on January 22, 2006 against the Toronto Raptors. His ankle was a little bit sore, but he gave it a go during a game that he felt the Lakers needed to win.

The game began with Bryant displaying his usual scoring greatness. He would make it to the basket several times and finish through contact. Bryant connected on jump shot after jump shot, as if a magnet was pulling the ball through the hoop. His ability to put points on the board was dazzling, and he ended the first half with a total of 26.

That's a really impressive half for any player, but it isn't anything that fans haven't seen before. Perhaps most important for Bryant personally was the fact that even though he was having a good night in the scoring column, his team was losing to Toronto by a large margin.

The Raptors were able to keep their foot on the gas and maintain a sizeable lead in the third quarter. With none of his teammates really shooting well that night, the onus remained on Kobe to keep his team in the game.

He did just that. It's not like the Raptors didn't know Bryant would be the focal point of the offense, but there wasn't much they could do to stop him. Bryant would make pull up three-pointers, difficult fade-aways, and pick-off passes that led to easy dunks on the other end of the floor.

The onslaught became too much for the Raptors to deal with. The significant lead that they had built up was completely erased, thanks to Bryant. Once the Lakers took the lead, they still needed Bryant to maintain his momentum to keep Toronto at bay.

The game script was perfect for Bryant to stay in aggressive point-seeking mode, because had the game been decided earlier, he likely would've been benched.

The crowd chanted Kobe's name throughout his 55-point second half barrage, and as he kept adding to his total at the free throw line.

While it is often said in sports that moments are groundbreaking or unique, this is one that will truly withstand the test of time, when Kobe Bryant made 81 points in a single game.

1993 WESTERN CONFERENCE SEMIFINALS GAME 6: PHOENIX SUNS AT SAN ANTONIO SPURS

NBC sports play-by-play commentator Dick Enberg put it best during the 1993 NBA Playoffs, when he said that Charles Barkley was having the year of a basketball lifetime.

Barkley hit the jackpot in so many different ways.

He'd started his career with the Philadelphia 76ers, as a young player learning from NBA legends like Julius Erving and Maurice Cheeks. However, as they got older and aged out of the league, the 76ers started to become less competitive, even though Barkley had developed into a clear-cut All-Star. He was in the prime of his career with the 76ers in the early 1990's, but his best years were being used up on a team that struggled to remain relevant.

In the summer of 1992, Barkley's NBA prospects would change dramatically. He was traded for three players to the Phoenix Suns, a team who was in the hunt to make the NBA Finals every year.

That wasn't all that was going right for Barkley. He was also named to the 1992 Olympic Team, which is more famously known in basketball history as The Dream Team. The collection of basketball greats would have a fun time hanging out on and off the court in Barcelona, Spain. Barkley got to see a different part of the world, and dominate the competition en route to winning a gold medal.

When he returned home for the NBA season, Barkley was motivated to remind people just how great he could be. In his first year with the Suns, Barkley was a man on a mission, along with the rest of his teammates. They finished with the best regular season record in the league, and had legitimate hopes of making the NBA Finals.

However, the Western Conference was loaded that year, and one obstacle in the Suns' way were the San Antonio Spurs. They were led by center David Robinson, whose physical gifts were as amazing as any player in the league. He could run the floor like a guard, had the athleticism of a dynamic small forward, but was also 7'1".

The two Dream Team teammates and All-Stars would square off in a memorable second round series in the 1993 NBA Playoffs. Both Robinson and Barkley would play phenomenally, carrying their teams for the first five games of the series. Phoenix held a 3-2 lead heading into a crucial Game 6.

At home, the Spurs seemed to be poised to force a Game 7. Robinson was excellent on both ends of the floor, and San Antonio got balanced scoring from the likes of Sean Elliot and Dale Ellis. The Suns were going to need to find an answer quickly if they wanted to end the series right there and then.

Phoenix made a great comeback, and evened up the score at 100 each. With 10 seconds left in regulation, the Suns would have a chance to officially continue their season in the Western Conference Finals.

Suns coach Paul Westphal put the ball in the hands of his best player. Barkley looked up at the clock, and then looked straight ahead to find the large Robinson hoping to shut him down.

Barkley milked the clock, wanting his final attempt at the hoop to be the last shot of the fourth quarter. He took a couple of dribbles towards Robinson, then quickly stepped back. The Spurs center was not as close to challenging Barkley's attempt as he would've hoped, and Barkley drilled the long two-pointer to give the Suns the win!

It was a great moment in NBA history because of the excitement of the finish, and because one player achieved their goal with another great directly in his way. To be the best, you have to beat the best, and Barkley did that on that night.

5

INCREDIBLE FACTS

There's no doubt that watching YouTube videos in the cafeteria and trying to find out which of your friends has the most delicious snack at lunch is a good time. It's always great to catch up with your buddies and laugh hysterically over the newest inside joke.

So while you've got your phones out (let's be honest, when are they not out!?), you might want to DM your friends about a bunch of amazing NBA facts I've included below. They're mostly about memorable performances, funny moments, great teams and notable people throughout the history of the game.

I hope you enjoy reading about this as much as I enjoyed putting them together for you!

100. Danny Biasone invented the 24-second shot clock in 1954, which meant teams could no longer hold the ball for several minutes.

99. Dallas Mavericks guard Bubba Wells once fouled out of an NBA game in three minutes.

98. The highest scoring game in NBA history was between the Detroit Pistons and Denver Nuggets in 1983. The Pistons won 186-184.

97. Seattle SuperSonics guard Dale Ellis once played 69 minutes in an NBA game. That's the most in league history.

96. Philadelphia Warriors center Wilt Chamberlain grabbed the most rebounds ever in an NBA game, with 55.

95. Orlando Magic point guard Scott Skiles made the most assists ever in an NBA game, with 30.

94. The Los Angeles Lakers franchise originated in Minneapolis, which has a lot of lakes surrounding the city. When the team moved to the West Coast, they kept the name.

93. The first three-point line in the NBA came in 1979. Before that, all shots from the court were worth two points or one point for a free throw.

92. Only four players have ever recorded a quadruple-double (10 or more of something in four different categories). They are Nate Thurmond, Alvin Robertson, Hakeem Olajuwon and David Robinson.

91. The Boston Celtics and Los Angeles Lakers have each won 17 championships, tied for the most of any team in NBA history.

90. Spalding was the official game ball partner of the NBA from 1983-2021. Today, Wilson provides the basketballs for NBA games.

89. Violet Palmer became the first female official to work an NBA game on October 30, 1997.

88. Toronto Raptors guard Jose Calderon set the record for free throw percentage in a season in 2008-2009. He made 98 percent of his attempts from the free throw line that year.

87. Minnesota Timberwolves guard Michael Williams made the most consecutive free throws in a row, with 97.

86. Golden State Warriors guard Klay Thompson scored 37 points in a quarter in 2015, which is the most points in any quarter in NBA history.

85. A.C. Green played in 1,192 consecutive NBA games, the longest streak in history.

84. The longest winning streak in NBA history belongs to the Los Angeles Lakers, who won 33 straight games in the 1971-1972 season.

83. The Larry O'Brien trophy is given to the team that wins the NBA title. It is over 25 inches tall, and weighs about 30 pounds.

82. The NBA schedule has consisted of 82 regular season games since the 1967-1968 season.

81. Utah Jazz point guard John Stockton has the most career assists and steals in NBA history.

80. The shortest player to ever play in an NBA game was Muggsy Bogues, who was 5'3".

79. The tallest players to ever play in an NBA game were Manute Bol and Gheorghe Muresan, who both stood at 7'7".

78. Phoenix Suns center Oliver Miller was the heaviest player to ever play in an NBA game, clocking in at 375 pounds.

77. The longest game in NBA history was six overtimes, played by the Indianapolis Olympians and Rochester Royals in 1951.

76. In the 2011 Slam Dunk Contest, Los Angeles Clippers forward Blake Griffin jumped over a car.

75. Richard Bavetta refereed 2,635 NBA games, the most of any official ever.

74. Boston Celtics shooting guard Chris Ford made the first three-point shot in NBA history in 1979.

73. 45-year-old Nat Hickey was the oldest player to play in an NBA game.

72. 18-year-old Andrew Bynum was the youngest player to play in an NBA game.

71. Dirk Nowitzki (Germany) scored the most career points of any non-American-born player.

70. Utah Jazz power forward Karl Malone has made the most career free throws, with 9,787.

69. The 1981-1982 Denver Nuggets averaged the most points per game for a team in a season, with 126.5.

68. Larry Brown is the only coach to win a college Division One championship and an NBA championship.

67. 430 players born in California have played in the NBA, the most of any state.

66. Canada has produced the most NBA players of any non-U.S. country, with 36.

65. Only one player ever born in New Hampshire made the NBA, and that was forward Matt Bonner.

64. Broadcaster Mike Breen has called more NBA Finals games on TV than anyone else.

63. Golden State Warriors forward Rick Barry used to shoot his free throws underhanded.

62. The NBA Finals MVP trophy is named after Bill Russell.

61. There are 11 NBA teams that have never won a championship. They are the Pacers, Hornets, Nets, Grizzlies, Jazz, Suns, Pelicans, Clippers, Nuggets, Magic and Timberwolves.

60. Jason Kidd and John Drew each had a game where they turned the ball over 14 times, which is an NBA record.

59. The New York Knicks have played the most games on Christmas than any team in NBA history.

58. The NBA has not scheduled a game on Thanksgiving since 2010.

57. Vince Carter is the only player to appear in an NBA game in four different decades.

56. The first game located outside of the U.S. took place in Israel in 1978 between the Washington Bullets and Maccabi Tel Aviv.

55. The most points ever scored in the first game of an NBA career was 43 by Wilt Chamberlain.

54. The first half record for most total points by a team is 107, achieved by the Phoenix Suns in 1990.

53. Michael Jordan had nine game-winning buzzer-beater shots in his career, the most of all-time.

52. Terrance Ross had only averaged 7.4 points a game when he scored 51 points in a game in 2014.

51. The first NBA teams based outside of the U.S. were the Vancouver Grizzlies and Toronto Raptors.

50. Kevin Durant scored the most points in a Game 7, dropping 48 in the 2021 playoffs against the Milwaukee Bucks.

49. NBA rules state that a player can only catch and shoot with 0.4 seconds left on the clock.

48. Rasheed Wallace holds the NBA record for technical fouls in a season, with 41.

47. Only five players in NBA history have gone undrafted, but made an All-Star team. They are Connie Hawkins, John Starks, Brad Miller, Ben Wallace and Fred VanVleet.

46. In the 1979-1980 season, NBA teams took an average of 2.8 three-pointers per game. In the 2021-2022 season, NBA teams took an average of 35.2 shots from long distance.

45. With 73 wins in the 2015-2016 regular season, the Golden State Warriors set the record for most victories.

44. In a league high six times, the Washington Wizards and Cleveland Cavaliers have picked first overall at the top of the NBA Draft.

43. Local broadcasters of teams that win NBA titles also receive championship rings.

42. Ping pong balls are used to determine the order in which teams that did not make the NBA playoffs select in the NBA Draft.

41. The NBA Replay Center is located in Secaucus, New Jersey.

40. Some fans in certain NBA arenas do not take their seats until the home team scores their first basket.

39. Halftime in the NBA lasts for 15 minutes.

38. Each NBA team is allowed to take up to seven timeouts per game, and no more than four in the fourth quarter. Two timeouts are allotted for each team if the game goes into overtime.

37. There was a time when the NBA Finals was not broadcast live on TV. Before the 1980's, it was common for games to be aired after the late local news.

36. Benny the Bull was the first NBA mascot. He started appearing at Chicago Bulls games in 1969.

35. Gregg Popovich is the winningest coach in NBA history, ahead of Don Nelson and Lenny Wilkens.

34. Three NBA players would go on to become NBA officials. Leon Wood, Haywoode Workman and Bernie Fryer all made this transition.

33. On average, NBA players run about two miles per game.

32. NBA teams are allowed to have a maximum of three assistant coaches on their staff.

31. If a player is hurt too badly to shoot free throws, the other team picks someone from the offensive team's bench to make the attempts. The injured player also cannot return to the game.

30. The Sacramento Kings have the most losses in NBA history.

29. The Boston Celtics have the most wins in NBA history.

28. Los Angeles Lakers center Elmore Smith set the single game record for blocks, with 17.

27. Unless it's for safety reasons, NBA players cannot hang on the rim after a dunk. If they do, they can be given a technical foul.

26. The NBA did not allow zone defenses (guarding an area of the court instead of guarding a player) until the 2001-2002 season.

25. The NBA provides each team with 72 official game balls at the beginning of each season. Referees will decide which basketballs are approved for game play on a given night.

24. In the 2021-2022 season, about two-thirds of NBA players wore Nike sneakers.

23. The NBA requires teams to replace court flooring once every 10 seasons.

22. An NBA game is automatically paused if a player is bleeding, and that player is allowed a maximum of 30 seconds to patch up the wound. If more time is needed, a substitute must replace him.

21. NBA forward Rick Fox was a teammate of both Larry Bird and Shaquille O'Neal. Bird retired in 1992, and O'Neal retired in 2011.

20. Miami Heat forward Udonis Haslem has played against both Karl Malone (drafted in 1985) and Keegan Murray (drafted in 2022).

19. The Anderson Packers were called for 60 fouls in a game against the Syracuse Nationals in 1949, which is still the record to this day.

18. The halfcourt line is sometimes known as "the timeline," since an offensive team has eight seconds to get the ball across it.

17. If the shot clock above the backboard stops working, portable clocks are placed on the floor out of bounds on each side of the court.

16. In 1972, the Phoenix Suns and Milwaukee Bucks played two exhibition games outdoors in Puerto Rico.

15. The 2022 Golden State Warriors' championship rings were made of 16-karat gold, to represent the team's 16 playoff wins en route to the title.

14. Forward Clyde Lovellette was the first player to win an NBA title, an NCAA college basketball title and an Olympic gold medal.

13. The final ballots used in the voting process for the Basketball Hall of Fame are eventually destroyed.

12. The Basketball Hall of Fame is located in Springfield, Massachusetts because that's where the game was invented.

11. Chicago Bulls forward Toni Kukoc would eat salad, pasta, chicken, an appetizer and dessert a few hours before every game.

10. Sacramento Kings fans set the record for being the loudest supporters in the league. They once reached 126 decibels of volume in a November 2013 game.

9. The NBA retired Bill Russell's number 6 across the entire league. This means no player will be able to wear the number 6 again in honor of the Celtics' legend.

8. The Los Angeles Clippers and Toronto Raptors are the only two teams without any jerseys retired (other than the league-enforced one of Russell's).

7. 11 NBA teams share their home arena with the local professional hockey team in their city. It can take as little as 90 minutes for workers to change a hockey rink into a basketball court.

6. Los Angeles Lakers guard Magic Johnson once signed a 25-year contract with the team in 1984, despite only playing in the NBA for a total of 13 seasons.

5. In the 2002-2003 regular season, 46 players played all 82 regular season games. In the 2021-2022 regular season, only five players appeared in all 82 games.

4. In the 2021-2022 season, Toronto Raptors forward Pascal Siakam led the league in minutes per game, at 37.9. In the 2001-2002 season, Philadelphia 76ers guard Allen Iverson led the league in minutes per game, at 43.7.

3. Kareem Abdul-Jabbar committed the most fouls in NBA history, with 4,657.

2. The University of Kentucky is the college program that has produced the most NBA players of all time.

1. 10 players have played 20 or more seasons in the NBA. Nine of those players played in over 1,300 games. Miami Heat forward Udonis Haslem is the only one who hasn't, with 877 games played so far.

Made in the USA
Las Vegas, NV
13 October 2023